THE
HUMAN
ADVENTURE

READINGS IN WORLD HISTORY

VOLUME ONE

Selected and Edited by
SYDNEY EISEN
MAURICE FILLER

General Editor: LEWIS PAUL TODD

HARCOURT BRACE JOVANOVICH

New York   Chicago   San Francisco   Atlanta   Dallas   and   *London*

ABOUT THE EDITORS

SYDNEY EISEN is Associate Professor of History and Humanities at York University in Toronto, Ontario. He formerly taught at Williams College and at The City College of New York, where he was also acting Assistant Dean of the College of Liberal Arts. Professor Eisen received his B.A. from the University of Toronto and his Ph.D. from The Johns Hopkins University. In 1953 he was the recipient of a Canadian Social Science Research Council Fellowship for study in England. He has taught history to high school students on the advanced placement level and has given courses and conducted seminars for secondary school teachers. Professor Eisen is a member of the CEEB Advanced Placement Committee in European History.

MAURICE FILLER is the Coordinator of the History Department at the Mt. Greylock Regional High School in Williamstown, Massachusetts. He received his Master's Degree from Boston University and has done additional graduate work in history at the University of Michigan and Columbia University. In the summer of 1960 he received a John Hay Fellowship for further study in the humanities. For the past fifteen years he has taught social studies courses at all levels from grade seven through grade twelve. He is a member of a number of professional organizations, among them the National Council for the Social Studies and the American Historical Association.

THE GENERAL EDITOR

LEWIS PAUL TODD is the editor of *Social Education*, the official journal of the National Council for the Social Studies. He has had many years of experience as a teacher in schools and colleges and has made many contributions to the professional literature of the social studies.

EDITORIAL CONSULTANTS

Consultation and advice on these volumes were given by Dr. Anatole G. Mazour and Dr. John M. Peoples. Dr. Mazour is Professor of History at Stanford University, and Dr. Peoples is a teacher of history at the Alameda High School, Alameda, California. They are co-authors of *Men and Nations: A World History*.

ISBN 0-15-371890-0

PREFACE

This collection of primary and secondary sources provides supplementary material for courses in world history. It is our hope that these readings will make the study of history a more exciting and meaningful experience, an experience that will help recapture the spirit of the past as well as reveal the complex nature of human development.

What is to be omitted and what is to be included in a collection of this nature often becomes a matter of individual preference. In our selection we have tried to choose documents that are both significant and interesting as well as to maintain a balance of political, social, and intellectual history. For the most part, documents that are summarized in every textbook have been omitted, though a few, such as Magna Carta and the Declaration of Independence, have been included so that the reader may get some sense of the original. We have sought to keep the collection small and manageable and yet provide a body of readings for each of the basic divisions of world history.

The collection is divided into two volumes, the first covering the period from the dawn of history to 1815, and the second from 1815 to the present. There are ten basic parts, of which Parts One through Six are included in Volume One and Parts Seven through Ten in Volume Two. The general order of the selections is chronological, but rather than adhere rigidly to chronology, we have grouped together within each of the appropriate sections those readings that pertain to the same topic.

The divisions used in Western history are not suitable for the civilizations of India, China, and Japan. The selections drawn from the histories of these areas before about the middle of the nineteenth century first appear at the end of Volume One as Part Six. For those who wish to use only the second volume and who meet the Asian civilizations for the first time in the Age of Imperialism in the nineteenth century, we have reprinted all the material on India, China, and Japan in Volume Two, Part Eight, together with material on Africa.

All documents, or groups of documents, are preceded by brief introductions that provide the historical setting against which the sources are to be read. In order to allow the reader the maximum freedom of interpretation, we have generally refrained from using the introductions to analyze the documents. Where necessary, footnotes and textual explanations have been added to make the meanings of the documents clear. We have followed accepted American spelling, capitalization, and punctuation. In a very few instances we have altered the word order to make a statement more comprehensible.

In preparing this book we have beset our friends and colleagues with numerous queries of fact and opinion; we are very grateful to them for their patience and advice. We appreciate the generous cooperation we received from the staff of the Stetson Library of Williams College, where much of the work was done over several summers. We are grateful to Emanuel S. Chill, Dante A. Puzzo, Conrad Schirokauer, and George Schwab, all in the Department of History of The City College, and to John W. Baldwin of the Department of History, The Johns Hopkins University, who read portions of the introductions and made valuable suggestions. We are indebted to the members of the Department of History at Mt. Greylock Regional High School, especially Lawrence Vadnais and John Good, and to Mrs. Doris Eisen and Mrs. Myril Filler, for reading the book and making perceptive comments. We also wish to acknowledge our obvious debt to those scholars who have previously made translations and compilations of sources for the study of history.

SYDNEY EISEN
MAURICE FILLER

CONTENTS

PART TWO   The Classical World

PART THREE The Middle Ages

PART FOUR The Emergence of Modern Europe

PART FIVE Enlightenment, Revolution, and Reaction

PART SIX India, China, and Japan

VOLUME TWO (for contents of Volume Two see pages 267–73)

PART ONE

The Emergence of Civilization

The Remains of Prehistoric Man

Although the history of man probably covers a period of more than one million years, the written evidence of his past goes back no more than five or six thousand years. For our knowledge and understanding of prehistory, that vast era preceding the invention of writing, we are dependent on the discovery and careful analysis of human and cultural remains. In spite of the great advances made in the scientific study of man's distant past, there is still disagreement among experts on both the age and meaning of these remains. New discoveries are constantly broadening our horizons and compelling us to revise our views.

L. S. B. Leakey, the author of the following selection, is a British anthropologist who has been conducting excavations in Tanganyika in East Africa for many years in his search of man's origins.

I want to try to answer a question which I am frequently asked. How do remains of Stone Age cultures, and sometimes of the men who made them, come to be preserved in caves and in geological deposits? It is of the greatest importance to understand the answer to this question, for unless we do we cannot hope to interpret correctly the results obtained by excavation.

Let us for a moment imagine that we can stand back and observe the sequence of events at a rock-shelter some twenty or thirty thousand years ago.

A Stone Age hunter is wandering down the valley in search of game when he espies a rock-shelter in the side of the rocky cliff above him. Carefully and with the utmost caution, he climbs up to it, fearful lest he may find that it is occupied by the members of some other Stone

Source: L. S. B. Leakey, *Adam's Ancestors: The Evolution of Man and His Culture*, London: Methuen & Co., Ltd., 1960, pp. 9–13. Reprinted by permission of the author and the publishers.

Age family who will resent his intrusion, or possibly even that it is the lair of a lion or a cave bear. At last he is close enough and he sees that it is quite unoccupied, and so he enters and makes a thorough examination. He decides that it is a much more suitable habitation than the little shelter where he and his family are living at present, and he goes off to fetch them.

Next we see the family arriving and settling into their new home. A fire is lit either from some embers carefully nursed and brought from the old home, or else by means of a simple wooden fire drill. (We cannot say for certain what methods Stone Age man used for obtaining fire, but we do know that from a very early period he did make use of fire, for hearths are a common feature in almost any occupation level in caves and rock-shelters.)

Probably some of the family then go off to collect grass or bracken [ferns] to make rough beds upon which they will sleep, while others break branches from bushes and trees in the nearby thicket and construct a rude wall across the front of the shelter. The skins of various wild animals are then unrolled and deposited in the new home, together with such household goods as they possess.

And now the family is fully settled in, and the day-to-day routine is resumed once more. The men hunt and trap animals for food, the women probably help in this and also collect edible fruits and nuts and roots. Gradually, rubbish starts to accumulate on the floor; decaying vegetation mingles with wood ash scraped from the hearth, and mixed with all this are the bones and teeth of the animals that have served as food. The stone and bone tools which comprise the weapons and domestic implements of the family break or become blunt through use, and they are discarded and new ones made. Blocks of suitable material collected during hunting expeditions have been brought to the new home, and from these, flakes are knocked off to make new tools. This process involves the scattering of many waste flakes and chips over the floor, and these soon become incorporated in the debris in the same way as the tools that have become too blunt for further use. When the weather is fine a great deal of the work is done on the platform outside the shelter, so that deposits accumulate there too.

Years pass, the older members of the family die and — according to custom — are buried in the floor of the shelter; the younger members of the family grow up and marry, and all the time the home continues to be used, so that more and more debris accumulates on the floor. A

3

large part of this debris is perishable material which by the process of decay turns into soil, throughout which imperishable objects of stone and bone are scattered.

Naturally enough, the deposits so formed do not accumulate evenly over the whole floor, and although the floor may have been level to start with (and even this is seldom the case), it very soon ceases to be so.

And so generations pass and a considerable depth of deposit is formed representing an occupation level, and then something happens which results in the shelter being vacated. When this occurs the shelter may perhaps be taken over almost immediately by some other Stone Age family — possibly of a different tribe and with a somewhat different culture — in which case we shall get a somewhat different occupation level superimposed upon the first one. On the other hand, the shelter may remain untenanted for a considerable period of time, in which case dust and leaves and other purely natural material will collect and gradually build up a sterile layer covering the occupation level until the place is once more selected as a living site.

And so the story goes on; occupation levels alternate with sterile layers, blocks of rock fall from the roof, and slowly but surely the floor level rises.

If the shelter happens to be in a limestone cliff and the site is unoccupied during a period when the climate is very moist, a hard deposit of stalagmite may form over the floor and seal in the underlying deposits. On the other hand, if the shelter is not very high above the level of the river, a spell of heavy floods may result in the partial or complete scouring out of the unconsolidated deposits. Or . . . a layer of water-laid sand may be formed.

Such occurrences and many other events will all leave their traces in the shelter, and if the eventual scientific excavation is carried out with patience and skill, the evidence can be recognized and interpreted and the story worked out. If, however, the excavator is not well trained, or if he works too fast, at least part of the evidence will be lost. Above all, the excavator must be very critical, taking care not to confuse facts with his own theoretical interpretation of them and seizing every opportunity to check and recheck each stage of his work.

Once the facts have been collected, it may be necessary to call in specialists in various branches of science before the data can be fully interpreted. The paleontologist will have to help identify the various animal bones and teeth and state what conclusions as to geological age and

4

climatic conditions may be drawn from them. The geologist and soil analyst may also be able to give aid in determining climatic conditions from soil samples of the deposits from different levels in the excavation, while the botanist may be able in some cases to identify certain trees and plants from well-preserved pieces of charcoal found in hearths. Even the physicist, by the latest methods of analysis of carbon 14, may be able to help to provide an approximate age from examination of the charcoal.

The stone and bone implements and even the waste flakes will also tell their own story, and so when all the necessary collaboration has been achieved, the prehistorian will be able to present a reasonably accurate story of the sequence of events in the rock-shelter. . . .

Let us . . . consider the case of river deposits such as gravels, clays, and sands. These, if they were formed during the period when Stone Age man lived, will often be found to contain stone implements, sometimes in great quantity.

It is not difficult to understand how remains of Stone Age cultures came to be incorporated in river deposits if we think in terms of what is happening today. Who has not stood upon a bridge and, looking down into the water beneath, has seen lying on the gravel in the bed of the stream broken bottles, tin cans, bits of china, bones, and other relics of our present-day culture? All of these objects are now being slowly incorporated in the sands and gravels and clays of the river, and they have reached their present position either because they have been thrown in or else washed in by flood waters.

Stone Age man — especially at certain stages of his history — was particularly fond of living close to the banks of streams and rivers, probably because he had no vessels in which to store and carry water and therefore liked to live as close as possible to his water supply. Living thus — and by analogy with what happens today — it is quite natural that many of his cultural objects as well as the bones thrown away after his meals got washed into the rivers and incorporated in the deposits. Owing to changes of climate and topography, . . . many of these old river deposits of the Stone Age lie today either on high-level terraces well above the present river levels, or in sunken channels; whole parts of these old deposits are sometimes washed into the present-day rivers, and in this way cultural material of a much earlier date that was originally incorporated in the old gravels gets redeposited in younger gravels, bringing about a mixture of elements in the newly forming gravels. . . .

Another type of geological deposit which is often found to contain

Stone Age man's tools is that formed under glacial conditions. Considerable areas of the zones that at the present time have a temperate climate were during the Stone Age covered from time to time by ice sheets. This was the result of world changes of climate. . . . Deposits formed under glacial conditions often consist of boulder clays and glacial outwash gravels.* When an ice sheet advances over the countryside it tends to plough up all the surface deposits that lie in its path and also to pick up most of this material and carry it forward. If the deposits so ploughed into and picked up already contained Stone Age tools of an earlier period, or if such implements were lying on the surface, they too were carried forward and churned up with the mass of other material. When further changes of climate resulted in the melting of the ice sheets, all the mass of rubble and rock and earth that had been caught up in the ice was deposited in the form of boulder clays and outwash gravels. Thus it often happens that such glacial deposits contain Stone Age implements. . . .

It is clear that ordinary common sense is a very important factor in the interpretation of the past. To this must be added a great deal of scientific knowledge if we are to obtain a proper picture of the climate, geography, and general environment which existed in the days when Stone Age man lived.

* **glacial outwash gravels:** deposits of gravel and sand left by streams coming from the melting ice.

Man Harnesses
the Forces of Nature

One of the distinguishing characteristics of man has been his ability to harness the forces of nature. In our day we have come to accept rapid material progress and new inventions as a matter of course. Early man's discoveries and inventions were made over a period of thousands of years; every step was extremely arduous and often not enduring because of the lack of communications.

Some of the greatest pioneers of all time will forever remain unknown. We owe a great debt to the men who first learned to make tools, to domesticate animals, to plant and to grow grain, to construct the wheel, and to smelt metals.

The late V. Gordon Childe, a leading British archaeologist, discusses below how man first learned to make and control fire and to smelt copper.

The Control of Fire

The control of fire was presumably the first great step in man's emancipation from the bondage to his environment. Warmed by the embers, man could endure cold nights and could thus penetrate into temperate and even arctic regions. The flames would give him light at night and allow him to explore the recesses of sheltering caves. Fire would scare away . . . wild beasts. By cooking, substances became edible that would be indigestible if eaten raw. Man is no longer restricted in his movements to a limited range of climates, and his activities need not be entirely determined by the sun's light.

But in mastery of fire man was controlling a mighty physical force and a conspicuous chemical change. For the first time in history a creature of Nature was directing one of the great forces of Nature. And the exercise of power must react upon the controller. The sight of the bright flame bursting forth when a dry bough was thrust into glowing embers, the transformation of the bough into fine ashes and smoke, must have stimulated man's rudimentary brain. What these phenomena suggested to him is unknowable. But in feeding and damping down the fire, in transporting and using it, man made a revolutionary departure from the behavior of other animals. He was asserting his humanity and making himself.

At first, of course, man just tamed and kept alight fires that had been produced by lightning or other natural agency. Even that presupposes some science — observation and comparison of experiences. Man had to learn what the effects of fire were, what it would " eat," and so on. And in tending and preserving the flames, man kept adding to his store of knowledge. Sacred fires that must never be allowed to die out,

Source: V. Gordon Childe, *Man Makes Himself*, London: C. A. Watts & Co., Ltd., 1951, pp. 46–47; 95–99. Reprinted by permission of the publishers.

like the fire of Vesta at Rome, were ritually tended by many ancient peoples and by modern savages. They are presumably survivals and reminiscences of a time when man had not yet learned to produce fire at will.

When that discovery was made is uncertain. Savage peoples produce fire by the spark from flint struck against iron pyrites or hematite, by the friction of two pieces of wood, or by the heat generated on compressing air in a tube of bamboo. The first device was being employed in Europe as early as the last Ice Age. . . . Perhaps the variety of methods used for kindling fire indicates that the trick was discovered only relatively late in human history, when our species had already been widely scattered into isolated groups.

In any case, the discovery was one of first-class significance. Man could thereafter not only control but also initiate the puzzling process of burning, the mysterious power of heat. He became consciously a creator.

The Discovery of Copper

Metalworking involved two groups . . . of discoveries: (1) that copper, when hot, melts and can be cast into any desired shape, but on cooling becomes as hard and will take on as good an edge as stone, and (2) that the tough . . . reddish metal can be produced by heating certain crystalline stones or earths in contact with charcoal. . . .

The discovery involved might easily be made. A prehistoric Egyptian may have dropped some malachite on the glowing ashes of his hearth and seen the gleaming globules of metallic copper run out. A campfire, lit . . . against the outcrop of a surface lode, might reduce some of the ore. In the Katanga district [of the Congo], prospectors have noticed beads of copper, thus accidentally smelted, among the ashes of campfires. . . .

The real superiority of metal is that it is fusible and can be cast. . . . A stone axhead, a flint spearpoint, or a bone harpoon can be made only by grinding, chipping, or cutting bits off the original piece. Molten copper is completely plastic and will adapt itself to fill any desired form; it can be run into a mold of any shape and will assume, and on cooling retain, precisely the form outlined by the mold. The only limit to size is the capacity of the mold; you can run into it as much copper as you like. And the molds themselves can be made of potter's clay. . . .

On the other hand, though so plastic when hot, the metal on cooling possesses the essential virtues of stone and bone; it is as solid, and will take as sharp an edge or as fine a point. Yet it has the additional advantage of being malleable. And finally, it is more permanent than stone or bone. A stone ax may easily be splintered by hard usage and is then done for; at best its edge will often need regrinding and it will soon be reduced to a useless size. But a copper ax can be remelted again and again, and will come out as good as new. The intelligent use of metal — let us say, simply, metallurgy — begins when these advantages have been realized. . . .

The change from tough solid copper to molten metal and back to the solid state again is dramatic, and must have seemed mysterious. The sameness between the shapeless lump of raw copper, the liquid in the crucible, and the well-formed casting must at first have been difficult to grasp. Man was here controlling a remarkable process of physical change. . . .

Moreover, the control of the process was only possible by means of a whole complex of discoveries and inventions. A temperature in the neighborhood of 1,200° C. is [required] to melt copper. That requires a blast. Some device had to be invented for forcing a current of air upon the flame; bellows are the correct solution. . . . Furnaces, crucibles, and tongs had to be invented. Casting requires molds. . . . A stout dagger with a ridge on both faces to strengthen it . . . required a two-piece mold, the halves of which must correspond exactly and must be bound or clamped together. By 3000 B.C. the ingenious cire-perdue * process was employed in Mesopotamia. A model of the desired object is first made in wax and then coated in clay; the clay is heated, becoming pottery, while the wax is allowed to run out; metal is then poured into the cavity, and finally the clay mold is broken, disclosing the metal casting reproducing the form of the wax model. . . .

The scientific and economic implications of the extraction of metal from its ores are perhaps more far-reaching than those of metal-working. Copper ores are crystalline or powdery minerals generally occurring as veins in hard ancient rocks. The transformation of the ores into copper is a fairly simple chemical change. But what an astonishing one to early man! The ore does not look the least like the metal. The change it un-

* **cire-perdue:** the method is explained in the following lines.

dergoes in contact with glowing carbon is miraculous. . . . Man learned enough practical chemistry to distinguish what sorts of stone would yield copper when heated with carbon. . . .

The first copper ores to be exploited were presumably derived from surface deposits. Many such lodes must once have existed but have been exhausted long before modern geological surveys were started. Eventually, however, men had to follow the vein beneath the ground and begin mining. The copper miner had to learn how to split hard rocks by kindling fires against them and throwing water on the heated surfaces. Systems of propping and timbering had to be devised to support the walls and roofs of the galleries. The ore had to be broken up, separated from the rock by washing, and transported to the surface. No records survive to illustrate the steps by which the science of mining was founded; but by 1000 b.c. copper miners, even in still-barbarous Europe, were applying a science that a layman today can admire but cannot attempt to expound. . . . And for production on a large scale a furnace had to be devised. . . .

Intelligent metallurgy must have been widely understood in the Ancient East soon after 4000 b.c. But metal ousted stone very slowly. The advantages . . . must not be exaggerated. For hoeing up the soil, stone blades serve the cultivator well; he will often have to replace them, but normally that is easy. A flint blade works excellently for cutting up carcasses, for reaping grains, for trimming leather, and even for shaving; it wears out quickly, but a new knife or razor can be fashioned in a few minutes where flint is abundant. Stone axes or adzes will fell trees, shape posts, or hew out a canoe almost as quickly and neatly as copper ones; only you will have to pause periodically and make a new ax from a convenient pebble. The chief defect of stone tools was that they wore out so quickly. But when the raw materials were lying about and time was not absurdly precious, it was not an intolerable hardship to have to make new tools from time to time. It needed the special geographical conditions of an alluvial plain,* where suitable stones were rare, to drive home the value of the new and more permanent material and to create an effective and general demand for metal. And to make the satisfaction of that demand possible, improved methods of transport were needed. That meant the harnessing of animal motive power and of the winds.

* **alluvial plain:** a level plain formed by river deposits containing topsoil and clay.

An Egyptian Vizier Instructs His Son

Egypt was the first large territory to be united under a central government. From the time of its unification, which took place somewhere between 3100 B.C. and 2900 B.C., Egypt had, in spite of some significant setbacks, a continuous history for about twenty-five centuries. One of the major sources of its unity and strength was the pharaoh, who was considered the son of the god Rē. As such, he ruled with absolute and divine authority. He owned all the land, his very word was law, and his subjects worshiped him as a god.

The pharaoh sought to employ able and honest men to help him govern his vast land. In order to secure the best officials, it was necessary to encourage men of talent and integrity. From the advice of the wise vizier Ptah-hotep to his son, we ascertain what personal qualities were rewarded in ancient Egypt. The aging vizier, hoping that his son would become his successor, had asked the pharaoh's permission to instruct him. Although the young man is warned to honor tradition, especially the obedience owed to one's parents, he is, at the same time, urged to get ahead by giving honest service.

Then he said to his son:

Let not thy heart be puffed up because of thy knowledge; be not confident because thou art a wise man. Take counsel with the ignorant as well as the wise. The full limits of skill cannot be attained, and there is no skilled man equipped to his full advantage. . . .

If thou art one of those sitting at the table of one greater than thyself, take what he may give when it is set before thy nose. Thou shouldst gaze at what is before thee. Do not pierce him with many stares. . . . Let thy face be cast down until he addresses thee, and thou shouldst speak only when he addresses thee. Laugh after he laughs and it will be

Source: J. B. Pritchard, editor, *Ancient Near Eastern Texts*, Princeton, N.J.: Princeton University Press, 1st ed., 1950, pp. 412–14. Reprinted by permission of the publishers.

very pleasing to his heart, and what thou mayest do will be pleasing to the heart. No one can know what is in the heart. . . .

If thou art a man of intimacy whom one great man sends to another, be thoroughly reliable when he sends thee. Carry out the errand for him as he has spoken. Do not be reserved about what is said to thee, and beware of any act of forgetfulness. Grasp hold of truth, and do not exceed it. . . . Struggle against making words worse, thus making one great man hostile to another through vulgar speech. . . .

If thou art a man of standing and foundest a household and producest a son who is pleasing to god, if he is correct and inclines toward thy ways and listens to thy instruction, while his manners in thy house are fitting, and if he takes care of thy property as it should be, seek out for him every useful action. He is thy son. . . . Thou shouldst not cut thy heart off from him. . . .

If he goes astray and transgresses thy plans and does not carry out thy instruction, so that his manners in thy household are wretched, and he rebels against all that thou sayest, while his mouth runs on in the most wretched talk, quite apart from his experience, while he possesses nothing, thou shouldst cast him off: he is not thy son at all. He was not really born to thee. . . .

Do not be greedy. . . . Do not be covetous against thy own kindred. Greater is the respect for the mild than for the strong. He is a mean person who exposes his kinfolk. . . .

If thou art a man of standing, thou shouldst found thy household and love thy wife at home as is fitting. . . . Make her heart glad as long as thou livest. . . . Thou shouldst not contend with her at law, and keep her far from gaining control. . : . Let her heart be soothed through what may accrue to thee; it means keeping her long in thy house. . . .

Bow thy back to thy superior, thy overseer from the palace. Then thy household will be established in its property, and thy recompense will be as it should be. Opposition to a superior is a painful thing, for one lives as long as he is mild. . . .

If thou art seeking out the nature of a friend, one whom thou questionest, draw near to him and deal with him alone, until thou art no longer troubled about his condition. Reason with him after a while. Test his heart with a bit of talk. If what he may have seen should come out of him or he should do something with which thou art displeased, behold, he is still a friend. . . . Do not answer in a state of turmoil; do not remove thyself from him; do not trample him down. . . .

If a son accepts what his father says, no project of his miscarries. He whom thou instructest as thy obedient son, who will stand well in the heart of the official, his speech is guided with respect to what has been said to him, one regarded as obedient. . . . The wise man rises early in the morning to establish himself, but the fool rises early in the morning only to agitate himself.

As for the fool who does not hearken, he cannot do anything. He regards knowledge as ignorance and profit as loss. He does everything blameworthy, so that one finds fault with him every day. He lives on that through which he should die, and guilt is his food. His character therefrom is told as something known to the officials: dying while alive every day.

Akhnaton Worships One God

The Egyptians worshiped many gods and goddesses. The priests, who were believed to possess the secret of everlasting life, wielded immense power. In the first half of the fourteenth century B.C., a religious revolution was inaugurated by Amenhotep IV (c. 1375–1358 B.C.), who proclaimed that the sun god, Aton, was the sole god. He changed his own name to Akhnaton * (he who is in the service of Aton). As a symbol of these changes and in order to escape the influence of the powerful priests, he left the ancient capital of Thebes and constructed a new capital city at Tell-el-Amarna.

Whether or not Akhnaton's new religion was an early form of monotheism remains debatable. Akhnaton and his family worshiped Aton, but everyone else was expected to worship the pharaoh. Evidence indicates that most people were unaffected by this religious revolution and continued in their old ways. On the death of Akhnaton, the priests restored the ancient faith and moved the capital back to Thebes.

The faith of Akhnaton is discussed in the following passage.

* **Akhnaton:** the name is also spelled Akhenaton, Akhenaten, or Ikhnaton.

Akhnaton, [then] a man of some twenty-two years, turned his thoughts fully to the development of his religion. . . .

Akhnaton's conception of God . . . was as the power which created the sun, the energy which penetrated to this earth in the sun's heat and caused all things to grow. . . . The Aton was the joy which caused the young sheep "to dance upon their legs," and the birds "to flutter in their marshes." He was the god of the simple pleasures of life. . . .

Akhnaton did not permit any graven image to be made of Aton. The True God, said the king, had no form. . . . The symbol of the religion was the sun's disk, from which there extended numerous rays, each ray ending in a hand; but this symbol was not worshiped. . . . [Akhnaton] boldly proclaimed God to be a life-giving [force] — the *heat* which is in the sun. He was "the living Aton,". . . the power which produced and sustained the energy and movement of the sun. . . . He was . . . defined as the "Master of the Aton.". . . But though so remote, the Aton was the tender, loving father of all men, ever-present and ever-mindful of his creatures. . . .

The Aton was the "Lord of love." His beams were "beauteous with love" as they fell upon His people and upon His city. . . . "Thy love is great and large," says one of Akhnaton's psalms, "Thou fillest the two lands of Egypt with Thy love."

The Aton was compassionate, was merciful, was gentle, was tender; He knew not anger, and there was no wrath in Him. . . . [Aton was] the idea of the beneficent Creator who though remote, spiritual, and impersonal, could love each of His creatures, great or small. . . .

The Aton was conceived as being without rivals. . . . "Thou art alone, but infinite vitalities [powers] are in Thee."

Aton was the "Lord of Peace," who could not tolerate battle and strife.

Above all things the Aton loved truth. Frankness, sincerity, straightforwardness, [and] honesty . . . were not always to be found in the heart of an Egyptian; and Akhnaton, . . . [despising] deception, . . . always spoke of himself as "living in truth." "I have set truth in my inward parts," says one of his followers, "and falsehood is my loathing; for I know that the King rejoiceth in truth."

Source: Arthur Weigall, *The Life and Times of Akhnaton, Pharaoh of Egypt*, New York: G. P. Putnam's Sons, 1923, pp. 99–111. Reprinted by permission of the publishers.

A Manual for the Dead

The death of the body, according to Egyptian belief, was the beginning of eternal life. It was essential, therefore, that careful preparation be made to assure a happy state of immortality for the individual. In the early days of Egyptian history, only the pharaoh and the men of wealth could receive the necessary funeral rites administered by the priests to assure eternal life. After hundreds of years, all people, regardless of wealth, were granted this right. Eventually this approach to the afterlife through ritual evolved into a system of rewards and punishments for behavior on earth. The dead were thought to be judged soon after death by Osiris and other gods.

The Book of the Dead is a collection of hymns, prayers, and petitions. The following excerpt is from the scene of judgment. This confession, which the dead were supposed to utter, gives us a good idea of the Egyptian moral code.

Hail to thee, O great god. . . . I have come to thee, my lord, I have been brought that I might see thy beauty. I know thee; I know thy name and the names of the forty-two gods who are with thee in the Broad-Hall of the Two Justices, who live on them who preserve evil and who drink their blood on that day of reckoning up character in the presence of Wennofer. Behold, "Sati-Mertifi, Lord of Justice," is thy name. I have come to thee; I have brought thee justice; I have expelled deceit for thee.

I have not committed evil against men. . . .
I have not committed sin in the place of truth. . . .
I have not seen evil. . . .
I have not blasphemed a god.
I have not done violence to a poor man.
I have not done that which the gods abominate.
I have not defamed a slave to his superior.
I have not made anyone sick.

Source: J. B. Pritchard, editor, *Ancient Near Eastern Texts*, Princeton, N.J.: Princeton University Press, 1st ed., 1950, p. 34. Reprinted by permission of the publishers.

I have not made anyone weep.
I have not killed.
I have given no order to a killer.
I have not caused anyone suffering.
I have not cut down on the food in the temples.
I have not damaged the bread of the gods. . . .
I have not taken milk from the mouths of children.
I have not driven cattle away from their pasturage. . . .
I have not built a dam against running water.

Dress and Sports in Ancient Egypt

The dry climate of Egypt has preserved for us monuments, written documents, and numerous and varied objects of Egyptian civilization. That the Egyptian, especially the man of means, thoroughly enjoyed life is evident from these sources. The man of wealth could own a spacious home provided with slaves and imported luxuries. His wife could furnish herself with a magnificent wardrobe, expensive jewelry, and a considerable amount of beautifying equipment. The masses of peasants, however, who were in a condition of semislavery, lived in squalid quarters and enjoyed none of these pleasures.

Margaret A. Murray, a British scholar, gives us a picture of dress and sports in ancient Egypt.

Dress

It is a curious fact that though needles are found, there are never any scenes of sewing, yet the women's dresses were certainly sewn. The invariable dress of the women was a long straight linen garment falling from the armpits to the ankles; it was held up by straps over the shoulders. . . .

Source: Margaret A. Murray, *The Splendor that Was Egypt*, new and revised edition, New York: Hawthorn Books, Inc., pp. 120–23. Copyright 1949, © 1963 by Margaret A. Murray. Reprinted by permission.

The men wore a short loincloth fastened with a belt round the waist, and reaching to about the knee. In the Old Kingdom the front fold of the loincloth was often pleated. In the Middle Kingdom the loincloth was much longer and reached to mid-calf, like a petticoat. At the end of the New Kingdom, under Akhnaton, the long loincloth came into fashion again, very closely pleated with a great many folds in the front. . . .

Decoration of the person was practiced from the earliest times. In prehistoric Egypt painting of the eyes with malachite was a common practice. . . . Ladies had beautiful . . . containers to hold their eye paint, . . . which was applied to the eyelids with a round-ended rod. . . . Under the Hyksos, when the country was poor, a piece of hollow reed was all that could be afforded as a container for the paint, and when in the New Kingdom Egypt again became wealthy, the ladies had the reed copied in more costly materials — ebony, alabaster, and multicolored glass. . . . Henna was used for staining the hands and nails, and there seems to have been some form of lipstick applied with a brush; . . . the coloring matter was probably red ocher. Tattooing was another form of personal decoration much in vogue in prehistoric Egypt, but there is nothing to show that it was practiced in historic times.

Except for the Pharaoh, fashions in hairdressing changed as often as fashions in dress. The royal mummies prove that the Pharaoh wore his hair short. . . . He was always clean shaven, but on state occasions he wore a long and narrow false beard of plaited hair held at the point of the chin by a strap on each side, which passed round the jaw and in front of the ear and was attached to the crown itself. . . . Men of high rank occasionally wore a false beard, but this was always short, little more than a tuft. In the Old Kingdom certain high officials wore moustaches, but this was rare. With these few exceptions the men were always clean shaven. Foreigners, especially Syrians and Libyans, wore natural beards trimmed to a point.

From early in the historic period both men and women wore wigs and cut their own hair short. . . . Few wigs have survived, for they were probably destroyed on the owner's death. Those that remain are of sheep's wool, black or very dark brown.

That the women of ancient Egypt were proud of their hair and cared for it is evidenced by the recipes for strengthening the hair and preventing its turning gray. . . . "Recipe for making the hair grow. . . . Paws of a dog, one part; kernels of dates, one part; hoof of a donkey, one part. Cook very thoroughly with oil in an earthen pot, and anoint therewith."

Mirrors . . . are known from the Old Kingdom. They were of copper or bronze highly polished, and usually set in a wooden handle; sometimes the handle was of ivory and often exquisitely decorated. As the polish on the mirror was important, ladies had leather cases lined with soft linen in which the mirror was kept when not in use.

Sports

Outdoor sports were much favored by men of all classes. For the wealthy there was hunting in the desert with bows and arrows and with hunting dogs, spearing big fish, or knocking down birds with a boomerang in the marshes. . . . After the introduction of horses, driving in chariots was very popular. There were, however, no outdoor games in the modern sense; the sportsman enjoyed himself alone or in company with his wife and daughter, who took no part in the man's actions. The chief amusement for lads and young men among the peasants was wrestling. It was evidently so popular that many scenes of wrestling are found in the tomb-chapels of the wealthy, especially in the Twelfth Dynasty. Sometimes the scraps of conversation between the two opponents are recorded: "By your leave," says one as he gets his arm round his adversary's leg. "And now," he adds, "you will find yourself on your nose! I'll make you do that.". . . In another scene two men are rolling on the ground in their struggle: "Don't talk so big," says the man on top. "See! Here we are! Now then, look out for yourself." But his apparently falling opponent thinks that, after all, he will turn the tables. . . . "Come, wretch," he [says], "I have wriggled round. See! It is you who are yielding."

For soldiers there were war dances, which were really a form of physical drill, and as probably the local prince enlisted all the able-bodied young men in his militia, these dances were part of the regular outdoor sports of a village.

Hammurabi
Issues a Law Code

If urban life and a knowledge of writing are considered the essential ingredients of civilization, then civilization first began in Mesopotamia. The Mesopotamians were, on the whole, more creative and inventive than the Egyptians. The first examples of the codification of law come from the Tigris-Euphrates Valley. Written laws, placed where all could see them, provided a measure of protection for everyone.

During the reign of Hammurabi (c. 1728–1686 B.C.), ruler of the Babylonian Empire, one of these codes of law was compiled. The Code of Hammurabi is the most comprehensive, though not the first, law code from this region. The complete code had 282 clauses dealing with every aspect of life. It is a very important source of information for understanding the civilization of the period.

Our best text of the code comes from a large stone discovered by French archaeologists at the beginning of the twentieth century. At the top of the stone there is a carving which shows Shamash, the god of justice, directing Hammurabi to issue the code.

If a seignior * accused another seignior and brought a charge of murder against him, but has not proved it, the accuser shall be put to death. . . .

If a seignior came forward with false testimony in a case, and has not proved the word which he spoke, if that case was a case involving life, that seignior shall be put to death. . . .

If a seignior stole the property of church or state, that seignior shall be put to death; also the one who received the stolen goods from his hand shall be put to death. . . .

* **seignior:** a free or semifree man.

Source: J. B. Pritchard, editor, *Ancient Near Eastern Texts*, Princeton, N.J.: Princeton University Press, 1st ed., 1950, pp. 166–67, 172–75, 176. Reprinted by permission of the publishers.

If a seignior has stolen the young son of another seignior, he shall be put to death.

If a seignior has helped either a male slave of the state or a female slave of the state or a male slave of a private citizen or a female slave of a private citizen to escape through the city gate, he shall be put to death. . . .

If a seignior caught a fugitive male or female slave in the open and has taken him to his owner, the owner of the slave shall pay him two shekels of silver. . . .

If a seignior committed robbery and has been caught, that seignior shall be put to death. . . .

If fire broke out in a seignior's house and a seignior who went to extinguish it cast his eye on the goods of the owner of the house and has appropriated the goods of the owner of the house, that seignior shall be thrown into that fire. . . .

In the case of . . . a private soldier . . . who was carried off while in the armed service of the king, if his son is able to look after the feudal obligations, the field and orchard shall be given to him and he shall look after the feudal obligations of his father. . . .

If a seignior cut down a tree in another seignior's orchard without the consent of the owner of the orchard, he shall pay one-half mina of silver. . . .

If a seignior wishes to divorce his wife who did not bear him children, he shall give her money to the full amount of her marriage price and he shall also make good to her the dowry which she brought from her father's house, and then he may divorce her. . . .

If a son has struck his father, they shall cut off his hand.

If a seignior has destroyed the eye of a member of the aristocracy, they shall destroy his eye.

If he has broken another seignior's bone, they shall break his bone.

If he has destroyed the eye of a commoner or broken the bone of a commoner, he shall pay one mina of silver. . . .

If a seignior has knocked out a tooth of a seignior of his own rank, they shall knock out his tooth. . . .

If a seignior hired an ox and has caused its death through carelessness or through beating, he shall make good ox for ox to the owner of the ox.

Gilgamesh Seeks
to Conquer Death

Among the best known tales in Mesopotamian literature is the ancient Epic of Gilgamesh, which has come down to us in several versions. According to the story, Gilgamesh, the hero, was the king of the city of Erech. Mighty and fearless in battle, he and his companion Enkidu enjoyed many glorious adventures. The death of Enkidu through illness depressed the carefree Gilgamesh. Overcome with grief and refusing to accept the fact of Enkidu's death, he set out to discover the secret of everlasting life.

The Mesopotamians did not have the simple, optimistic view of immortality held by the Egyptians. Gilgamesh, in spite of many disappointments, stubbornly pursues his course, but in vain. The advice he generally receives is similar to that in the second passage below. The long poem ends on a note of pessimism. The problem of death is not solved, and the secret of immortality not discovered.

"My friend, my younger brother — who with me . . .
hunted . . . panther in the plains;
Enkidu, my friend, my younger brother — who with me . . .
hunted . . . panther in the plains;
who with me could do all, who climbed the crags. . . .
Now — what sleep is this that seized you?
You have grown dark and cannot hear me."
He did not raise his eyes.
Gilgamesh touched his heart, it was not beating.
Then he covered his friend. . . .
His voice roared out. . . .
Again and then again he turned toward his friend,
tearing his hair and scattering the tufts,
stripping and flinging down the finery off his body.

Source: H. and H. A. Frankfort, John A. Wilson, Thorkild Jacobsen, *The Intellectual Adventure of Ancient Man*, Chicago: University of Chicago Press, 1946, pp. 209–11. Reprinted by permission of the publishers.

Gilgamesh, whither are you wandering?
Life, which you look for, you will never find.
For when the gods created man, they let
death be his share, and life
withheld in their own hands.
Gilgamesh, fill your belly —
day and night make merry,
let days be full of joy,
dance and make music day and night.
And wear fresh clothes,
and wash your head and bathe.
Look at the child that is holding your hand. . . .
These things alone are the concern of men.

Assyrian Expansion
Under Sargon II

Mesopotamia, unlike Egypt, lacked natural geographic barriers
to discourage invaders. Consequently the empires of the Tigris-
Euphrates Valley rose and fell in fairly rapid succession. The
country was conquered and ruled, in turn, by the Babylonians,
the Assyrians, and the Persians. By about 900 B.C., the Assyrians were the dominant power in the region. By 700 B.C.
they ruled a vast empire which, for a short time, even included
Egypt.

The Assyrians were probably the most brutal conquerors of
ancient times. Their army was the finest of its day — disciplined,
well trained, and professional. No enemy could withstand the
assault of their bowmen, who used deadly iron-tipped arrows.
They had a superb cavalry and a magnificent fleet of chariots.
Toward the defeated they practiced a deliberate policy of
terror. It may be surprising, in the light of all this, that they
built fine libraries and collected writings from all over the ancient world.

The empire eventually grew too big for the small military
ruling clique. After 700 B.C. it began to decline, and with the

destruction of the capital, Nineveh, by the Medes and Babylonians in 612 B.C. it fell apart. Sargon II (722–705 B.C.), who ruled the Assyrian Empire at its height, discusses his conquests.

Iamani from Ashdod, afraid of my armed force, left his wife and children and fled to the frontier . . . and hid there like a thief. I installed an officer of mine as governor over his entire large country and its prosperous inhabitants, thus aggrandizing again the territory belonging to Ashur, the king of the gods. The terror-inspiring glamor of Ashur, my lord, overpowered . . . the king of Meluhha [Ethiopia] and he threw Iamani . . . in fetters on hands and feet and sent him to me, to Assyria. I conquered and sacked the towns Shinuhtu and Samaria, and all Israel. I caught, like a fish, the Greek Ionians who live on islands amid the Western Sea. . . .

Ia'ubidi from Hamath, a commoner without claim to the throne, a cursed Hittite, schemed to become king of Hamath, induced the cities Arvad, Simirra, Damascus, and Samaria to desert me, made them collaborate, and fitted out an army. I called up the masses of the soldiers of Ashur and besieged him and his warriors in Qarqar, his favorite city. I conquered it and burnt it. Himself I flayed; the rebels I killed in their cities and established peace and harmony again. A contingent of two hundred chariots and six hundred men on horseback I formed from among the inhabitants of Hamath and added them to my royal corps. . . .

Asuri, king of Ashdod, had schemed not to deliver tribute any more and sent messages full of hostilities against Assyria to the kings living in his neighborhood. On account of these acts which he committed, I abolished his rule over the people of his country and made Ahimiti, his younger brother, king over them. But these Hittites, always planning evil deeds, hated his reign and elevated to rule over them a Greek who, without any claim to the throne, had no respect for authority — just as they themselves. In a sudden rage, I did not wait to assemble the full might of my army or to prepare the camping equipment, but started out toward Ashdod only with those of my warriors who, even in friendly areas, never leave my side. But this Greek heard about the advance of

Source: J. B. Pritchard, editor, *Ancient Near Eastern Texts*, Princeton, N.J.: Princeton University Press, 1st ed., 1950, pp. 285–86. Reprinted by permission of the publishers.

my expedition from afar, and he fled into the territory of Musru — which belongs now to Ethiopia — and his hiding place could not be detected. I besieged and conquered the cities; . . . I declared his images, his wife, his children, all the . . . treasures of his palace as well as the inhabitants of his country as booty. I reorganized the administration of these cities and settled therein people from the regions of the East which I had conquered personally. I installed an officer of mine over them and declared them Assyrian citizens. . . . The king of Ethiopia, who lives in a distant country in an inapproachable region, . . . whose fathers never — from remote days until now — had sent messengers to inquire after the health of my royal forefathers, he did hear, even that far away, of the might of Ashur, Nebo, and Marduk. The awe-inspiring glamor of my kingship blinded him and terror overcame him. He threw . . . the Greek in fetters, shackles, and iron bands, and they brought him to Assyria, a long journey.

The First Case of Juvenile Delinquency

Samuel Noah Kramer is an American archaeologist who has spent his life studying the history and culture of ancient Sumer (c. 4000–2000 B.C.). "The Sumerologist," he remarked, "more than most other scholars and specialists, is in a position to satisfy man's universal quest for origins — for 'firsts' in the history of civilization." Kramer's History Begins at Sumer recounts twenty-seven of these "firsts."

The father begins by asking his son:
"Where did you go?"
"I did not go anywhere."
"If you did not go anywhere, why do you idle about? Go to school,

Source: Samuel N. Kramer, *From the Tablets of Sumer*, Indian Hills, Colorado: The Falcon's Wing Press; and reprinted as *History Begins at Sumer*, New York: Doubleday Anchor Books, 1959, pp. 13–16. Reprinted by permission of The Falcon's Wing Press.

24

stand before your 'school-father,' recite your assignment, open your schoolbag, write your tablet, let your 'big brother' write your new tablet for you. After you have finished your assignment and reported to your monitor, come to me, and do not wander about in the street. Come now, do you know what I said?"

"I know, I'll tell it to you."

"Come, now, repeat it to me."

"I'll repeat it to you."

"Tell it to me. Come on, tell it to me."

"You told me to go to school, recite my assignment, open my schoolbag, write my tablet, while my 'big brother' is to write my new tablet. After finishing my assignment, I am to proceed to my work and to come to you after I have reported to my monitor. That's what you told me."

The father now continues with a long monologue:

"Come now, be a man. Don't stand about in the public square, or wander about the boulevard. When walking in the street, don't look all around. Be humble and show fear before your monitor. When you show terror, the monitor will like you.

"You who wander about in the public square, would you achieve success? Then seek out the first generations. Go to school, it will be of benefit to you. My son, seek out the first generations, inquire of them. . . .

"I never sent you to work, to plow my field. I never sent you to work to dig up my field. I never sent you to work as a laborer. 'Go, work and support me,' I never in my life said to you.

"Others like you support their parents by working. If you spoke to your kin and appreciated them, you would emulate them. They provide ten gur (seventy-two bushels) barley each — even the young ones provided their fathers with ten gur each. They multiplied barley for their father, maintained him in barley, oil, and wool. But you, you're a man when it comes to perverseness, but compared to them you are not a man at all. You certainly don't labor like them — they are the sons of fathers who make their sons labor, but me — I didn't make you work like them.

"Perverse one with whom I am furious — who is the man who can really be furious with his son — I spoke to my kin and found something hitherto unnoticed. The words which I shall relate to you, fear them and be on your guard because of them. Your partner, your yokemate —

25

you failed to appreciate him; why do you not emulate him? Your friend, your companion — you failed to appreciate him; why do you not emulate him? Emulate your older brother. Emulate your younger brother. Among all mankind's craftsmen who dwell in the land, as many as Enki [the god of arts and crafts] called by name [brought into existence], no work as difficult as the scribal art did he call by name. For if not for song — like the banks of the sea, the banks of the distant canals, is the heart of song distant — you wouldn't be listening to my counsel, and I wouldn't be repeating to you the wisdom of my father. It is in accordance with the fate decreed by Enlil [the god of storms] for man that a son follows the work of his father.

"Night and day am I tortured because of you. Night and day you waste in pleasures. You have accumulated much wealth, have expanded far and wide, have become fat, big, broad, powerful, and puffed. But your kin waits expectantly for your misfortune, and will rejoice at it because you looked not to your humanity."

The Hebrews Hear the Word of God

The major contribution of the early Hebrews to Western tradition was in the field of religion. According to the biblical account, the development of Hebrew monotheism begins with Abram, the eldest son of a Mesopotamian family that moved to Canaan in the twentieth century b.c. Abram broke from his family's religion of many gods and devoted himself to the worship of the one God. The Bible further states that God had chosen to give the land of Canaan to Abram and his descendants — a promise that was sealed by a covenant between God and Abram. Abram's name was changed to Abraham, implying "father of many nations." The covenant was reaffirmed by God with Isaac and Jacob, Abraham's son and grandson.

To escape famine conditions in Canaan, Jacob and his family moved to Egypt. After some time there, the Hebrews began to suffer cruel treatment at the hands of the Egyptians, who enslaved and oppressed them. Between the fifteenth and thirteenth centuries B.C. (the exact date is uncertain) the Hebrews, under the leadership of Moses, who came to them as the agent of God, rebelled against their masters and fled.

After the Exodus from Egypt, Moses prepared the people for receiving God's law. At the foot of Mount Sinai an extraordinary event took place. God made another covenant with the people of Israel. They would be a "kingdom of priests" and a "holy nation," but they must keep God's commandments. The Hebrews willingly accepted this burden. Though they frequently returned to idolatry, the idea of one God, all powerful, demanding obedience to His laws, remained central to the Hebrew faith.

The first selection deals with the covenant with Abraham; the second is the story of the Ten Commandments, followed by excerpts from the Law of Moses.

The Covenant with Abraham

When Abram was ninety-nine years old the Lord appeared to Abram, and said to him, "I am God Almighty; walk before me, and be blameless. And I will make my covenant between me and you, and will multiply you exceedingly." Then Abram fell on his face; and God said to him, "Behold, my covenant is with you, and you shall be the father of a multitude of nations. No longer shall your name be Abram, but your name shall be Abraham; for I have made you the father of a multitude of nations. I will make you exceedingly fruitful; and I will make nations of you, and kings shall come forth from you. And I will establish my covenant between me and you and your descendants after you throughout their generations for an everlasting covenant, to be God to you and to your descendants after you. And I will give to you, and to your descendants after you, the land of your sojournings, all the land of Canaan, for an everlasting possession; and I will be their God."

The Ten Commandments

On the morning of the third day there were thunders and lightnings, and a thick cloud upon the mountain, and a very loud trumpet

THE COVENANT WITH ABRAHAM. Source: Gen. 17:1–8, from the Revised Standard Version of the Bible, copyright 1946, 1952, by the Division of Christian Education, National Council of Churches, and used by permission.

blast, so that all the people who were in the camp trembled. Then Moses brought the people out of the camp to meet God; and they took their stand at the foot of the mountain. And Mount Sinai was wrapped in smoke, because the Lord descended upon it in fire; and the smoke of it went up like the smoke of a kiln, and the whole mountain quaked greatly. And as the sound of the trumpet grew louder and louder, Moses spoke, and God answered him in thunder. And the Lord came down upon Mount Sinai, to the top of the mountain; and the Lord called Moses to the top of the mountain, and Moses went up. And the Lord said to Moses, "Go down and warn the people, lest they break through to the Lord to gaze and many of them perish. And also let the priests who come near to the Lord consecrate themselves, lest the Lord break out upon them." And Moses said to the Lord, "The people cannot come up to Mount Sinai; for thou thyself didst charge us, saying, 'Set bounds about the mountain, and consecrate it.' " And the Lord said to him, "Go down, and come up bringing Aaron with you; but do not let the priests and the people break through to come up to the Lord, lest he break out against them." So Moses went down to the people and told them.

And God spoke all these words, saying,

"I am the Lord your God, who brought you out of the land of Egypt, out of the house of bondage.

"You shall have no other gods before me.

"You shall not make yourself a graven image, or any likeness of anything that is in heaven above, or that is in the earth beneath, or that is in the water under the earth; you shall not bow down to them or serve them; for I the Lord your God am a jealous God, visiting the iniquity of the fathers upon the children to the third and the fourth generation of those who hate me, but showing steadfast love to thousands of those who love me and keep my commandments.

"You shall not take the name of the Lord your God in vain; for the Lord will not hold him guiltless who takes his name in vain.

"Remember the sabbath day, to keep it holy. Six days you shall labor, and do all your work; but the seventh day is a sabbath to the Lord

THE TEN COMMANDMENTS. Source: Exod. 19:16—20:17; 21:1, 12–15, 17; 22:1, 7, 8, 21, 22; 23:1, 2, 6, 8, from the Revised Standard Version of the Bible, copyright 1946, 1952, by the Division of Christian Education, National Council of Churches, and used by permission.

your God; in it you shall not do any work, you, or your son, or your daughter, your manservant, or your maidservant, or your cattle, or the sojourner who is within your gates; for in six days the Lord made heaven and earth, the sea, and all that is in them, and rested the seventh day; therefore the Lord blessed the sabbath day and hallowed it.

"Honor your father and your mother, that your days may be long in the land which the Lord your God gives you.

"You shall not kill.

"You shall not commit adultery.

"You shall not steal.

"You shall not bear false witness against your neighbor.

"You shall not covet your neighbor's house; you shall not covet your neighbor's wife, or his manservant, or his maidservant, or his ox, or his ass, or anything that is your neighbor's."

[The Lord said to Moses:]
"Now these are the ordinances which you shall set before them [the children of Israel]. . . .

"Whoever strikes a man so that he dies shall be put to death. But if he did not lie in wait for him, but God let him fall into his hand, then I will appoint for you a place to which he may flee. But if a man willfully attacks another to kill him treacherously, you shall take him from my altar, that he may die.

"Whoever strikes his father or his mother shall be put to death. . . .

"Whoever curses his father or his mother shall be put to death. . . .

"If a man steals an ox or a sheep, and kills it or sells it, he shall pay five oxen for an ox, and four sheep for a sheep. . . .

"If a man delivers to his neighbor money or goods to keep, and it is stolen out of the man's house, then, if the thief is found, he shall pay double.

"If the thief is not found, the owner of the house shall come near to God, to show whether or not he has put his hand to his neighbor's goods. . . .

"You shall not wrong a stranger or oppress him, for you were strangers in the land of Egypt. You shall not afflict any widow or orphan. . . .

"You shall not utter a false report. You shall not join hands with a wicked man, to be a malicious witness. You shall not follow a multitude to do evil. . . .

"You shall not pervert the justice due to your poor in his suit. . . . And you shall take no bribe, for a bribe blinds the officials, and subverts the cause of those who are in the right."

Isaiah Counsels the Hebrews

The Hebrew idea of God and God's relationship to man is fully developed and majestically expressed in the writings of the prophets. The prophets were individuals who felt called upon to speak the word of God and to warn the people of the terrible punishment in store for them for their transgressions against God. At the same time they were astute political advisors.

Of all ancient people it is only among the Hebrews that we find the institution of the prophet. Isaiah was one of the most eloquent of the prophets. He cried out against useless political alliances and implored the Hebrews to seek strength by putting their faith in the Lord.

But now thus says the Lord, he who created you, O Jacob,
    he who formed you, O Israel:
"Fear not, for I have redeemed you;
    I have called you by name, you are mine.
When you pass through the waters I will be with you;
    and through the rivers, they shall not overwhelm you;
when you walk through fire you shall not be burned,
    and the flame shall not consume you.
For I am the Lord your God, the Holy One of Israel,
    your Savior.
I give Egypt as your ransom,
    Ethiopia and Seba in exchange for you.

Source: Isa. 43:1–7; 44:6–8, from the Revised Standard Version of the Bible, copyright 1946, 1952, by the Division of Christian Education, National Council of Churches, and used by permission.

Because you are precious in my eyes,
        and honored, and I love you,
I give men in return for you,
        peoples in exchange for your life.
Fear not, for I am with you;
        I will bring your offspring from the east,
        and from the west I will gather you;
I will say to the north, Give up,
        and to the south, Do not withhold;
bring my sons from afar
        and my daughters from the end of the earth,
every one who is called by my name,
        whom I created for my glory,
        whom I formed and made.". . .
Thus says the Lord, the King of Israel
        and his Redeemer, the Lord of hosts:
"I am the first and I am the last;
        besides me there is no god.
Who is like me? Let him proclaim it,
        let him declare and set it forth before me.
Who has announced from of old the things to come?
        Let them tell us what is yet to be.
Fear not, nor be afraid; have I not told you from of old
        and declared it?
        And you are my witnesses!
Is there a God besides me?
        There is no Rock; I know not any."

PART TWO

The Classical World

The Severity of
Spartan Life and Training

Greek political and cultural life was centered in the city-state,
which was intensely patriotic and often geographically isolated
from its neighbors. One of the strongest city-states was Sparta,
the capital of Laconia.

The laws of Sparta were designed to isolate it from outside
influence, to render it immune from internal corruption, and
to protect it from its large, oppressed slave population. The
Spartiates, or citizens, who numbered no more than ten per-
cent of the total population, had to undergo long and vigorous
military training. Moreover, the lives of the citizens were closely
controlled by the government.

Sparta's austerity, its civic patriotism, its athletic and military feats, and its "laconic" manner made it an object of admiration, especially in the days when corruption destroyed
political life in other city-states. Sparta, for a long time, was
able to maintain an efficient government and an almost unbeatable army, but its cultural contributions were very few.

The following selection is from the writings of Xenophon
(431–354 B.C.), an Athenian historian and soldier, who was a
friend and pupil of Socrates.

I recall the astonishment with which I first noted the unique
position of Sparta among the states of Hellas [Greece], the relatively
sparse population, and at the same time the extraordinary power and
prestige of the community. I was puzzled to account for the fact. It was
only when I came to consider the peculiar institutions of the Spartans
that my wonderment ceased. Or rather, it is transferred to the legislator who gave them those laws, obedience to which has been the secret

Source: Francis R. B. Godolphin, editor, *The Greek Historians*, New York:
Random House, Inc., 1942, Vol. I, pp. 648–53. Reprinted by permission of the
publishers.

of their prosperity. This legislator, Lycurgus, I admire, and hold him to have been one of the wisest of mankind. . . .

Take for example — and it is well to begin at the beginning — the whole topic of the . . . rearing of children. Throughout the rest of the world, the young girl who will one day become a mother (and I speak of those who may be held to be well brought up) is nurtured on the plainest food attainable, with the scantiest addition of meat or other condiments; while as to wine they train them either to total abstinence or to take it highly diluted with water. And . . . we, the rest of the Hellenes, are content that our girls should sit quietly and work wools. That is all we demand of them. But how are we to expect that women nurtured in this fashion should produce a splendid off-spring?

Lycurgus pursued a different path. . . . He insisted on the training of the body as incumbent no less on the female than the male, and in pursuit of the same idea instituted rival contests in running and feats of strength for women as for men. His belief was that where both parents were strong, their progeny [children] would be found to be more vigorous. . . .

I wish now to explain the systems of education in fashion here and elsewhere. Throughout the rest of Hellas the custom on the part of those who claim to educate their sons in the best way is as follows. As soon as the children are of an age to understand what is said to them, they are immediately placed under the charge of *paidogogoi* (or tutors) who are also attendants, and sent off to the school of some teacher to be taught grammar [and] music. . . . Besides this they are given shoes to wear which tend to make their feet tender, and their bodies are [softened] by various changes of clothing. And as for food, the only measure recognized is that which is fixed by appetite.

But when we turn to Lycurgus, instead of leaving it to each member of the state privately to appoint a slave to be his son's tutor, he set over the young Spartans a public guardian . . . with complete authority over them. This guardian was selected from those who filled the highest magistracies. He had authority to hold musters of the boys and as their overseer, in case of any misbehavior, to chastise severely. The legislator further provided the pastor with a body of youths in the prime of life, and bearing whips, to inflict punishment when necessary, with this happy result that in Sparta modesty and obedience ever go hand in hand, nor is there lack of either.

Instead of softening their feet with shoe or sandal, his rule was to make them hardy through going barefoot. This habit . . . would, . . . he believed, enable them to scale heights more easily and clamber down precipices with less danger. In fact, with his feet so trained, the young Spartan would leap and spring and run faster unshod than another shod in the ordinary way.

Instead of making them effeminate with a variety of clothes, his rule was to habituate them to a single garment the whole year through, thinking that so they would be better prepared to withstand the variations of heat and cold.

Again, as regards food, according to his regulation the prefect, or head of the flock, must see that his messmates gathered to the club meal, with such moderate food as to avoid that heaviness which is engendered by repletion [having one's fill], and yet not to remain altogether unacquainted with the pains of penurious [poor] living. His belief was that by such training in boyhood they would be better able when occasion demanded to continue toiling on an empty stomach. They would be all the fitter, if the word of command were given, to remain on the stretch for a long time without extra dieting. The craving for luxuries would be less, the readiness to take any victual set before them greater, and in general the regime would be found more healthy. . . .

Furthermore, and in order that the boys should not [lack] a ruler, even in case the guardian himself were absent, he gave to any citizen who chanced to be present authority to lay upon them injunctions for their good, and to chastise them for any trespass committed. By so doing he created in the boys of Sparta a most rare modesty and reverence. And indeed there is nothing which, whether as boys or men, they respect more highly than the ruler. . . .

Furthermore, in his desire firmly to implant modesty in them he imposed a special rule. In the streets they were to keep their hands within the folds of the cloak; they were to walk in silence and without turning their heads to gaze, but rather to keep their eyes fixed upon the ground before them. And hereby it would seem to be proved conclusively that even in the matter of quiet bearing and sobriety the masculine type may claim greater strength than that which we attribute to the nature of women. At any rate, you might sooner expect a stone image to find voice than one of those Spartan youths; to divert the eyes of some bronze statue were less difficult. . . .

It would be hard to discover a healthier or more completely developed human being, physically speaking, than the Spartan. Their gymnastic training, in fact, makes demands alike on the legs, arms, and neck equally.

There are other points in which this legislator's views run counter to those commonly accepted. Thus: in other states the individual citizen is master over his own children, servants, and belongings generally; but Lycurgus, whose aim was to secure to all the citizens a considerable share in one another's goods without mutual injury, enacted that each one should have an equal power over his neighbor's children as over his own. The principle is this. When a man knows that this, that, and the other person are fathers of children subject to his own authority, he must perforce deal by them even as he desires his own children to be dealt by. And if a boy chance to have received a whipping, not from his own father but some other, and goes and complains to his own father, it would be thought wrong on the part of that father if he did not inflict a second whipping on his son. A striking proof, in its way, how completely they trust each other not to impose dishonorable commands upon their children. . . .

There are yet other customs in Sparta which Lycurgus instituted in opposition to those of the rest of Hellas, the following among them. We all know that in the generality of states everyone devotes his full energy to the business of making money: one man as a tiller of the soil, another as a mariner, a third as a merchant, while others depend on various arts to earn a living. But at Sparta Lycurgus forbade his freeborn citizens to have anything whatsoever to do with the concerns of moneymaking. As freemen, he enjoined upon them to regard as their concern exclusively those activities upon which the foundations of civic liberty are based.

And indeed, one may well ask, for what reason should wealth be regarded as a matter for serious pursuit in a community where, partly by a system of equal contributions to the necessaries of life, and partly by the maintenance of a common standard of living, the lawgiver placed so effectual a check upon the desire for riches for the sake of luxury? What inducement, for instance, would there be to make money, even for the sake of wearing apparel, in a state where personal adornment is held to lie not in the costliness of the clothes they wear, but in the healthy condition of the body to be clothed?

The Glory of Athens

Few great states have made so brilliant and lasting a contribution to our civilization as the city-state of Athens in the sixth and fifth centuries B.C. In sculpture, in architecture, in drama, and in government, the accomplishments of Athens were spectacular. For the Athenian citizen, life was a splendid and enriching experience.

This is not the whole picture, however. Much of the leisure of Athenians was built on the work of slaves, who made up about half the population of the city. Most of the slaves were well treated, but those who worked for the state, especially in the mines, lived hard and short lives. A considerable portion of Athenian splendor of the fifth century B.C. was built with tribute money levied on the hundreds of subject states in the Athenian empire.

Athens, the great sea power of Greece and the leader in Greek culture, was the envy and natural antagonist of conservative Sparta, the great land power. In 431 B.C. a war broke out between them; it lasted until 404 B.C. and involved nearly all Greece. Sparta emerged the victor, but Greece as a whole was the loser, for the city-states were exhausted and were never able to regain their former vitality.

In 429 B.C. the leading Athenian statesman, Pericles, in a funeral oration over the Athenian dead, gave us a most vivid portrait of the Athenian ideal in life. The speech is recorded in the History of the Peloponnesian War by Thucydides, who was in many ways a model historian. Though he himself was an Athenian general, Thucydides strove for impartiality and accuracy in his account.

Of the military exploits by which our various possessions were acquired, or of the energy with which we or our fathers drove back the tide of war, Hellenic or barbarian,* I will not speak; for the tale would

* **barbarian:** The Greeks referred to all non-Greek peoples as barbarians. The word literally means "foreigners."

Source: Francis R. B. Godolphin, editor, The Greek Historians, New York: Random House, Inc., 1942, Vol. II, pp. 658–66. Reprinted by permission of the publishers.

be long and is familiar to you. But before I praise the dead, I should like to point out by what principles of action we rose to power, and under what institutions and through what manner of life our empire became great. For I conceive that such thoughts are not unsuited to the occasion, and that this numerous assembly of citizens and strangers may profitably listen to them.

Our form of government does not enter into rivalry with the institutions of others. We do not copy our neighbors but are an example to them. It is true that we are called a democracy, for the administration is in the hands of the many and not of the few. But while the law secures equal justice to all alike in their private disputes, the claim of excellence is also recognized; and when a citizen is in any way distinguished, he is preferred to the public service, not as a matter of privilege, but as the reward of merit. Neither is poverty a bar, but a man may benefit his country whatever be the obscurity of his condition. There is no exclusiveness in our public life, and in our private [life] we are not suspicious of one another, nor angry with our neighbor if he does what he likes; we do not put on sour looks at him which, though harmless, are not pleasant. While we are thus unconstrained in our private [lives], a spirit of reverence pervades our public acts; we are prevented from doing wrong by respect for authority and for the laws, having an especial regard to those which are ordained for the protection of the injured as well as to those unwritten laws which bring upon the transgressor of them the reprobation [disapproval] of the general sentiment.

And we have not forgotten to provide for our weary spirits many relaxations from toil; we have regular games . . . throughout the year; at home the style of our life is refined; and the delight which we daily feel in all these things helps to banish melancholy. Because of the greatness of our city, the fruits of the whole earth flow in upon us, so that we enjoy the goods of other countries as freely as of our own.

Then again, our military training is in many respects superior to that of our adversaries. Our city is thrown open to the world, and we never expel a foreigner or prevent him from seeing or learning anything of which the secret if revealed to an enemy might profit him. We rely not upon management or trickery, but upon our own hearts and hands. And in the matter of education, whereas they from early youth are always undergoing laborious exercises which are to make them brave, we live at ease and yet are equally ready to face the perils which they face. And here is the proof. The Lacedaemonians come into Attica not by themselves but with their whole confederacy following; we go alone into a neighbor's country; and although our opponents are fighting for their homes and we on a foreign soil, we have seldom any difficulty in overcoming them. . . .

If then we prefer to meet danger with a light heart but without laborious training, and with a courage which is gained by habit and not enforced by law, are we not greatly the gainers? We do not anticipate the pain, [but] when the hour comes, we can be as brave as those who never allow themselves to rest; and thus too our city is equally admirable in peace and in war. . . .

We are lovers of the beautiful, yet with economy, and we cultivate the mind without loss of manliness. Wealth we employ not for talk and ostentation, but when there is a real use for it. To avow poverty with us is no disgrace; the true disgrace is in doing nothing to avoid it. An Athenian citizen does not neglect the state because he takes care of his own household; and even those of us who are engaged in business have a very fair idea of politics. We alone regard a man who takes no interest in public affairs not as a harmless but as a useless character; and if few of us are originators, we are all sound judges of a policy. The great impediment to action is, in our opinion, not discussion, but the want of that knowledge which is gained by discussion preparatory to action. . . . We have a peculiar power of thinking before we act and of acting too, whereas other men are courageous from ignorance but hesitate upon reflection. And they are surely to be esteemed the bravest spirits who, having the clearest sense both of the pains and pleasures of life, do not on that account shrink from danger. In doing good, again, we are unlike others; we make our friends by conferring, not by receiving favors. Now he who confers a favor is the firmer friend, because he would fain by kindness keep alive the memory of an obligation; but the recipient is colder in his feelings, because he knows that in [repaying] another's generosity he will not be winning gratitude but only paying a debt. We alone do good to our neighbors not upon calculation of interest, but in the confidence of freedom and in a frank and fearless spirit.

To sum up: I say that Athens is the school of Hellas, and that the individual Athenian in his own person seems to have the power of adapting himself to the most varied forms of action with the utmost versatility and grace. This is no passing and idle word, but truth and fact; and the assertion is verified by the position to which these qualities have raised the state. . . . In the hour of trial Athens alone among her contemporaries is superior to the report of her. No enemy who comes against her is indignant at the reverses which he sustains at the hands of such a city; no subject complains that his masters are unworthy of him. And we shall assuredly not be without witnesses; there are mighty monuments of our power which will make us the wonder of this and of succeeding ages. . . . We have compelled every land and every sea to open a path for our valor, and have everywhere planted eternal memorials of our friendship and of our enmity. Such is the city for whose sake these men nobly fought and died; they could not bear the thought that she might be taken from them; and every one of us who survives should gladly toil on her behalf.

I have dwelt upon the greatness of Athens because I want to show you that we are contending for a higher prize than those who enjoy none of these privileges, and to establish by manifest proof the merit of these men whom I am now commemorating. Their loftiest praise has been already spoken. . . . In magnifying the city, I have magnified them, and men like them whose virtues made her glorious. And of how few Hellenes can it be said as of them, that their deeds when weighed in the balance have been found equal to their fame! It seems to me that a death such as theirs has been gives the true measure of a man's worth. . . . None of these men . . . hesitated to resign the pleasures of life; none of them put off the evil day in the hope, natural to poverty, that a man, though poor, may one day become rich. But, deeming that the punishment of their enemies was sweeter than any of these things, and that they could fall in no nobler cause, they determined at the hazard of their lives to be honorably avenged, and to leave the rest. They resigned to hope their unknown chance of happiness; but in the face of death they resolved to rely upon themselves alone. And when the moment came they were minded to resist and suffer, rather than to fly and save their lives; . . . on the battlefield their feet stood fast, and in an instant, at the height of their fortune, they passed away from the scene, not of their fear, but of their glory. . . .

I have paid the required tribute in obedience to the law, making use of such fitting words as I had. The tribute of deeds has been paid in part; for the dead have been honorably interred, and it remains only that their children should be maintained at the public charge until they are grown up: this is the solid prize with which, as with a garland,

Athens crowns her sons living and dead, after a struggle like theirs. . . .
Where the rewards of virtue are greatest, there the noblest citizens are
enlisted in the service of the state. And now, when you have duly la-
mented, everyone his own dead, you may depart.

The Defense and
Execution of Socrates

*The Greek mind was extraordinarily inquisitive. Greeks asked
basic questions about the nature of man, society, and the universe, and they were the first to search for rational answers.*

*However, not all Athenians appreciated the prodding in-
quisitiveness of the philosopher Socrates (c. 469–399 B.C.). The
great loss sustained by Athens in the Peloponnesian War had
made her especially touchy and suspicious of so unsettling an
influence. When the ruling clique in Athens indicted Socrates
for "impiety," Socrates refused to treat his accusers with respect.
After he was found guilty, he had the opportunity, according
to custom, of suggesting an alternative to the death penalty.
His proposal that he be given the equivalent of the key to the
city left his jurors little choice but to condemn him to death.
When his disciples offered to help him escape, he turned them
down on the grounds that he could not put himself above
the law.*

*The account of Socrates' defense and subsequent execution
is recorded by his pupil Plato, from whom we get most of our
information about Socrates.*

His Defense

"And here, O men of Athens, I must beg you not to interrupt
me, even if I seem to say something extravagant, for the word which
I will speak is not mine. I will refer you to a witness who is worthy of
credit; that witness shall be the god of Delphi — he will tell you about

HIS DEFENSE. Source: Plato, *Apology*, in *The Dialogues of Plato*, translated
by Benjamin Jowett, 3rd ed., London: Oxford University Press, 1892, Vol. II, pp.
112–15.

my wisdom, if I have any, and of what sort it is. You must have known Chaerephon; he was early a friend of mine, and also a friend of yours. . . . Well, Chaerephon, as you know, was very impetuous in all his doings, and he went to Delphi and boldly asked the oracle to tell him whether — as I was saying, I must beg you not to interrupt — he asked the oracle to tell him whether anyone was wiser than I was, and the Pythian [Delphic] prophetess answered that there was no man wiser. . . .

"Why do I mention this? Because I am going to explain to you why I have such an evil name. When I heard the answer, I said to myself, 'What can the god mean? and what is the interpretation of his riddle? for I know that I have no wisdom, small or great. What then can he mean when he says that I am the wisest of men? And yet he is a god, and cannot lie; that would be against his nature.' After long consideration, I thought of a method of trying the question. I reflected that if I could only find a man wiser than myself, then I might go to the god with a refutation in my hand. I should say to him, 'Here is a man who is wiser than I am; but you said that I was the wisest.' Accordingly I went to one who had the reputation of wisdom, and observed him — his name I need not mention; he was a politician whom I selected for examination — and the result was as follows: When I began to talk with him, I could not help thinking that he was not really wise, although he was thought wise by many, and still wiser by himself; and thereupon I tried to explain to him that he thought himself wise, but was not really wise; and the consequence was that he hated me, and his enmity was shared by several who were present and heard me. So I left him, saying to myself, as I went away: 'Well, although I do not suppose that either of us knows anything really beautiful and good, I am better off than he is, for he knows nothing, and thinks that he knows; I neither know nor think that I know. In this latter particular, then, I seem to have slightly the advantage of him. . . .'

"Then I went to one man after another, being not unconscious of the enmity which I provoked. . . . And I swear to you, Athenians . . . — for I must tell you the truth — the result of my mission was just this: I found that the men most in repute were all but the most foolish; and that others less esteemed were really wiser and better. . . .

"This inquisition has led to my having enemies of the worst and most dangerous kind, and has given occasion also to many calumnies. And I am called wise, for my hearers always imagine that I myself possess the wisdom which I find wanting in others; but the truth is, O men of Athens, that God only is wise; and by his answer he intends to show that the wisdom of men is worth little or nothing; he is not speaking of Socrates, he is only using my name by way of illustration, as if he said, 'He, O men, is the wisest, who, like Socrates, knows that his wisdom is in truth worth nothing. . . .' "

His Execution

Now the hour of sunset was near, for a good deal of time had passed while he was within. When he came out, he sat down with us again after his bath, but not much was said. Soon the jailer . . . entered and stood by him, saying: "To you, Socrates, whom I know to be the noblest and gentlest and best of all who ever came to this place, I will not impute the angry feelings of other men, who rage and swear at me, when, in obedience to the authorities, I bid them drink the poison — indeed, I am sure that you will not be angry with me; for others, as you are aware, and not I, are to blame. And so fare you well, and try to bear lightly what must needs be — you know my errand." Then bursting into tears he turned away and went out.

Socrates looked at him and said, "I return your good wishes, and will do as you bid." Then turning to us, he said: "How charming the man is. Since I have been in prison he has always been coming to see me, and at times he would talk to me, and was as good to me as could be, and now see how generously he sorrows on my account. We must do as he says . . . and therefore let the cup be brought, if the poison is prepared: if not, let the attendant prepare some.". . .

Crito made a sign to the servant who was standing by; and he went out, and having been absent for some time, returned with the jailer carrying the cup of poison. Socrates said, "You, my good friend, who are experienced in these matters, shall give me directions how I am to proceed." The man answered, "You have only to walk about until your legs are heavy and then to lie down, and the poison will act." At the same time he handed the cup to Socrates, who in the easiest and gentlest manner, without the least fear or change of color or feature . . . took the cup. . . . Then raising the cup to his lips, quite readily and

HIS EXECUTION. Source: Plato, *Phaedo*, in *The Dialogues of Plato*, translated by Benjamin Jowett, 3rd ed., London: Oxford University Press, 1892, Vol. II, pp. 264–66.

cheerfully he drank off the poison. Hitherto most of us had been able to control our sorrow, but now, when we saw him drinking, and saw too that he had finished the draught, we could no longer forbear, and in spite of myself my own tears were flowing fast, so that I covered my face and wept, not for him, but at the thought of my own calamity in having to part from such a friend. Nor was I the first, for Crito, when he found himself unable to restrain his tears, had got up, and I followed; and at that moment, Apollodorus, who had been weeping all the time, broke out in a loud and passionate cry which made cowards of us all. Socrates alone retained his calmness: "What is this strange outcry?" he said. "I sent away the women mainly in order that they might not misbehave in this way, for I have been told that a man should die in peace. Be quiet then, and have patience." When we heard his words we were ashamed, and refrained our tears; and he walked about until, as he said, his legs began to fail, and then he lay on his back, according to the directions. . . .

Such was the end . . . of our friend, concerning whom I may truly say that of all the men of his time whom I have known, he was the wisest and justest and best.

Hippocrates Advances the Science of Medicine

The curiosity of the Greeks and their rational approach to knowledge resulted in the accumulation of both interesting and useful data. This was especially true in the science of medicine as taught by Hippocrates (c. 460–377 B.C.). Hippocrates rejected both supernatural causes and magical cures of disease. In his medical school on the Island of Cos, he taught his students to observe with care and to keep accurate records of case histories. A pioneer in his field, and lacking proper instruments, he was bound to make serious errors, but his approach was fundamentally correct. Hippocrates also formulated a lofty code of behavior for medical practitioners. Graduating medical students still take the Oath of Hippocrates.

Prognostic

I hold that it is an excellent thing for a physician to practice forecasting. . . . If he discover and declare unaided by the side of his patients the present, the past, and the future, and fill in the gaps in the account given by the sick, he will be the more believed to understand the cases, so that men will confidently entrust themselves to him for treatment. . . .

In acute diseases the physician must conduct his inquiries in the following way. First he must examine the face of the patient, and see whether it is like the faces of healthy people, and especially whether it is like its usual self. Such likeness will be the best sign, and the greatest unlikeness will be the most dangerous sign. The latter will be as follows: nose sharp, eyes hollow, temples sunken, ears cold and contracted with their lobes turned outwards, the skin about the face hard and tense and parched, the color of the face as a whole being yellow or black.

Aphorisms

Life is short, art long, opportunity fleeting, experience treacherous, judgment difficult. The physician must be ready not only to do his duty himself, but also to secure the cooperation of the patient, [and] of the attendants. . . .

One ought to have an eye to season, district, age, and disease, to see if the treatment is, or is not, proper in the circumstances. . . .

Old men endure fasting most easily, then men of middle age, youths very badly, and worst of all children, especially those of a liveliness greater than the ordinary. . . .

A sloppy [liquid] diet is beneficial in all fevers, especially in the case of children and of those used to such a diet.

To some, food should be given once, to others twice; in greater quantity or in less quantity; a little at a time. Something too must be conceded to season, district, habit, and age. . . .

A disease in which sleep causes distress is a deadly one; but if sleep is beneficial, the disease is not deadly. . . .

Source: *Hippocrates*, translated by W. H. S. Jones, Cambridge, Mass.: Harvard University Press, Vol. I, pp. 299–301; Vol. II, pp. 7, 9; Vol. IV, pp. 99–131. Reprinted by permission of the publishers and the Loeb Classical Library.

Sleep or sleeplessness, in undue measure, these are both bad symptoms. . . .

In the case of acute diseases to predict either death or recovery is not quite safe. . . .

When a convalescent has a good appetite without improving his bodily condition it is a bad sign. . . .

In every disease it is a good sign when the patient's intellect is sound and he enjoys his food; the opposite is a bad sign. . . .

Those who are constitutionally very fat are more apt to die quickly than those who are thin. . . .

It is chiefly the changes of the seasons which produce diseases, and in the seasons the great changes from cold or heat, and so on according to the same rule.

Of constitutions some are well or ill adapted to summer, others are well or ill adapted to winter. . . .

All diseases occur at all seasons, but some diseases are more apt to occur and to be aggravated at certain seasons. . . .

In winter occur pleurisy, pneumonia, lethargus, colds, sore throat, coughs, pains in the sides, chest, and loins, headache, dizziness, apoplexy.

The Hippocratic Oath

I swear by Apollo Physician, by Asclepius, by Health, by Panacea, and by all the gods and goddesses, making them my witnesses, that I will carry out, according to my ability and judgment, this oath and this indenture. To hold my teacher in this art equal to my own parents; to make him partner in my livelihood; when he is in need of money to share mine with him; to consider his family as my own brothers, and to teach them this art, if they want to learn it, without fee or indenture; to impart precept, oral instruction, and all other instruction to my own sons, the sons of my teacher, and to indentured pupils who have taken the physician's oath, but to nobody else. I will use treatment to help the sick according to my ability and judgment, but never with a view to injury and wrongdoing. Neither will I administer poison to anybody when asked to do so, nor will I suggest such a course. . . . But I will keep pure and holy both my life and my art. . . . Into whatsoever houses I enter, I will enter to help the sick, and I will abstain from all

intentional wrongdoing and harm. . . . And whatsoever I shall see or
hear in the course of my profession, as well as outside my profession . . .
if it be what should not be published abroad, I will never divulge, holding such things to be holy secrets. Now if I carry out this oath and break
it not, may I gain forever reputation among all men for my life and for
my art; but if I transgress it and forswear myself, may the opposite be-
fall me.

The Political Ideals
of Aristotle

*The best students are not always those who accept without
question the word of their teachers. Plato's most brilliant pupil
was Aristotle (384–322 B.C.), whose ideas differed markedly
from those of his master.*

*Aristotle had a much greater interest than Plato in the
physical and biological world. Plato sought to discover the
world of ideas above and beyond the facts, whereas Aristotle
was interested in the facts themselves. Aristotle became one of
the first collectors and classifiers of knowledge. He stressed the
importance of observation and made original contributions in
such areas of thought as logic, ethics, poetry, biology, and phys-
ics. So great was his reputation that later scholars tended to accept his works uncritically.*

The following selections are from Aristotle's Politics.

The Origin and Nature of the State

He who considers things in their first growth and origin, whether
a state or anything else, will obtain the clearest view of them. . . . The
family is the association established by nature for the supply of men's
everyday wants. . . . But when several families are united, and the

Source: Aristotle, *Politics*, translated by Benjamin Jowett, in *The Works of
Aristotle*, edited by W. D. Ross, Oxford: The Clarendon Press, 1921, Vol. X, sections 1252, 1253, 1295, 1336, 1337.

association aims at something more than the supply of daily needs, the first society to be formed is the village. . . .

When several villages are united in a single complete community, large enough to be nearly or quite self-sufficing, the state comes into existence, originating in the bare needs of life, and continuing in existence for the sake of a good life. And therefore, if the earlier forms of society are natural, so is the state, for it is the end of them, and the nature of a thing is its end. . . .

Hence it is evident that the state is a creation of nature, and that man is by nature a political animal. And he who by nature and not by mere accident is without a state is either a bad man or above humanity; he is like the "Tribeless, lawless, heartless one," whom Homer denounces — the natural outcast is forthwith a lover of war. . . .

Now, that man is more of a political animal than bees or any other gregarious animals is evident. Nature, as we often say, makes nothing in vain, and man is the only animal whom she has endowed with the gift of speech. And whereas mere voice is but an indication of pleasure or pain, and is therefore found in other animals, . . . the power of speech is intended to set forth . . . the just and the unjust. And it is a characteristic of man that he alone has any sense of good and evil, of just and unjust, and the like, and the association of living beings who have this sense makes a family and a state. . . . A social instinct is implanted in all men by nature, and yet he who first founded the state was the greatest of benefactors. For man, when perfected, is the best of animals, but when separated from law and justice, he is the worst of all; since armed injustice is the more dangerous, and he is equipped at birth with arms, meant to be used by intelligence and virtue, which he may use for the worst ends. . . .

We have now to inquire what is the best constitution for most states and the best life for most men, neither assuming a standard of virtue which is above ordinary persons nor an education which is exceptionally favored by nature and circumstances, nor yet an ideal state which is an aspiration only, but having regard to the life in which the majority are able to share and to the form of government which states in general can attain. . . .

Now in all states there are three elements: one class is very rich, another very poor, and a third in a mean [the middle]. It is admitted that moderation and the mean are best . . . for in that condition of life men are most ready to follow rational principle. But he who greatly excels in beauty, strength, birth, or wealth, or on the other hand who is very poor, or very weak, or very much disgraced, finds it difficult to follow rational principle. Of these two the one sort grow into violent and great criminals, the others into rogues and petty rascals. . . . The middle class is least likely to shrink from rule, or to be overambitious for it; both of which are injuries to the state. . . . But a city ought to be composed, as far as possible, of equals and similars; and these are generally the middle classes. . . .

Thus it is manifest that the best political community is formed by citizens of the middle class, and that those states are likely to be well administered in which the middle class is large, and stronger if possible than both the other classes, or at any rate than either singly; for the addition of the middle class turns the scale, and prevents either of the extremes from being dominant. . . .

The Education of Youth

After the children have been born, the manner of rearing them may be supposed to have a great effect on their bodily strength. It would appear from the example of animals, and of those nations who desire to create the military habit, that the food which has most milk in it is best suited to human beings; but the less wine the better, if they would escape diseases. Also all the motions to which children can be subjected at their early age are very useful. But in order to preserve their tender limbs from distortion, some nations have had recourse to mechanical appliances which straighten their bodies. To accustom children to the cold from their earliest years is also an excellent practice, which greatly conduces to health, and hardens them for military service. Hence many barbarians have a custom of plunging their children at birth into a cold stream; others, like the Celts, clothe them in a light wrapper only. . . . Human nature should be early habituated to endure all which by habit it can be made to endure; but the process must be gradual. And children, from their natural warmth, may be easily trained to bear cold. Such care should attend them in the first stage of life.

The next period lasts to the age of five; during this no demand should be made upon the child for study or labor, lest its growth be impeded; and there should be sufficient motion to prevent the limbs from being inactive. . . . The directors of education, as they are termed, should be careful what tales or stories the children hear, for all such things are designed to prepare the way for the business of later life, and should be for the most part imitations of the occupations which they will hereafter pursue in earnest. . . .

No one will doubt that the legislator should direct his attention above all to the education of youth; for the neglect of education does harm to the constitution. The citizen should be molded to suit the form of government under which he lives, for each government has a peculiar character which originally formed and which continues to preserve it. The character of democracy creates democracy, and the character of oligarchy creates oligarchy; and always the better the character, the better the government.

Again, for the exercise of any faculty or art a previous training and habituation are required; clearly therefore for the practice of virtue. And since the whole city has one end, it is manifest that education should be one and the same for all, and that it should be public, and not private — not as at present, when everyone looks after his own children separately, and gives them separate instruction of the sort which he thinks best; the training in things which are of common interest should be the same for all. Neither must we suppose that any one of the citizens belongs to himself, for they all belong to the state, and are each of them a part of the state, and the care of each part is inseparable from the care of the whole. In this particular as in some others the Lacedaemonians are to be praised, for they take the greatest pains about their children, and make education the business of the state.

Alexander Calls for Harmony and Fellowship

Fact and myth will forever be mingled in our knowledge of Alexander of Macedon (356–323 B.C.). At his death at the age of thirty-three, he was ruler of an enormous empire and already a legendary figure. What he wished to accomplish, however, and how much he would have been able to accomplish had he lived are still matters of debate and conjecture.

His father Philip left him an orderly state and a superb army, which had already subdued the Greek cities. Alexander himself was an imaginative general and an inspiring leader. As a young man he had been tutored by the philosopher Aristotle. On his voyages and campaigns he invited along teams of scientists to collect data.

In the area of human relations, Alexander did not adhere to Aristotle's teaching, which drew so sharp a distinction between Greek and non-Greek. He was an admirer of Greek culture and spread it throughout the world. He also came to appreciate the culture of the East. What has intrigued men most about Alexander was his attempt to fuse the two cultures and to inaugurate an era where all men would be brothers and all would live in harmony as citizens of one world.

The following account by Arrian, written in the second century A.D., *was based on earlier sources.*

On reaching Opis, Alexander summoned his Macedonians and announced that those who from old age or from mutilations were unfit for service be there discharged from the army; and he sent them to their own homes. He promised to give them on departure enough to make them objects of greater envy to those at home, and also stir up the rest of the Macedonians to a zeal for sharing his own dangers and toils. Alexander . . . said this no doubt to flatter the Macedonians; they, however, feeling that Alexander rather despised them by this time and regarded them as altogether useless for warfare, quite naturally . . . were annoyed at his remarks, having been annoyed during this whole campaign with a great deal else, since he caused them indignation frequently by his Persian dress . . . and the Macedonian equipment . . . and the importation of cavalry of foreign tribes into the ranks of the Companions.* They did not, then, restrain themselves and keep silence, but called upon him to release them all from the army. . . . When . . . Alexander heard this — for he had grown worse-tempered at that time — he leaped down from the platform with the officers that were about him and bade them arrest the foremost of those

* **Companions:** personal troops of the king.

Source: Arrian, *The Anabasis of Alexander*, translated by E. Iliff Robson, Cambridge, Mass.: Harvard University Press, Vol. II, pp. 225–41. Reprinted by permission of the publishers and the Loeb Classical Library.

who had disturbed the multitude, himself with his finger pointing out to the guards whom they were to arrest; they were in number thirteen. These he ordered to be marched off to die; but as the others, amazed, remained in dead silence, he remounted the platform and spoke thus:

"I now propose to speak, Macedonians, not with a view to checking your homeward impulse (so far as I am concerned, you may go where you will) but that you may know, if you do so go away, how you have behaved to us, and how we have behaved to you. . . .

"I set forth from that country [Macedon] which hardly maintained you in comfort and at once opened to you the strait of the Hellespont, though the Persians were then masters of the sea; then . . . I added to your empire all Ionia, all Aeolia, Upper and Lower Phrygia, and Lydia; Miletus I took by siege; all else I took by surrender and gave to you to reap the fruits thereof. All good things from Egypt and Cyrene, which I took without striking a blow, come to you; the Syrian Valley and Palestine and Mesopotamia are your own possessions; Babylon is yours, Bactria, and Susa; the wealth of Lydia, the treasures of Persia, the good things of India, the outer ocean, all are yours. . . . So what is left for myself from all these toils save the purple * and this diadem? † I have taken nothing to myself, nor can anyone show treasures of mine, save these possessions of yours or what is being safeguarded for you. For there is nothing as concerns myself for which I should reserve them, since I eat the same food that you eat, and have such sleep as you have — and yet I hardly think that I do eat the same food as some of you who live delicately; I know, moreover, that I wake before you, that you may sleep quietly in your beds.

"Yet you may feel that while you were enduring the toils and distresses, I have acquired all this without toil and without distress. But who of you is conscious of having endured more toil for me than I for him? Or see here, let any who carries wounds strip himself and show them; I too will show mine. For I have no part of my body, in front at least, that is left without scars; there is no weapon, used at close quarters or hurled from afar, of which I do not carry the mark. Nay, I have been wounded by the sword, hand to hand; I have been shot with arrows, I have been struck from a catapult, smitten many a time with stones and clubs, for you, for your glory, for your wealth; I led you

---

* **the purple:** imperial rank or power. A purple robe was worn as an emblem of rank or authority.
† **diadem:** crown.

conquerors through every land, every sea, every river, mountain, plain. I married as you married; * the children of many of you will be blood relations of my children. Moreover, if any had debts, I, being no busybody to inquire how they were made when you were winning so much pay and acquiring so much plunder whenever there was plunder after a siege — I have canceled them all. . . . Whosoever has died, his death has been glorious; and splendid has been his burial; . . . [his] parents are held in esteem, and have been freed from all services and taxes. . . . While I have led you, not one of you has fallen in flight.

"And now I had in mind to send away those of you who are no longer equal to campaigning, to be the envy of all at home; but since you all wish to go home, depart, all of you; and when you reach home, tell them there that this your King, Alexander, victor over Persians, Medes, Bactrians . . . — tell them, I say, that you deserted him, that you took yourselves off, leaving him to the care of the wild tribes you had conquered. This, when you declare it, will be, no doubt, glorious among men, and pious in the sight of heaven. Begone!"

When Alexander had finished, he leaped down swiftly from his platform and passed into the palace, . . . nor was he seen by any of the Companions; and indeed, not even on the day following. But on the third day he summoned within the picked men among the Persians, and divided among them the command of the different brigades. . . . The Macedonians, however, were at the time much moved on hearing his speech, and remained in silence there around the platform; yet no one followed the King when he departed save his personal Companions and the bodyguards; but the mass while remaining there neither had anything to do or say, nor were willing to depart. But when they heard about the Persians and the Medes, and the handing of commands to the Persians, and the Oriental force being drafted into the various ranks, and a Persian squadron called by a Macedonian name, and of Persian "infantry Companions," and others too, and a Persian company of "silver shields," and "cavalry of the Companions," and a new royal squadron: . . . they could no longer contain [themselves], but running all together to the palace they threw their arms before the doors as signs of supplication to the King; they themselves standing shouting before the doors begging to be let in. The instigators of the late disturbance and those who began the cry . . . said they would

* Alexander's wife was a Persian princess and it is this marriage to which he refers.

give up; in fact they would depart from the doors neither day nor night unless Alexander would have some pity on them.

When this was reported to Alexander, he at once came out; and seeing them so humble, and hearing most of the number crying and lamenting, he also shed tears. Then he came forward as if to speak, and they continued beseeching. And one of them, a notable officer of the Companions' cavalry both by age and rank, called Callines, said thus: "This, O King, is what grieves the Macedonians, that you have made Persians your kinsmen and Persians are called 'Alexander's kinsmen,' and they are permitted to kiss you; but no Macedonian has tasted this privilege."

On this Alexander broke in: "But all of you I regard as my kinsmen, and so from henceforth I call you." When thus he had spoken, Callines approached and kissed him, and any other who desired to kiss him. And thus they took up their arms again and returned shouting and singing their victory song to the camp. But Alexander in gratitude for this sacrificed to the gods to whom he was wont to sacrifice, and gave a general feast, sitting himself there, and all the Macedonians sitting round him; and then next to them Persians, and next any of the other tribes who had precedence in reputation or any other quality, and he himself and his comrades drank from the same bowl and poured the same libations, while the Greek seers . . . began the ceremony. And Alexander prayed for all sorts of blessings, and especially for harmony and fellowship in the empire between Macedonians and Persians.

Archimedes Discovers the Principle of Specific Gravity

Greek culture grew and flourished in the Mediterranean world long after the political life of the ancient city-states had decayed and their freedom had been lost. The intellectual center of this wider Hellenistic world was Alexandria, a wealthy and cosmopolitan commercial city with a magnificent library and museum. The Greek mind continued to be creative, especially

*in the sciences, where specialization and experimentation pro-
duced rich results.*

*The most inventive of the Hellenistic scientists was Archi-
medes of Syracuse, who conducted numerous experiments and
calculations, often with an eye to their practical application.
Archimedes (c. 287–212 B.C.) was responsible for a number of
inventions as well as many discoveries, including the law of the
pulley and the value of "pi." The remarkable story of his discovery of the law of specific gravity, which became known as
Archimedes' Principle, is told by Vitruvius, who wrote in the
first century A.D.*

In the case of Archimedes, although he made many wonderful
discoveries of diverse kinds, yet of them all, the following, which I shall
relate, seems to have been the result of a boundless ingenuity. Hiero,
after gaining the royal power in Syracuse, resolved, as a consequence of
his successful exploits, to place in a certain temple a golden crown
which he had vowed to the immortal gods. He contracted for its making at a fixed price, and weighed out a precise amount of gold to the
contractor. At the appointed time the latter delivered to the king's satisfaction an exquisitely finished piece of handiwork, and it appeared that
in weight the crown corresponded precisely to what the gold had
weighed.

But afterward a charge was made that gold had been abstracted
and an equivalent weight of silver had been added in the manufacture
of the crown. Hiero, thinking it an outrage that he had been tricked
and yet not knowing how to detect the theft, requested Archimedes
to consider the matter. The latter, while the case was still on his mind,
happened to go to the bath, and on getting into a tub observed that
the more his body sank into it the more water ran out over the tub. As
this pointed out the way to explain the point in question, without a
moment's delay, and transported with joy, he jumped out of the tub
and rushed home, . . . [and] as he ran he shouted repeatedly in Greek,
"Eureka! Eureka!"

Taking this as the beginning of his discovery, it is said that he
made two masses of the same weight as the crown, one of gold and the

Source: Vitruvius, *The Ten Books of Architecture*, translated by Morris H.
Morgan, Cambridge, Mass.: Harvard University Press, Book IX, pp. 253–54. Reprinted by permission of the publishers and the Loeb Classical Library.

other of silver. After making them he filled a large vessel with water to the very brim, and dropped the mass of silver into it. As much water ran out of it as was equal in bulk to that of the silver sunk in the vessel. Then, taking out the mass, he poured back the lost quantity of water, using a pint measure, until it was level with the brim as it had been before. Thus he found the weight of silver corresponding to a definite quantity of water. After this experiment, he likewise dropped the mass of gold into the full vessel and, on taking it out and measuring as before, found that not so much water was lost but a smaller quantity, namely, as much loss as a mass of gold lacks in bulk compared to a mass of silver of the same weight. Finally, filling the vessel again and dropping the crown itself into the same quantity of water, he found that more water ran over for the crown than for the mass of gold of the same weight. Hence, reasoning from the fact that more water was lost in the case of the crown than in that of the mass, he detected the mixing of silver with the gold, and made the theft of the contractor perfectly clear.

Camillus—a Roman Hero

The early history of Rome is shrouded in legend. Since the ancient records were destroyed when the Gauls captured and plundered Rome in 390 B.C., the later Roman historians had to rely on hearsay and on their own imagination in writing about the origin and expansion of the city. Being patriots, these historians painted the early heroes of Rome in glowing colors and attributed to them qualities of character such as courage, honesty, and patriotism. Camillus was one of these heroes. He served Rome as a general in the campaign against a town north of Rome in about 394 B.C.

The following story is told by the historian Livy, who wrote during the reign of Augustus (31 B.C.–A.D. 14).

At Falerii it was the custom to employ the same person as schoolteacher and companion, and many boys were entrusted to his sole care, as is done in Greece to this day. The nobles' children, as was

Source: Moses Hadas, *A History of Rome*, New York: Doubleday & Co., Inc., 1956, pp. 21–22. © 1956 by Moses Hadas. Reprinted by permission of the publishers.

natural, were taught by their most eminent scholar. In peacetime this man had instituted the practice of taking the boys out into the country for play and exercise, and during the war he continued it. He would entertain them in short or long walks with games and stories, until one day he managed to bring them to the enemy outposts, then into the Roman camp, and then to Camillus' headquarters. His infamous deed he topped with a more infamous speech, saying that he was putting Falerii in the power of the Romans by delivering to them the children of the most influential Faliscans. Upon hearing this Camillus replied: "Neither the people to whom you bring this blackguard's gift, you blackguard, nor their general is of your stripe. With the Faliscans we have no fellowship founded on men's covenants; but there is and there will continue to be between us the fellowship implanted by nature. War as well as peace has its laws, and we wage it with justice as well as vigor. Our arms we bear not against children, who are spared even when cities are stormed, but against men armed like ourselves, who attacked our camp at Veii without provocation. You have conquered them, as you think, by a scoundrel's trick; I shall conquer them, as I did Veii, in the Roman way, by courage, effort, and weapons." He stripped the fellow, tied his hands behind his back, and gave him to the boys to drive back to Falerii, putting rods in their hands to scourge him as he went. . . .

At Falerii, senate and market place rang with Roman integrity and their commander's justice. Unanimously they dispatched emissaries to Camillus' camp, and then by his permission to the Senate at Rome, to surrender Falerii. This is reported to be their speech when they were introduced into the Senate: "Senators, a victory which neither god nor man could begrudge, you and your general have won over us. We surrender to you because we believe (and what could be handsomer for a victor?) that life will be better under your administration than under our own laws."

Roman Law

Roman law is the most enduring of the cultural achievements of Rome. Originally the law of the city-state of Rome was closely associated with religion. It was not written down and it tended to be administered to the advantage of the patricians. At the demand of the plebeians a written code was drawn up in the middle of the fifth century B.C. This code, known as the Law of the Twelve Tables, was displayed for all to see. It became the foundation of the "civil law," which in the process of expansion and interpretation became almost entirely nonreligious.

The Romans did not subject foreigners to their civil law. From the middle of the third century B.C. they appointed a special official (later the number of these officials was increased) to handle cases involving foreigners. In judging such cases a number of broad factors were considered — the customs of the foreigner, the intentions of the defendant, Roman principles, and common sense. Out of these cases there grew up a new and humane code of law known as "the law of nations." As citizenship was extended throughout the Empire, these two systems of law (the civil law and the law of nations), which had already influenced each other, were gradually blended into one system of law that applied to the whole Roman world.

As Roman law developed over the centuries, it also incorporated much that was confusing and contradictory. The enormous task of clarifying, codifying, and summarizing was undertaken in the reign of the Emperor Justinian (A.D. 527–565), when the Corpus Juris Civilis (Body of Civil Law) was compiled.

The following selection is from the Roman Law of the Twelve Tables.

If plaintiff summons defendant to court, he shall go. If he does not go, plaintiff shall call witness thereto. Then only shall he take defendant by force.

If defendant shirks or takes to his heels, plaintiff shall lay hands on him.

When a debt has been acknowledged, or judgment about the matter has been pronounced in court, thirty days must be the legitimate time of grace. After that, the debtor may be arrested by laying on of

Source: *Remains of Old Latin*, translated by E. H. Warmington, Cambridge, Mass.: Harvard University Press, Vol. III, reprinted by permission of the publishers and the Loeb Classical Library; and from *Selected Readings in the History of Civilization*, edited by Bailey W. Diffie and Aaron Noland, pp. 158–61, by permission of the Department of History of the City College of New York.

hands. Bring him into court. If he does not satisfy the judgment, . . . the creditor may take the defaulter with him. . . .

Unless they make a settlement, debtors shall be held in bonds for sixty days. During that time they shall be brought before the . . . court in the meeting place on three successive market days, and the amount for which they are judged liable shall be announced; on the third market day they shall suffer capital punishment or be delivered up for sale abroad, across the Tiber. On the third market day creditors shall cut pieces [from the debtor's body]. Should they cut more or less than their due, it shall be with impunity. . . .

If a father thrice surrender a son for sale, the son shall be free from the father. . . .

Females shall remain in guardianship even when they have attained their majority. . . .

A spendthrift is forbidden to exercise administration over his own goods. . . .

Persons shall mend roadways. If they do not keep them laid with stone, a person may drive his beasts where he wishes.

Should a tree on a neighbor's farm be bent crooked by a wind and lean over your farm, action may be taken for removal of that tree.

It is permitted to gather up fruit falling down on another man's farm.

If any person has sung or composed against another person a song such as was causing slander or insult to another, he shall be clubbed to death.

If a person has maimed another's limb, let there be retaliation in kind unless he makes agreement for settlement with him. . . .

For pasturing on, or cutting secretly by night, another's crops acquired by tillage, there shall be capital punishment in the case of an adult malefactor: . . . he shall be hanged and put to death as a sacrifice. . . . In the case of a person under the age of puberty, at the discretion of the praetor either he shall be scourged or settlement shall be made for the harm done by paying double damages.

If theft has been done by night, if the owner kill the thief, the thief shall be held lawfully killed. It is forbidden that a thief be killed by day . . . unless he defend himself with a weapon; even though he has come with a weapon, unless he use his weapon and fight back, you shall not kill him. And even if he resists, first call out. . . .

The penalty shall be capital punishment for a judge or arbiter legally appointed who has been found guilty of receiving a bribe for giving a decision.

A dead man shall not be buried or burned within the city. Women must not tear cheeks or hold chorus of "Alas!" [during] a funeral.

Putting to death . . . of any man who has not been convicted, whosoever he might be, is forbidden.

The Qualities of Hannibal

No enemy of the Roman Republic left so deep and lasting an impression on the Roman mind as did the Carthaginian Hannibal. Burning to avenge the defeat of Carthage at the hands of Rome, Hannibal, in 218 B.C., led an army of men, horses, and elephants over the perilous Alps into Italy. In some of the most perfectly executed military campaigns known to history, he eliminated three Roman armies of superior strength.

Only the discipline and steadfastness of the Roman people saved them from destruction. They would not surrender, nor would they meet Hannibal in pitched battle. Under the cautious generalship of Fabius, who became renowned for his delaying tactics, Roman forces sapped Hannibal's strength by harassing his forces and cutting off his supplies. Finally in 204 B.C. a Roman army under Scipio invaded Africa and forced Hannibal to return there. Scipio defeated the Carthaginians decisively at the Battle of Zama. Hannibal himself fled, and after being pursued by the Romans for two decades committed suicide to avoid capture.

The qualities of Hannibal and his descent into Italy are described by Livy.

Upon his first arrival in Spain, Hannibal became the center of attention in the whole army. . . . They saw the same energetic expression, the same piercing eyes, the same features and visage [in Hannibal as were characteristic of his father Hasdrubal]. But very quickly

Source: Moses Hadas, A *History of Rome*, New York: Doubleday & Co., Inc., 1956, pp. 31–33. © 1956 by Moses Hadas. Reprinted by permission of the publishers.

his resemblance to his father was a negligible factor in winning approval. Never were high aptitudes for obeying and commanding — very different qualities — combined to such a degree in a single character. It was not easy to decide whether the general or the army loved him best. It was Hannibal that Hasdrubal chose to put in charge of any business that required courage and energy, and it was under Hannibal that the soldiers displayed greatest confidence and daring. He was fearless in undertaking dangerous enterprises; he was prudent in discharging them. Toil could not weary his body or subdue his spirit. Heat and cold he endured alike. He ate and drank to satisfy nature, not pleasure. Hours for sleeping and waking were not determined by the clock; whatever time was left after work was done he devoted to sleep. Nor was sleep wooed by soft couches and stillness; often he could be seen lying on the ground among the sentries and pickets, covered with a soldier's cape. His dress was no different from his contemporaries', but his arms and horses were preeminent. Among horse and foot alike he was far the best; he was the first to engage in a battle, the last to leave the engagement. But great as the man's merits were, his enormous faults were as great — inhuman cruelty, . . . no scruple for truth or sanctity, no fear of gods, no respect for oaths or religion. . . .

The Romans thought the war would be waged in Spain, and the consul Publius Cornelius Scipio proceeded toward that country; but Hannibal was determined to carry the war to Italy and had brought his army across the Pyrenees to the Rhone before Scipio reached Massilia. Scipio sent his brother on to Spain and returned to Italy to meet Hannibal. Despite hostile nature and difficult terrain Hannibal reached the summit of the Alps, where he heartened his dispirited soldiers by showing them the Po Valley stretching before them. . . .

But the descent was even more trying than the ascent, for on the Italian side the Alps fall sheer. The whole way was precipitous, narrow, and slippery, so that they could not keep from slipping nor stick to their tracks if they stumbled: men and beasts rolled one on top of another. A cliff they reached was so narrow and perpendicular that a soldier without pack could scarcely lower himself by feeling his way and holding onto bushes and roots. A recent landslip had deepened the precipice to nearly a thousand feet. At this impasse the cavalry halted; and when Hannibal wondered what was delaying the column, he was told that the rock was impassable. He went to inspect the situation in person and found the column would have to detour through a pathless and untrodden tract. But this was found impracticable. The first few who attempted to pass could find footing in the new snow which covered that hard-packed below, but when the tramp of men and beasts ground this to slush they trod on the naked ice below. Men floundered and struggled. The slippery ice afforded no traction, and was the more treacherous as it was downhill; if a man rose on his hands or braced himself on his knees he would collapse together with his supports, and there were no stumps or roots against which he could buttress himself. They kept wallowing in the slush on the smooth ice. Sometimes the pack animals, stamping their hoofs against falling, broke through and were stuck in the hard, deep-frozen ice as if trapped and fettered. [Hannibal cut through the rock with hot vinegar, enabling his forces to make their way down the mountains.]

The Slave Revolt
Under Spartacus

Slaves made up as much as half of the population of the city of Rome and a considerable proportion of the entire Empire. Most slaves had been captured in war. Those who were lucky enough to be employed in households, as craftsmen, or on the farm could hope for fairly good treatment. Less fortunate were those who worked in mines or in large groups under the whip of an overseer. A relatively small number were trained for gladiatorial combat for the amusement of the citizens.

Slave revolts were common, but they were easily crushed. The slave revolt (73–71 B.C.) led by Spartacus, a Thracian gladiator, was of a very different magnitude. Spartacus was a man of great organizing and fighting ability. His goal, to lead the slaves to freedom across the Alps, was less frustrated by his enemies than by his own followers, who were content to terrorize the countryside and live off booty. One Roman army after another was beaten back by the untrained slaves, until they were finally defeated in a supreme effort on the part of the Romans. Spartacus was killed in battle and the revolt was brutally crushed.

This account is by Appian, an Egyptian in the Roman civil service in the second century A.D.

Spartacus, a Thracian by birth, who had once served as a soldier with the Romans but had since been a prisoner and sold for a gladiator and was in the gladiatorial training school at Capua, persuaded about seventy of his comrades to strike for their own freedom rather than for the amusement of spectators. They overcame the guards and ran away, arming themselves with clubs and daggers that they took from people on the roads, and took refuge on Mount Vesuvius. There many fugitive slaves and even some freemen from the fields joined Spartacus, and he plundered the neighboring country, having for subordinate officers two gladiators named Oenomaus and Crixus. As he divided the plunder impartially, he soon had plenty of men. Varinius Glaber was first sent against him and afterward Publius Valerius, not with regular armies but with forces picked up in haste and at random, for the Romans did not consider this a war as yet but a raid, something like an outbreak of robbery. They attacked Spartacus and were beaten. . . .

After this still greater numbers flocked to Spartacus till his army numbered 70,000 men. For these he manufactured weapons and collected equipment. . . . One of [the Roman consuls] overcame Crixus near Mount Garganus with 30,000 men, two thirds of whom perished together with himself. Spartacus endeavored to make his way through the Apennines to the Alps and the Gallic country, but [another consul] anticipated him and hindered his flight. . . . He turned upon them one after the other and beat them in detail. They retreated in confusion in different directions. Spartacus sacrificed 300 Roman prisoners to the shade [spirit] of Crixus, and marched on Rome with 120,000 foot [infantry], having burned all his useless material, killed all his prisoners, and butchered his pack animals in order to [hasten] his movement. . . . The consuls again met him in the country of Picenum. Here there was fought another great battle, and there was, too, another great defeat for the Romans.

Spartacus changed his intention of marching on Rome. He did not consider himself ready as yet for that kind of a fight, as his whole force was not suitably armed, for no city had joined him, but only slaves, deserters, and riffraff. However, he occupied the mountains around Thurii and took the city itself. . . . When this war, so formid-

Source: Appian, *The Civil Wars*, Vol. III of Appian, *Roman History*, translated by Horace White, Cambridge, Mass.: Harvard University Press, pp. 215–23. Reprinted by permission of the publishers and the Loeb Classical Library.

able to the Romans (although ridiculed and despised in the beginning as being merely the work· of gladiators), had lasted three years . . . Licinius Crassus assumed the praetorship and marched against Spartacus with six new legions.

Spartacus . . . invited Crassus to come to terms with him. When his proposals were rejected with scorn, he resolved to risk a battle, and as his cavalry had arrived he made a dash with his whole army through the lines of the besieging force and pushed on . . . with Crassus in pursuit. . . . Spartacus . . . brought his forces, which were even then very numerous, to close quarters with Crassus. The battle was long and bloody, as might have been expected with so many thousands of desperate men. Spartacus was wounded in the thigh with a spear and sank upon his knee, holding his shield in front of him and contending in this way against his assailants until he and the great mass of those with him were surrounded and slain. The remainder of his army was thrown into confusion and butchered in crowds. So great was the slaughter that it was impossible to count them. . . . The body of Spartacus was not found. A large number of his men fled from the battlefield to the mountains, and Crassus followed them thither. They divided themselves in four parts and continued to fight until they all perished except 6,000, who were captured and crucified along the whole road from Capua to Rome.

Misgovernment
in the Roman Provinces

Great fortunes were quickly accumulated by Roman citizens who obtained official positions in the provinces of the Empire. The governors, the moneylenders, and the tax collectors all combined to drain the helpless provincials. Roman government officials who had contracted enormous debts eagerly sought a lucrative governorship in order to reimburse their creditors and to secure their own future political careers. The provincials cried out against these parasites, but usually in vain. The men who robbed them wielded immense power in Rome, and the senators, before whom these cases of corruption were tried, were themselves deeply involved in this practice. *The result was poverty and demoralization in the provinces and degradation in Rome.*

The Cicero mentioned in this passage was a lawyer and statesman of the late Roman Republic. During civil war and in the face of tyranny, he staunchly defended republican institutions. With compelling oratory he spoke out for honest government. His successful prosecution of Verres, a notoriously corrupt governor of Sicily, won him much popular acclaim.

Below, a modern historian discusses how the Roman provinces were ruled.

The governors sent to rule the most important . . . provinces were Roman senators. . . . They . . . belonged to the inner circle of people and families who shared, at first absolutely and then under imperial supervision, the control of Rome's destinies.

When the East had received its first Roman governors in the second century B.C., their ability to keep their hands off public funds was noted to exceed that of the Greeks. . . .

A famous example and model of such integrity [honesty] was Cato the Elder. . . . As Cicero said:

The most eminent men in the country, during the best period of our history, counted it among their most honorable and splendid achievements to protect from injury and to maintain in prosperity those guests and retainers of theirs — the foreign nations who had been received as friends into the Roman Empire. That wise and distinguished man Marcus Cato Sapiens, history tells us, made many and lasting enemies by standing up for the unfortunate Spaniards, among whom he had served as consul [195 B.C.].

In the first century B.C., on the other hand, . . . the standard of honesty and responsibility among governors was very low; they were mostly corrupt and [grasping], regarding their year of office as a period for making large, illegitimate profits. . . .

During the second and first centuries B.C., the Roman government initiated and elaborated laws aimed at limiting and controlling the im-

Source: Michael Grant, *The World of Rome,* Cleveland, Ohio: The World Publishing Company, 1960, pp. 32–35. Copyright © 1960 by Michael Grant. Reprinted by permission of The World Publishing Company and George Weidenfeld and Nicolson, Ltd., London.

proprieties of its representatives in the provinces. But the Extortion Court thus established was all too often totally incapacitated by bribery; and Cicero, in his courageous attack upon one of the most unscrupulous — and best protected — governors, Verres, in Sicily (70 B.C.), deplores the discredit which had fallen upon the institution in the eyes of provincials:

I asserted my belief that, one of these days, communities from the provinces would send deputations to the people of Rome requesting that the extortion law and its court should be abolished. For if no such court existed, they suppose that each governor would only take away with him enough for himself and his children. At present, on the other hand, with the courts as they are, a governor takes enough for himself, and his protectors, and his counsel, and the president of the court, and the judges! In other words, there is no end to it. A greedy man's lust for gain they could satisfy, but they cannot afford a guilty man's acquittal. How peculiarly glorious our courts have become, how scintillating is the prestige of our Senatorial Order, when Rome's allies pray that the courts which our ancestors created for their benefit should be struck out of existence!

The provincials suffered also from the onslaughts of Roman financiers belonging to, or depending on, the important Order of Knights. In the immensely wealthy province of Asia, corporations directed by knights, with their own couriers, banks, and probably shareholders, were authorized by the Roman authorities to farm the taxation. . . . The corporations of tax collectors made bids to the Roman government for four years' income, and the successful bidders guaranteed an agreed sum to the treasury; what more they collected was their margin of profit. The state itself could not have collected this money since it did not yet possess a civil service capable of doing so. . . .

Cicero was a hesitant, timid man, but occasionally he was so moved by a cause that he showed determination; and he showed it here. This was in keeping with his own conduct as governor of Cilicia, which at that time extended far into the interior of Asia Minor. He worked strenuously, fought to maintain public security, . . . and . . . was in a position to claim that he had extracted no improper gains from his province. . . . Cicero also proved unwilling to help Caelius Rufus, the fashionable young man who was his political informant at Rome, either with a free gift of panthers for his electioneering show, or with a financial contribution from the provincials. Cicero describes the situation in his Cilician province . . . with a typical mixture of vanity, the human desire to criticize one's predecessor, and real humanity:

So I sit down on the high road to scribble you a summary of what really calls for a long epistle. You must know that my arrival in this province, which is in a state of lasting ruin and desolation, was expected eagerly. I got here on July 31. . . . Everywhere I heard the same tale. People could not pay their taxes: they were forced to sell out their investments; groans and lamentations in the towns, and awful conduct of one who is some kind of savage beast rather than a man. All the people are, as you may suppose, tired of life. However, the poor towns are relieved that they have had to spend nothing on me. . . . You must know that I not only refused to accept pay . . . but that none of us will take firewood or anything beyond four beds and a roof; and in many places we do not accept even a roof, but remain mostly under canvas. Thus, extraordinary throngs of people have come to meet me from farms and villages and every homestead. Upon my word, my very coming seems to revive them. Your friend Cicero has won all hearts by his justice and self-restraint and kind bearing.

Even with Cicero, however, the overriding consideration was, too often, the effect of his actions on his Roman career. . . .

During the later Republic, governors were generally bad; from the time of Augustus onward they were generally conscientious. When Tiberius told them that "a good shepherd shears his flock but does not flay them," he was instructing them to maintain what had already . . . become current practice.

The Deeds of Augustus

A century of class conflict, military dictatorship, and civil war came to an end when young Octavian, the great-nephew and adopted heir of Julius Caesar, defeated the fleet of Anthony and Cleopatra at Actium in 31 B.C. Both Anthony and Cleopatra committed suicide. In 29 B.C. Octavian returned to Rome in triumph. After a period of transition from a state of war to peace, Octavian formally proclaimed the restoration of the republican constitution at a meeting of the Senate in 27 B.C. While this won him great acclaim, as did his offer to surrender his power to the Senate, everyone knew that the ancient Republic was beyond restoration and that a strong imperial government under a powerful ruler was essential to prevent a return of the chaos that had almost destroyed Rome. Augustus — a title bestowed upon him at the time he restored the constitution — pretended to rule as a republican official by sharing his power with the Senate. In reality he was an absolute monarch.

This first Roman Emperor proved to be a farsighted statesman with extraordinary administrative ability. Concentrating his strength on internal problems, he established a system of government which became the foundation of the Pax Romana for two centuries. Before his death in A.D. 14 he had his numerous accomplishments inscribed in bronze.

At the age of nineteen, on my own initiative and at my own expense, I raised an army by means of which I restored liberty to the Republic, which had been oppressed by the tyranny of a faction. For this service the Senate . . . enrolled me in its order . . . [and] gave me the imperium.* As propraetor † it ordered me, along with the consuls, "to see that the Republic suffered no harm." In the same year, moreover, as both consuls had fallen in war, the people elected me consul and a triumvir for settling the constitution.

Those who slew my father I drove into exile, punishing their deed by due process of law, and afterward when they waged war upon the Republic I twice defeated them in battle.

Wars, both civil and foreign, I undertook throughout the world, on sea and land, and when victorious I spared all citizens who sued for pardon. The foreign nations which could with safety be pardoned I preferred to save rather than to destroy. The number of Roman citizens who bound themselves to me by military oath was about 500,000. Of these I settled in colonies or sent back into their own towns, after their term of service, something more than 300,000, and to all I assigned lands or gave money as a reward for military service. . . .

Twice I triumphed with an ovation, . . . and was saluted as im-

* **imperium:** the right to command soldiers. Augustus, in fact, already had the power to command the army.
† **propraetor:** an official of high rank.

Source: *Res Gestae Divi Augusti*, bound with Velleius Paterculus, *History of Rome*, translated by Frederick W. Shipley, Cambridge, Mass.: Harvard University Press, pp. 345–401. Reprinted by permission of the publishers and the Loeb Classical Library.

perator twenty-one times. Although the Senate decreed me additional triumphs I set them aside. . . . For successful operations on land and sea, . . . the Senate on fifty-five occasions decreed that thanks should be rendered to the immortal gods. . . . At the time of writing these words I have been thirteen times consul. . . .

The dictatorship offered me by the people and the Roman Senate, in my absence and later when present, . . . I did not accept. I did not decline at a time of the greatest scarcity of grain the charge of the grain supply, which I so administered that within a few days I freed the entire people, at my own expense, from the fear and danger in which they were. The consulship, either yearly or for life, then offered me I did not accept. . . .

When the Senate and the Roman people unanimously agreed that I should be elected overseer of laws and morals, without a colleague and with the fullest power, I refused to accept any power offered me which was contrary to the traditions of our ancestors. . . .

The Senate decreed that every fifth year vows should be undertaken for my health by the consuls and the priests. . . .

By the decree of the Senate . . . it was enacted by law that my person should be sacred. . . .

Four times I aided the public treasury with my own money. . . .

I restored the channels of the aqueducts which in several places were falling into disrepair through age. . . .

Three times in my own name I gave a show of gladiators, and five times in the name of my sons or grandsons; in these shows there fought about ten thousand men. . . .

I gave the people the spectacle of a naval battle beyond the Tiber [River]. . . .

I freed the sea from pirates. . . .

I extended the boundaries of all the provinces. . . .

Embassies were often sent to me from the kings of India, a thing never seen before in the camp of any general of the Romans.

In my sixth and seventh consulships, when I had extinguished the flames of civil war, after receiving by universal consent the absolute control of affairs, I transferred the Republic from my own control to the will of the Senate and the Roman people. For this service on my part I was given the title of Augustus by decree of the Senate; and the doorposts of my house were covered with laurels by public act; and a civic crown was fixed above my door; and a golden shield was placed in the Curia Julia whose inscription testified that the Senate and the Roman people gave me this in recognition of my valor, my clemency, my justice, and my piety. After that time I took precedence of all in rank, but of power I possessed no more than those who were my colleagues in any magistracy.

While I was administering my thirteenth consulship, the Senate and the Equestrian Order and the entire Roman people gave me the title of Father of my Country.

The Depravity of Roman Society

The rule of Augustus ushered in a long period of peace and prosperity. There was now more opportunity than ever to concentrate on pleasures and luxuries. Depravity and debauchery infected every class, including the aristocracy. More than others perhaps, the freedmen — the freed slaves — some of whom had amassed great fortunes, indulged their whims and vices. One of the most vivid portraits of the vulgarity of the period is the tale of the sumptuous dinner party of Trimalchio, a wealthy freedman. The author is Petronius, an aristocrat who was not immune to the pleasures of the senses. A close companion of Emperor Nero for some years, he fell from royal favor and committed suicide during the purge of A.D. 66.

I cannot linger over details. We went into the bath. We stayed till we ran with sweat, and then at once passed through into the cold water. Trimalchio was now anointed all over and rubbed down, not with towels, but with blankets of the softest wool. Three masseurs sat there drinking Falernian wine under his eyes. . . . Trimalchio said they were drinking his health. Then he was rolled up in a scarlet woolen coat and put in a litter. Four runners decked with medals went before him. . . . As he was being driven off, a musician with a tiny pair of

Source: Petronius, *Satyricon*, translated by Michael Heseltine, Cambridge, Mass.: Harvard University Press, pp. 41–59. Reprinted by permission of the publishers and the Loeb Classical Library.

pipes arrived, and played the whole way as though he were whispering secrets in his ear.

We followed, lost in wonder, and came with Agamemnon to the door. A notice was fastened on the doorpost: "No slave to go out of doors except by the master's orders. Penalty, one hundred stripes." Just at the entrance stood a porter in green clothes, with a cherry-colored belt, shelling peas in a silver dish. A golden cage hung in the doorway, and a spotted magpie in it greeted visitors. I was gazing at all this when I nearly fell backwards and broke my leg. For on the left hand as you went in, not far from the porter's office, a great dog on a chain was painted on the wall, and over him was written in large letters "Beware of the Dog." My friends laughed at me, but I plucked up courage and went on to examine the whole wall. It had a picture of a slave market on it, with the persons' names. Trimalchio was there with long hair, holding a Mercury's staff.*. . . Then the painstaking artist had given a faithful picture of his whole career with explanations: how he had learned to keep accounts, and how at last he had been made steward. At the point where the wall space gave out, Mercury had taken him by the chin, and was whirling him up to his high official throne. . . . I also observed a company of runners practicing in the gallery under a trainer, and in a corner I saw a large cupboard containing a tiny shrine wherein were silver house gods, and a marble image of Venus, and a large golden box, where, they told me, Trimalchio's first beard was laid up. . . .

We tried to get into the dining room, when one of the slaves, who was entrusted with this duty, cried, "Right foot first!" For a moment we were naturally nervous, for fear any of us had broken the rule in crossing the threshold. But just as we were all taking a step with the right foot together, a slave stripped for flogging fell at our feet, and began to implore us to save him from punishment. It was no great sin which had put him in such peril; he had lost the steward's clothes in the bath, and the whole lot were scarcely worth ten sesterces. So we drew back our right feet and begged the steward, who sat counting gold pieces in the hall, to let the slave off. He looked up haughtily, and said, "It is not the loss I mind so much as the villain's carelessness. He lost my dinner dress. . . . Well, well, I make you a present of the fellow.". . .

* **long hair . . . Mercury's staff**: long hair was the mark of a slave. Mercury, as the god of business, was Trimalchio's patron.

At last then we sat down, and boys from Alexandria poured water cooled with snow over our hands. Others followed and knelt down at our feet and proceeded with great skill to pare our hangnails. Even this unpleasant duty did not silence them, but they kept singing at their work. I wanted to find out whether the whole household could sing, so I asked for a drink. A ready slave repeated my order in a chant not less shrill. They all did the same if they were asked to hand anything. It was more like an actor's dance than a gentleman's dining room. But some rich and tasty [morsels] were brought on. . . .

Trimalchio . . . in a loud voice invited any of us who wished to take a second glass of mead. Suddenly, the music gave the sign and the light dishes were swept away by a troop of singing servants. . . .

We complimented our host on his arrangements. "Mars loves a fair field," said he, "and so I gave orders that everyone should have a separate table. In that way these filthy slaves will not make us so hot by crowding past us."

Trimalchio . . . ground out a tune. . . . We came to such an evil entertainment rather depressed. "Now," said Trimalchio, "let us have dinner. This is sauce for the dinner." As he spoke, four dancers ran up in time with the music and took off the top part of the dish. Then we saw in the well of it fat fowls and sows' bellies. . . . They let a spiced sauce run from their wineskins over the fishes. . . . We all took up the clapping which the slaves started, and attacked these delicacies with hearty laughter. Trimalchio was delighted with the trick he had played us, and said, "Now, carver." The man came up at once and, making flourishes in time with the music, pulled the dish to pieces; you would have said that a gladiator in a chariot was fighting to the accompaniment of a water organ. . . .

I was now unable to eat any more, so I turned to my neighbor to get as much news as possible. I began to seek for farfetched stories, and to inquire who the woman was who kept running about everywhere. "She is Trimalchio's wife Fortunata," he said, "and she counts her money by the bushel. And what was she a little while ago? You will pardon me if I say that you would not have taken a piece of bread from her hand. Now without why or wherefore she is queen of heaven, and Trimalchio's all in all. In fact, if she tells him that it is dark at high noon, he will believe it. He is so enormously rich that he does not know himself what he has; but this lynx-eyed woman has a plan for everything, even where you would not think it. She is temperate, sober, and prudent, but she has a nasty tongue, and henpecks him. . . . Whom she likes, she likes; whom she dislikes, she dislikes. Trimalchio has estates wherever a kite can fly in a day, is millionaire of millionaires. There is more plate lying in his steward's room than other people have in their whole fortunes. And his slaves! My word! I really don't believe that one out of ten of them knows his master by sight. . . . You must not suppose either that he buys anything. Everything is homegrown: wool, citrons, pepper. . . . He had bees brought from Athens to give him Attic honey on the premises. . . . Within the last few days, I may say, he has written for a cargo of mushroom spawn from India. . . . But do not look down on the other freedmen who are his friends. They are very juicy people. That one you see lying at the bottom of the end sofa has his eight hundred thousand. He was quite a nobody. A little time ago he was carrying loads of wood on his back."

The Culture of the Barbarians

For centuries, German barbarian tribes pressed against the northern borders of the Roman Empire. Until the end of the fourth century A.D. the Roman legions were strong enough to keep them in check. Peaceful infiltration of small groups was not blocked. The barbarians found work on the large Roman estates or in the legions themselves. A mixture of motives, including admiration for the Empire, population pressure, the advance of external enemies, and hunger for land, impelled the barbarians to press against Roman territory.

In the days when corruption had set into Roman political life, the institutions of the barbarians seemed rather admirable to many Romans. Barbarian loyalty, courage, and love of freedom contrasted sharply with the greed and absolutism within the Empire. The anti-imperial sentiments of the historian Tacitus may have colored his description of the barbarians in his Germania (A.D. 98) from which the first selection is taken. In the second selection, Ammianus Marcellinus, who lived in the fourth century, portrays the savage character of the Huns, who swept into Europe from Central Asia, terrorizing the German tribes and forcing them south and west against the Roman frontier in their desperate struggle to escape.

The Germans

Their physique, in spite of their vast numbers, is identical: fierce blue eyes, red hair, tall frames, . . . impatient at the same time of labor and hard work, and by no means habituated to bearing thirst and heat; to cold and hunger, thanks to the climate and the soil, they are accustomed. . . .

Iron is not plentiful among them, as may be gathered from the style of their weapons. Few have swords or the longer kind of lance: they carry short spears . . . with a narrow and small iron head, so sharp and so handy in use that they fight with the same weapon, as circumstances demand, both at close quarters and at a distance. The mounted man is content with a shield and [spear]: the infantry launch showers of missiles in addition, each man a volley, and hurl these to great distances, for they wear no outer clothing, or at most a light cloak. .·. .

Few have breastplates; scarcely one or two at most have metal or hide helmets. The horses are conspicuous neither for beauty nor speed; but then neither are they trained like our horses to run in shifting circles. . . . The battle line itself is arranged in wedges: to retire, provided you press on again, they treat as a question of tactics, not of cowardice: they carry off their dead and wounded even in drawn battles. To have abandoned one's shield is the height of disgrace; the man so disgraced cannot be present at religious rites nor attend a council. . . .

They take their kings on the ground of birth, their generals on the basis of courage: the authority of their kings is not unlimited or arbitrary; their generals control them by example rather than command, and by means of the admiration which attends upon energy and a conspicuous place in the front of the line. . . . The strongest incentive to courage lies in this, that neither chance nor casual grouping makes the squadron or the wedge, but family and kinship: close at hand are their dearest, whence is heard the wailing voice of woman and the child's cry: here are the witnesses who are in each man's eyes most precious; here the praise he covets most: they take their wounds to mother and wife, who do not shrink from counting the hurts and demanding a sight of them: they minister to the combatants food and exhortation. . . .

THE GERMANS. Source: Tacitus, *Germania*, translated by Maurice Hutton, Cambridge, Mass.: Harvard University Press, pp. 269–83. Reprinted by permission of the publishers and the Loeb Classical Library.

They have . . . a method of taking divinations by means of which they probe the issue of serious wars. A member of the tribe at war with them is . . . captured and pitted against a selected champion of their own. . . . The victory of one or the other is taken as a [sign].

On small matters the chiefs consult, on larger questions the community; but with this limitation, that even the subjects, the decision of which rests with the people, are first handled by the chiefs. . . .

It is a foible of their freedom that they do not meet at once and when commanded, but a second and a third day are wasted by dilatoriness in assembling; when the mob is pleased to begin, they take their seats carrying arms. Silence is called for by the priests, who thenceforward have power also to coerce; then a king or a chief is listened to, in order of age, birth, glory in war, or eloquence. . . . If the advice tendered be displeasing, they reject it with groans; if it please them, they clash their spears. . . .

They do no business, public or private, without arms in their hands; yet the custom is that no one take arms until the state has endorsed his competence. Then in the assembly itself one of the chiefs or his father or his relatives equip the young man with shield and spear; this corresponds with them to the toga and is youth's first public distinction: hitherto he seems a member of the household, now a member of the state.

The Huns

The origin of all the ruin . . . we have found to be this. . . . The people of the Huns, but little known from ancient records, . . . exceed every degree of savagery. Since there the cheeks of the children are deeply furrowed with the steel [blades] from their very birth, in order that the growth of hair, when it appears at the proper time, may be checked by the wrinkled scars, they grow old without beards and without any beauty. . . . They all have compact, strong limbs and thick necks, and are so monstrously ugly and misshapen that one might take them for two-legged beasts or for the stumps, roughhewn into images, that are used in putting sides to bridges. But although they have the form of men, however ugly, they are so hardy in their mode of life that they

THE HUNS. Source: Ammianus Marcellinus, *Roman History*, translated by J. C. Rolfe, Cambridge, Mass.: Harvard University Press, Vol. III, pp. 381–87. Reprinted by permission of the publishers and the Loeb Classical Library.

have no need of fire nor of savory food, but eat the roots of wild plants and the half-raw flesh of any kind of animal whatever, which they put between their thighs and the backs of their horses, and thus warm it a little. They are never protected by any buildings but they avoid these like tombs, which are set apart from everyday use. For not even a hut thatched with reed can be found among them. But roaming at large amid the mountains and woods, they learn from the cradle to endure cold, hunger, and thirst. When away from their homes they never enter a house unless compelled by extreme necessity; for they think they are not safe when staying under a roof. They dress in linen cloth or in the skins of field mice sewn together, and they wear the same clothing indoors and out. But when they have once put their necks into a faded tunic, it is not taken off or changed until by long wear and tear it has been reduced to rags and fallen from them bit by bit. They cover their heads with round caps and protect their hairy legs with goatskins. . . . For this reason they are not at all adapted to battles on foot but they are almost glued to their horses, which are hardy, it is true, but ugly, and sometimes they sit on them woman-fashion. . . . From their horses . . . everyone of that nation buys and sells, eats and drinks, and, bowed over the narrow neck of the animal, relaxes into a sleep. . . . They enter the battle drawn up in wedge-shaped masses, while their medley of voices makes a savage noise. And as they are lightly equipped for swift motion and unexpected in action, they purposely divide suddenly into scattered bands and attack, rushing about in disorder here and there, dealing terrific slaughter. . . . You would not hesitate to call them the most terrible of all warriors, because they fight from a distance with missiles having sharp bone, instead of their usual points, joined to the shafts with wonderful skill; then they gallop over the intervening spaces and fight hand to hand with swords, regardless of their own lives; and while the enemy are guarding against wounds from the saber thrusts, they throw strips of cloth plaited into nooses over their opponents and so entangle them that they fetter their limbs and take from them the power of riding or walking. No one in their country ever plows a field or touches a plow handle. They are all without fixed abode, without hearth, or law, or settled mode of life, and keep roaming from place to place, like fugitives, accompanied by the wagons in which they live; in wagons their wives weave for them their hideous garments, in wagons they . . . bear children and rear them. . . . In truces they are faithless and unreliable, . . . sacrificing every feeling to the mad impulse of the moment. Like unreasoning beasts, they are utterly ignorant of the difference between right and wrong; they are deceitful and ambiguous in speech, never bound by any reverence for religion or for superstition. They burn with an infinite thirst for gold, and they are so fickle and prone to anger that they often quarrel with their allies without provocation more than once on the same day, and make friends with them again without a mediator.

The Message of Jesus

Who could have imagined at the beginning of the first century A.D. that within a few hundred years the glorious Roman Empire would be lying in ruins and that the handful of disciples of Jesus of Nazareth, who was crucified as a rebel by the Romans, would have made hundreds of thousands of converts throughout the world?

Jesus was born at a time when Judea was smarting under the oppression of Rome. Jewish rebellions against Rome were crushed with brutality and terminated in crucifixions. Some Jews thought it best to get along with their powerful rulers; others longed for deliverance and recalled the miracles of old when God had destroyed the enemies of Israel. Jesus was accepted as the hoped-for Messiah by some groups of Jews, but was rejected by most. He disappointed revolutionary elements, who were awaiting political deliverance, by directing the minds of men toward the everlasting Kingdom of Heaven. He frightened conservative elements by spreading doctrines that seemed both blasphemous and seditious.

The message of Jesus is expressed in the following passages from the New Testament.

Eternal Life

And as he was setting out on his journey, a man ran up and knelt before him, and asked him, "Good Teacher, what must I do to inherit eternal life?" And Jesus said to him, "Why do you call me good?

ETERNAL LIFE. Source: Mark 10:7–22, from the Revised Standard Version of the Bible, copyright 1946, 1952, by the Division of Christian Education, National Council of Churches, and used by permission.

No one is good but God alone. You know the commandments: 'Do not kill, Do not commit adultery, Do not steal, Do not bear false witness, Do not defraud, Honor your father and mother.'" And he said to him, "Teacher, all these I have observed from my youth." And Jesus looking upon him loved him, and said to him, "You lack one thing; go, sell what you have, and give to the poor, and you will have treasure in heaven; and come, follow me." At that saying his countenance fell, and he went away sorrowful; for he had great possessions.

The Sermon on the Mount

Seeing the crowds, he went up on the mountain, and when he sat down his disciples came to him. And he opened his mouth and taught them, saying:

Blessed are the poor in spirit, for theirs is the kingdom of heaven.

Blessed are those who mourn, for they shall be comforted.

Blessed are the meek, for they shall inherit the earth.

Blessed are those who hunger and thirst for righteousness, for they shall be satisfied.

Blessed are the merciful, for they shall obtain mercy.

Blessed are the pure in heart, for they shall see God.

Blessed are the peacemakers, for they shall be called sons of God.

Blessed are those who are persecuted for righteousness' sake, for theirs is the kingdom of heaven.

Blessed are you when men revile you and persecute you and utter all kinds of evil against you falsely on my account. Rejoice and be glad, for your reward is great in heaven, for so men persecuted the prophets who were before you.

You are the salt of the earth; but if salt has lost its taste, how shall its saltness be restored? It is no longer good for anything except to be thrown out and trodden under foot by men.

You are the light of the world. A city set on a hill cannot be hid. Nor do men light a lamp and put it under a bushel, but on a stand, and it gives light to all in the house. Let your light so shine before men, that

THE SERMON ON THE MOUNT. Source: Matt. 5:1–17, 21–22, 38–48; 6:1, 14, 15, from the Revised Standard Version of the Bible, copyright 1946, 1952, by the Division of Christian Education, National Council of Churches, and used by permission.

they may see your good works and give glory to your Father who is in heaven.

Think not that I have come to abolish the law and the prophets; I have come not to abolish them but to fulfil them. . . .

You have heard that it was said to the men of old, "You shall not kill; and whoever kills shall be liable to judgment." But I say to you that every one who is angry with his brother shall be liable to judgment; whoever insults his brother shall be liable to the council, and whoever says, "You fool!" shall be liable to the hell of fire.". . .

You have heard that it was said, "An eye for an eye and a tooth for a tooth." But I say to you, Do not resist one who is evil. But if any one strikes you on the right cheek, turn to him the other also; and if any one would sue you and take your coat, let him have your cloak as well; and if anyone forces you to go one mile, go with him two miles. Give to him who begs from you, and do not refuse him who would borrow from you.

You have heard that it was said, "You shall love your neighbor and hate your enemy." But I say to you, Love your enemies and pray for those who persecute you, so that you may be sons of your Father who is in heaven; for he makes his sun rise on the evil and on the good, and sends rain on the just and on the unjust. For if you love those who love you, what reward have you? Do not even the tax collectors do the same? And if you salute only your brethren, what more are you doing than others? Do not even the Gentiles do the same? You, therefore, must be perfect, as your heavenly Father is perfect.

Beware of practicing your piety before men in order to be seen by them; for then you will have no reward from your Father who is in heaven. . . .

For if you forgive men their trespasses, your heavenly Father also will forgive you; but if you do not forgive men their trespasses, neither will your Father forgive your trespasses.

The Persecution of Christians

The Romans were most considerate of the religions of other peoples, though they would not tolerate human sacrifice or beliefs that undermined civic loyalty. Even the Jews, who abso-

lutely and stubbornly rejected emperor worship and the state cults, were given special treatment. The Christian groups, however, raised more serious questions. Christians not only refused to worship the emperor and serve in the army, but they also extended their influence everywhere, caused riots, and insisted that Jesus, who had been executed as a rebel of the state, was the Lord and thus was above all emperors on earth. Their refusal to take part in state ceremonies was considered as a sign of their disloyalty.

At the beginning of the second century, the persecution of Christians was neither systematized nor organized, as the letters between Pliny the Younger, Governor of Bithynia, and the Emperor Trajan illustrate. The fears, the indecision, and the tolerance of the Romans can be seen in this correspondence. Christian leaders, nevertheless, did not escape torture and martyrdom. Roman brutality and the heroism of the martyrs, as portrayed by the Christian historian Eusebius (c. 260–c. 340), brought many converts to the new faith.

The Correspondence Between Pliny and Trajan

Pliny's Letter to the Emperor Trajan

It is a rule, Sir, which I inviolably observe, to refer myself to you in all my doubts; for who is more capable of guiding my uncertainty or informing my ignorance? Having never been present at any trials of the Christians, I am unacquainted with the method and limits to be observed either in examining or punishing them. Whether any difference is to be made on account of age, or no distinction allowed between the youngest and the adult; whether repentance admits to a pardon, or if a man has once been a Christian it avails him nothing to recant; whether the mere profession of Christianity, . . . or only the crimes associated therewith are punishable — in all these points I am greatly doubtful.

In the meanwhile, the method I have observed toward those who have been denounced to me as Christians is this: I interrogated them whether they were Christians; if they confessed it, I repeated the question twice again, adding the threat of capital punishment; if they still

THE CORRESPONDENCE BETWEEN PLINY AND TRAJAN. Source: Pliny, *Letters*, translated by William Melmoth, Cambridge, Mass.: Harvard University Press, Vol. II, pp. 401–05, 407. Reprinted by permission of the publishers and the Loeb Classical Library.

persevered, I ordered them to be executed. For whatever the nature of their creed might be, I could at least feel no doubt that . . . inflexible obstinacy deserved chastisement. . . .

These accusations spread (as is usually the case) from the mere fact of the matter being investigated, and several forms of the mischief came to light. A placard was put up, without any signature, accusing a large number of persons by name. Those who denied they were, or had ever been, Christians, who repeated after me an invocation to the gods, and offered adoration, with wine and frankincense, to your image, which I had ordered to be brought for that purpose, together with those of the gods, and who finally cursed Christ — none of which acts, it is said, those who are really Christians can be forced into performing — these I thought it proper to discharge. Others who were named by that informer at first confessed themselves Christians, and then denied it; true, they had been of that persuasion but they had quitted it, some three years, others many years, and a few as much as twenty-five years ago. . . .

They affirmed, however, the whole of their guilt or their error was that they were in the habit of meeting on a certain fixed day before it was light, when they sang in alternate verses a hymn to Christ as to a god, and bound themselves by a solemn oath not to any wicked deeds, but never to commit any fraud [or] theft or . . . to falsify their word, nor deny a trust when they should be called upon to deliver it up; after which it was their custom to separate and then reassemble to partake of food — but food of an ordinary and innocent kind. . . . I judged it so much the more necessary to extract the real truth with the assistance of torture from two female slaves who were styled deaconesses: but I could discover nothing more than depraved and excessive superstition. . . .

The matter seemed to me well worth referring to you — especially considering the numbers endangered. Persons of all ranks and ages and of both sexes are, and will be, involved in the prosecution. For this contagious superstition is not confined to the cities only, but has spread through the villages and rural districts; it seems possible, however, to check and cure it. . . .

Trajan's Reply

The method you have pursued, my dear Pliny, in sifting the cases of those denounced to you as Christians is extremely proper. It is not possible to lay down any general rule which can be applied as the fixed standard in all cases of this nature. No search should be made for these people; when they are denounced and found guilty they must be punished, with the restriction, however, that when the party denies himself to be a Christian and shall give proof that he is not (that is, by adoring our gods), he shall be pardoned on the ground of repentance, even though he may have formerly incurred suspicion. Informations without the accuser's name subscribed [affixed] must not be admitted in evidence against anyone, as it is introducing a very dangerous precedent and by no means agreeable to the spirit of the age.

Martyrs for the Faith

There were also arrested certain heathen slaves of our members, since the governor had publicly commanded that we should all be prosecuted, and these, by the snare of Satan, fearing the tortures which they saw the saints suffering, when the soldiers urged them, falsely accused us of . . . things which it is not right for us either to speak of or to think of or even to believe that such things could ever happen among men. When this rumor spread all men turned like beasts against us, so that even if any had formerly been lenient for friendship's sake they then became furious and raged against us, and there was fulfilled that which was spoken by our Lord that "the time will come when whosoever killeth you will think that he doeth God service." Then at last the holy martyrs endured sufferings beyond all description, for Satan was striving to wring some blasphemy even from them, and all the fury of the mob and of the governor and of the soldiers was raised beyond measure against Sanctus, the deacon from Vienne, and against Maturus, who was a novice but a noble contender, and against Attalus, a Pergamene by race, who had always been a pillar and support of the Christians there, and against Blandina. . . .

Maturus and Sanctus and Blandina and Attalus were led forth to the wild beasts, to the public, and to a common exhibition of the inhumanity of the heathen, for the day of fighting with beasts was specially appointed for the Christians. Maturus and Sanctus passed again through all torture in the amphitheater as though they had suffered nothing

MARTYRS FOR THE FAITH. Source: Eusebius, *Ecclesiastical History*, translated by Kirsopp Lake, Cambridge, Mass.: Harvard University Press, Vol. I, pp. 413–33. Reprinted by permission of the publishers and the Loeb Classical Library.

before, but rather as though, having conquered the opponent in many bouts, they were now striving for his crown. Once more they ran the gauntlet in the accustomed manner, endured the worrying of the wild beasts and everything which the maddened public, some in one way, some in another, were howling for and commanding, finally, the iron chair on which the roasting of their own bodies clothed them with its reek. Their persecutors did not stop even here, but went on growing more and more furious, wishing to conquer their endurance, yet gained nothing from Sanctus beyond the sound of the confession which he had been accustomed to make from the beginning.

Thus after a long time, when their life still remained in them through the great contest, they were at last sacrificed, having been made a spectacle to the world throughout that day as a substitute for all the variations of gladiatorial contests; but Blandina was hung on a stake and offered as a prey to the wild beasts that were let in. She seemed to be hanging in the shape of a cross, and by her continuous prayer gave great zeal to the combatants while they looked on during the contest and with their outward eyes saw in the form of their sister Him who was crucified for them, to persuade those who believe in Him that all who suffer for the glory of Christ have forever fellowship with the living God. Then when none of the beasts would touch her she was taken down from the stake and brought back into the jail, and was thus preserved for another contest. . . .

In addition to all this, on the last day of the gladiatorial sports, Blandina was again brought in with Ponticus, a boy of about fifteen years, and they had been brought in every day to see the torture of the others, and efforts were made to force them to swear by the idols, and the mob was furious against them because they had remained steadfast and disregarded them, so that there was neither pity for the youth of the boy nor respect for the sex of the woman. They exposed them to all the terrors and put them through every torture in turn, trying to make them swear but not being able to do so. For Ponticus was encouraged by the Christian sister, so that even the heathen saw that she was exhorting and strengthening him, and after nobly enduring every torture he gave up his spirit. But the blessed Blandina, last of all, like a noble mother who had encouraged her children and sent them forth triumphant to the king, having herself endured all the tortures of the children, hastened to them, rejoicing and glad at her departure as though invited to a marriage feast rather than cast to the beasts. And after scourging, after the beasts, after the gridiron, she was at last put in a net and thrown to a bull. She was tossed about a long time by the beast, having no more feeling for what happened to her through her hope and hold on what had been entrusted to her and her converse with Christ. And so she too was sacrificed, and the heathen themselves confessed that never before among them had a woman suffered so much and so long.

The Triumph of Christianity

Christianity spread and flourished amid the waves of imperial persecution. At the beginning of the fourth century, after another period of fierce repression, it was granted tolerance. Henceforth, with the exception of one, all Roman emperors favored Christianity. As the old state religion began to lose ground, the emperors withdrew from it their official support. Not interested in religion as such, they wanted only to unite the Empire, and unity could now be more effectively accomplished with the help of the Christians. Under the Emperor Theodosius I (379–395) the edict given below was issued, proclaiming Christianity the official religion of the Empire and making all other faiths illegal and subject to punishment.

It is our desire that all the various nations which are subject to our clemency and moderation should continue in the profession of that religion which was delivered to the Romans by the divine Apostle Peter, as it hath been preserved by faithful tradition; and which is now professed by the Pontiff Damasus and by Peter, Bishop of Alexandria, a man of apostolic holiness. According to the apostolic teaching and the doctrine of the Gospel, let us believe the one deity of the Father, the Son, and the Holy Spirit, in equal majesty and in a holy Trinity. We authorize

Source: Henry Bettenson, editor, *Documents of the Christian Church*, London: Oxford University Press, 1947, pp. 31–32; and from *Documents of the Continental Reformation*, edited by the Reverend B. J. Kidd, Oxford: The Clarendon Press, 1911. Reprinted by permission of the publishers.

85

the followers of this law to assume the title of Catholic Christians; but as for the others, since in our judgment they are foolish madmen, we decree that they shall be branded with the ignominious name of heretics, and shall not presume to give to their conventicles * the name of churches. They will suffer in the first place the chastisement of the divine condemnation, and in the second the punishment which our authority, in accordance with the will of Heaven, shall decide to inflict.

* **conventicles:** meeting places.

PART THREE

The Middle Ages

The Byzantine Empire

The Eastern Roman Empire survived the disintegration of the Empire in the West by about one thousand years. Though the Eastern Empire became increasingly Greek in its culture, its citizens continued to call themselves Romans, and the emperors retained the title "King of the Romans." To the people of this region, Constantinople was the legitimate successor to Rome.

Justinian, who was Emperor from 527 to 565, ruled as an oriental autocrat. Every area of life, including religion, trade, and industry, was under his control. His dream to unite and reestablish the ancient Roman Empire was ruinous in cost and ended in failure. The oppressiveness of the autocracy resulted in numerous uprisings, the most dangerous of which was the Nike Rebellion in 532. The greatest monuments of Justinian's reign are the codification of Roman law and the construction of the glorious Church of Holy Wisdom (Hagia Sophia).

The following account of the reign of Justinian was written by Procopius, who was the aide of Belisarius, the most famous general of his day. Procopius knew Justinian and the Empress Theodora from personal observation, and most of his writings about them are full of praise. Later in life, however, he wrote a Secret History in which he claimed to portray the real nature of the Emperor and Empress. It is generally agreed that he exaggerated their vices.

In the second selection the city of Constantinople in A.D. 1000 is vividly described by W. S. Davis.

The Character of Justinian and Theodora

All that has befallen the Roman nation in its wars up to the present day has been narrated by me, as far as it proved possible, on the plan of arranging all the accounts of its activities in accordance with their

THE CHARACTER OF JUSTINIAN AND THEODORA. Source: Procopius, *Secret History*, XIII, XV, translated by H. B. Dewing, Cambridge, Mass.: Harvard University Press, Vol. VI, pp. 3, 99, 101, 131, 177–81. Reprinted by permission of the publishers and the Loeb Classical Library.

proper time and place. Henceforth, however, this plan of composition will be followed by me no longer, for here shall be set down everything that came to pass in every part of the Roman Empire. The reason for this is that it was not possible, as long as the actors were still alive, for these things to be recorded in the way they should have been. For neither was it possible to elude the vigilance of multitudes of spies, nor, if detected, to escape a most cruel death. Indeed, I was unable to feel confidence even in the most intimate of my kinsmen. . . .

This Emperor was insincere, crafty, hypocritical, dissembling [hiding] his anger, doubledealing, clever, a perfect artist in acting out an opinion which he pretended to hold, and even able to produce tears, not from joy or sorrow, but . . . according to the need of the moment, always playing false yet not carelessly, but adding both his signature and the most terrible oaths to bind his agreements. . . . But he departed straightway from his agreements and his oaths, just like the vilest slaves, who, through fear of the tortures hanging over them, are induced to make confession of acts which they had denied on oath. He was a fickle friend, a truceless enemy, an ardent devotee of assassination and of robbery. . . . And in addition to his other shortcomings, while he was very easygoing as to lending an ear to slanders, yet he was severe as to inflicting punishment. . . . He never paused for a thorough investigation before reaching a decision, but straightway upon hearing what the slanderer said, he would make his decision and order it published. And he did not hesitate to write orders that called for the capture of towns and the burning of cities and the enslavement of whole peoples, for no reason whatever. . . .

And after he had slain perhaps myriads for no good reason, he straightway embarked on plans for the ruin of many more. So then, the Romans being at peace with the whole world, and he by reason of his lust for blood not knowing what to do with himself, Justinian kept bringing all the barbarians into collision with one another. . . .

Such, then, was Justinian. As for Theodora, she had a mind fixed firmly and persistently upon cruelty. For she never did anything at any time as the result of persuasion or compulsion by another person, but she herself, applying a stubborn will, carried out her decisions with all her might, no one daring to intercede for the victim who had given offense. . . . And to state the matter briefly, no one ever saw Theodora reconciled with one who had given offense, even after the person had died, but the son of the deceased received the Empress' enmity as an inheritance from him, just as he received anything else that had been his father's, and passed it on to the third generation. . . .

She claimed the right to administer the whole Roman Empire. And if the Emperor should impose any task upon a man without her consent, that man's affairs would suffer such a turn of fortune that not long thereafter he would be dismissed from his office with the greatest indignities and would die a most shameful death.

The Magnificence of Constantinople

Size and Population

Around A.D. 1000 Christian Constantinople undoubtedly boasted over 500,000 inhabitants and may well have approximated 1,000,000. It was incomparably the largest city in Christendom, and, since the waning of the splendors of Baghdad, probably surpassed any other in the known world. . . .

Strangers were lost in . . . eloquence when describing the magnificence of New Rome and the impression which a visit to it produced upon them. Its denizens [residents] took this homage as a matter of course. To them their capital was not only "The City guarded by God," it was "*The City*" — as if all other communities in the world were merely secondary towns. . . .

Wealth and Commerce

Its income largely rested upon the teeming commerce and tireless industry of Constantinople and the other wealthy sections of the Empire. In the twelfth century Benjamin of Tudela [in Spain] visited Constantinople and recorded his admiration and wonder: "Hither come the merchants from all sides — from Babylonia, from Media, from Persia; from Egypt, from Canaan, from Russia; from Hungary, from Lombardy, from Spain. . . . There is no other city in the world to which I can compare it save only Baghdad." He is in ecstasies over "the richness of Hagia Sophia," and of the imperial palace, "whither they bear the tribute of all Greece. The towers are filled with garments of silk, of purple, and of gold. . . . The native Greeks are rich in gold and

THE MAGNIFICENCE OF CONSTANTINOPLE. Source: W. S. Davis, A *Short History of the Near East, From the Founding of Constantinople* (330 A.D. to 1922), New York: The Macmillan Company, 1922, pp. 59, 68–69, 70–71. Copyright 1922 by The Macmillan Company; renewed 1950 by Alice R. Davis. Reprinted by permission.

pearls; they are clothed in garments of silk fringed with gold or elaborate embroideries. . . ."

Industries and Control of Trade

The gains of Constantinople came partly of course in a heavy import and export tax which took its toll from every article bought and sold in the great marts and exchanges lining the plazas and the quays. . . . But a large part of the wealth of the Empire came not by way of her middlemen but through her industrialists. The greatest silk manufactures were largely located in Greece, but Constantinople herself boasted her thousands of looms and forges. The old arts and handicrafts of antiquity had still their . . . disciples. Jewel work of all varieties, enamels and religious ornaments so indispensable in the churches, bronzes, elegant glass work, furs beautifully dyed — in short, practically everything that could pass as luxuries in the Middle Ages — was manufactured beside the Bosporus and distributed afar. Besides these works there were produced a great supply of weapons, tools, and other metal wares, tasteful or useful. . . .

The state fixed prices, wages, terms of sale, and the actual processes of manufacturing. The importation of certain articles, e.g., soap from southern France, was carefully forbidden lest they compete with native products. On the other hand, the export of certain articles was as carefully prohibited. Thus it was a grave offense to send from the Empire garments dyed with that superior purple which was reserved for the imperial family. The government inspector or tax gatherer had his eye on every transaction, and the imposts doubtless often ate . . . into the margin of profit.

The Rise and Spread of Islam

The Moslem faith, which now embraces four hundred million people, or about one eighth of the world's population, traces its origins to the commercial town of Mecca located in the dry and barren region of western Arabia. About the early life of Mohammed (570–632), the founder of Islam,* we know very little. He

* **Islam:** the word means "submitting oneself to God." A follower of the Islamic faith is called a Muslim. "Moslem" is a Western version of Muslim.

became an orphan while young, worked hard for his living, and received scant education. His marriage to a wealthy widow gave him the leisure to meditate. At the age of forty, while reflecting in a lonely cave near Mecca, he received the first of a series of revelations from God through the angel Gabriel. These revelations are included in the Moslem "bible" — the Koran (the Recitation). The fundamental article of the Moslem faith is "there is no god but Allah (the one God), and Mohammed is His Prophet."

Success in gaining converts came very slowly at first. To avoid local persecution, Mohammed and his followers left Mecca in 622 and settled in nearby Medina. (The date of the Hegira, or Emigration, later became the first year of the Moslem calendar.) In Medina the Prophet's influence began to grow. Within the ten years of life which remained to Mohammed, his religion gained numerous converts, and by 630 he was able to re-enter and win Mecca. From such humble beginnings grew the great Islamic civilization.

The Teachings of Mohammed

Praise be to God, Lord of the worlds!
The compassionate, the merciful!
King on the day of reckoning!
Thee only do we worship, and to Thee do we cry for help.
Guide Thou us on the straight path,
The path of those to whom Thou hast been gracious — with whom
    thou art not angry, and who go not astray.

Say: He is God alone:
God the eternal!
He begetteth not, and He is not begotten;
And there is none like unto Him.

What thinkest thou of him who treateth our religion as a lie?
He it is who thrusteth away the orphan,

THE TEACHINGS OF MOHAMMED. Source: The Koran, translated by J. M. Rodwell, Everyman's Library Edition, 1937, pp. 28, 29, 31, 40–41, 61, 378–79. Reprinted by permission of E. P. Dutton & Co., Inc. and J. M. Dent & Sons, Ltd., London.

And stirreth not others up to feed the poor.
Woe to those who pray,
But in their prayer are careless;
Who make a show of devotion,
But refuse help to the needy.

The desire of increasing riches occupieth you,
Till ye come to the grave,
Nay! but in the end ye shall know —
Nay! once more, in the end ye shall know your folly.
Nay! would that ye knew it with knowledge of certainty!
Surely ye shall see hellfire.
Then shall ye surely see it with the eye of certainty;
Then shall ye on that day be taken to task concerning pleasures.

Praise the name of thy Lord the Most High,
Who hath created and balanced all things,
Who hath fixed their destinies and guideth them,
Who bringeth forth the pasture,
And reduceth it to dusky stubble.
We will teach thee to recite the Koran, nor aught shalt thou forget,
Save what God pleaseth; for he knoweth alike things manifest and
     hidden; . . .
Happy he who is purified by Islam,
And who remembereth the name of his Lord and prayeth.
But ye prefer this present life,
Though the life to come is better and more enduring.
This truly is in the Books of old,
The Books of Abraham and Moses.

Perish the liars,
Who are bewildered in the depths of ignorance!
They ask, "When this day of judgment?"
On that day they shall be tormented at the fire.
"Taste ye of this your torment, whose speedy coming ye challenged."
But the God-fearing shall dwell amid gardens and fountains,
Enjoying what their Lord hath given them, because aforetime they were
     well-doers:

But little of the night was it that they slept,
And at dawn they prayed for pardon,
And gave due share of their wealth to the suppliant and the outcast.

The infidels spend their riches with intent to turn men aside from the way of God: spend it they shall; then shall sighing be upon them, and then shall they be overcome.

And the infidels shall be gathered together into hell,

That God may separate the bad from the good, and put the bad one upon the other, and heap them all up and put them into hell! These are they who shall be lost.

Say to the infidels: If they desist from their unbelief, what is now past shall be forgiven them; but if they return to it, they have already before them the doom of the ancients!

Fight then against them till strife be at an end, and the religion be all of it God's. If they desist, verily God beholdeth what they do:

But if they turn their back, know ye that God is your protector: Excellent protector! excellent helper!

And know ye that when ye have taken any booty, a fifth part belongeth to God and to the Apostle, and to the near of kin, and to orphans, and to the poor, and to the wayfarer, if ye believe in God. . . .

Believers! when you confront a troop, stand firm and make frequent mention of the name of God, that it may fare well with you:

And obey God and his Apostle; and dispute not, lest ye become fainthearted and your success go from you; but endure with steadfastness, for God is with the steadfastly enduring.

Holy War

What made Islam so militant a faith? The explanation is clearly to be sought in the career of Mohammed. His preaching failed to convert Mecca; the hostility he aroused was the signal for an armed conflict between the two rival towns [Mecca and Medina]. To spur on his followers to overcome the "idolators" of Mecca, a Koranic revelation

HOLY WAR. Source: "The Caliph Omar: Arab Imperialist," J. J. Saunders, in *History Today*, Vol. XI, No. 3, March, 1961, pp. 180–81. Reprinted by permission of the author and *History Today*, London.

enjoined [commanded] them to "Fight in the cause of God against those who fight you, but do not be the aggressors." The early Moslems thus fought their heathen enemies in the same spirit as the Israelites of old fought the Canaanites. Mecca was won by the sword, and the Prophet resolved to extirpate [uproot] idolatry from the whole land. But many Arabs were Jews or Christians: what was to be done with them? Mohammed respected the older monotheistic faiths, from which he had learned so much; their adherents could not be classed among the pagans; he styled them "People of the Book" (they possessed sacred scriptures), and commanded that they were not to be forced into Islam but were to be allowed to retain their ancestral religion on payment of tribute. In 628 or 629, his messengers appeared among the Christian tribes on the Syrian frontier, some of whom owed allegiance to the Byzantine emperor. They met with an unfriendly reception; one messenger is alleged to have been killed, whereupon a new Koranic revelation proclaimed war against "those who do not believe in Allah nor in the Last Day and do not forbid what Allah and his Apostle have forbidden and do not practice the religion of truth, until they pay tribute and are subdued." On these texts, the first directed against the Meccan pagans, the second against the Christian Bedouins of the northern borderlands, was based the whole theory of *jihad*, or holy war. Doubtless Mohammed had no idea of world conquest. He conceived it his duty to give all his fellow countrymen the chance of embracing Islam. If the summons was resisted by violence, then he must fight back. But the Arab nomads who ranged the Syrian desert from the Dead Sea to the lower reaches of the Euphrates were mostly Christian tribes under the protection of one of the two great powers, the Byzantine Empire and the Persian Kingdom. Any attempt to subdue them would almost certainly involve the Moslems in hostilities with these states; indeed, a force sent by Mohammed in 629 against the tribesmen of the Syrian border was cut to pieces at Mu'ta, a village to the east of the Dead Sea, by a mixed body of Arabs and Byzantines. The Prophet swore revenge, but he did not live to fulfill his vow. A precedent had, however, been set; what God and his Apostle had commanded must be carried out; war against unbelievers was sanctioned by divine revelation and the example of the Prophet.

The Reign of Charlemagne

The dream of reviving the Roman Empire died hard even among the barbarian invaders. Roman traditions were maintained in barbarian courts and the Roman pattern was imitated to some degree in administration. There was no startling break between the late Empire and the early barbarian kingdoms.

The most successful attempt to unite the West was made by Charlemagne (768–814), who was crowned Emperor of the Romans by the Pope in the year 800 on Christmas Day. Historians are still debating whether Charlemagne wanted and expected the crown to be placed on his head while he was kneeling at Mass. Considering the power which Charlemagne wielded over the papacy, it seems unlikely that the Pope would have taken such a step without Charlemagne's silent approval, and Charlemagne gave every indication of enjoying the title.

Charlemagne extended his realm in all directions, imposing Christianity by force on his conquered victims. He organized a loyal, fair, and efficient administration. Though he had enormous energy and personal prestige, it was still difficult for him to rule effectively throughout his vast dominions.

Intellectual life had been seriously disrupted by the barbarian invaders. In a valiant attempt to cope with ignorance and poverty of learning, Charlemagne made his court at Aix-la-Chapelle a center of culture. Scholars were invited there from all over Europe.

The best description of Charlemagne was written by his friend Einhard, from whose work the first selection is taken. The second selection consists of excerpts from letters written by Charlemagne to Church officials.

The Character of Charlemagne

He was by nature most ready to contract friendships, and not only made friends easily, but clung to them persistently, and cherished most fondly those with whom he had formed such ties. He was so care-

THE CHARACTER OF CHARLEMAGNE. Source: Einhard, *Life of Charlemagne*, translated by Samuel E. Turner, New York: American Book Co., 1880, pp. 52–64.

ful of the training of his sons and daughters that he never took his meals without them when he was at home. . . . Strange to say, although his daughters were very handsome women and he loved them very dearly, he was never willing to marry any of them to a man of their own nation or to a foreigner, but kept them all at home until his death, saying that he could not dispense with their society. . . .

He liked foreigners and was at great pains to take them under his protection. There were often so many of them, both in the palace and the kingdom, that they might reasonably have been considered a nuisance; but he, with his broad humanity, was very little disturbed by such annoyances. . . .

Charles was large and strong and of lofty stature, though not disproportionately tall (his height is well known to have been seven times the length of his foot); the upper part of his head was round, his eyes very large and animated, nose a little long, hair fair, and face laughing and merry. Thus his appearance was always stately and dignified, whether he was standing or sitting, although his neck was thick and somewhat short and his belly rather prominent; but the symmetry of the rest of his body concealed these defects. His gait was firm, his whole carriage manly, and his voice clear, but not so strong as his size led one to expect. . . .

He used to wear the national, that is to say the Frank, dress: next to his skin a linen shirt and linen breeches and above these a tunic fringed with silk, while hose fastened by bands covered his lower limbs, and shoes his feet; and he protected his shoulders and chest in winter by a close-fitting coat of otter or marten skins. Over all he flung a blue cloak, and he always had a sword girt about him, usually one with a gold or silver hilt and belt; he sometimes carried a jeweled sword, but only on great feast days or at the reception of ambassadors from foreign nations. He despised foreign costumes, however handsome, and never allowed himself to be robed in them, except twice in Rome. . . .

Charles was temperate in eating, and particularly so in drinking, for he abominated drunkenness in anybody, much more in himself and those of his household; but he could not easily abstain from food, and often complained that fasts injured his health. He very rarely gave entertainments, only on great feast days, and then to large numbers of people. His meals ordinarily consisted of four courses, not counting the roast, which his huntsmen used to bring in on the spit; he was more fond of this than of any other dish. While at table, he listened to reading or music. The subjects of the readings were the stories and deeds of olden time; he was fond, too, of St. Augustine's books, and especially of the one entitled *The City of God*. . . .

Charles had the gift of ready and fluent speech, and could express whatever he had to say with the utmost clearness. He was not satisfied with command of his native language merely, but gave attention to the study of foreign ones, and in particular was such a master of Latin that he could speak it as well as his native tongue; but he could understand Greek better than he could speak it. . . . He most zealously cultivated the liberal arts, held those who taught them in great esteem, and conferred great honors upon them. . . . The King spent much time and labor . . . studying rhetoric, dialectics, and especially astronomy; he learned to reckon, and used to investigate the motions of the heavenly bodies most curiously, with an intelligent scrutiny. He also tried to write, and used to keep tablets and blanks in bed under his pillow, that at leisure hours he might accustom his hand to form the letters; however, as he did not begin his efforts in due season, but late in life, they met with ill success.

He cherished with the greatest fervor and devotion the principles of the Christian religion, which had been instilled into him from infancy. . . .

He was very forward in succoring [aiding] the poor, and in that gratuitous generosity which the Greeks call alms, so much so that he not only made a point of giving in his own country and his own kingdom, but when he discovered that there were Christians living in poverty in Syria, Egypt, and Africa, at Jerusalem, Alexandria, and Carthage, he had compassion on their wants, and used to send money over the seas to them.

The Revival of Learning

Although correct conduct may be better than knowledge, nevertheless knowledge precedes conduct. Therefore each one ought to study what he desires to accomplish, so that so much the more fully the mind may know what ought to be done, as the tongue hastens in the praises

THE REVIVAL OF LEARNING. Source: *Translations and Reprints from the Original Sources of European History*, Philadelphia: University of Pennsylvania Press, 1900, Vol. VI, No. 5, pp. 13–15.

of omnipotent God without the hindrances of errors. . . . For when in the years just passed letters were often written to us from several monasteries in which it was stated that the brethren who dwelt there offered up in our behalf sacred and pious prayers, we have recognized in most of these letters both correct thoughts and uncouth expressions; because what pious devotion dictated faithfully to the mind, the tongue, uneducated on account of the neglect of study, was not able to express in the letter without error. Whence it happened that we began to fear lest perchance, as the skill in writing was less, so also the wisdom for understanding the Holy Scriptures might be much less than it rightly ought to be. And we all know well that, although errors of speech are dangerous, far more dangerous are errors of the understanding. Therefore we exhort you not only not to neglect the study of letters, but also with most humble mind, pleasing to God, to study earnestly in order that you may be able more easily and more correctly to penetrate the mysteries of the divine Scriptures. . . . For we desire you to be, as it is fitting that soldiers of the Church should be, devout in mind, learned in discourse, chaste in conduct, and eloquent in speech.

Therefore, because we take care constantly to improve the condition of our churches, we have striven with watchful zeal to advance the cause of learning, which has been almost forgotten by the negligence of our ancestors; and by our example also, we invite those whom we can to master the study of the liberal arts. Accordingly, God aiding us in all things, we have already corrected carefully all the books of the Old and New Testaments, corrupted by the ignorance of the copyists.

And we also demand of your holiness that the ministers of the altar of God shall adorn their ministry by good manners, and likewise the other orders, . . . and let them join and associate to themselves not only children of servile condition, but also sons of free men. And let schools be established in which boys may learn to read. Correct carefully the Psalms, the signs in writing, the songs, the calendar, the grammar, in each monastery or bishopric, and the Catholic books; because often some desire to pray to God properly, but they pray badly because of the incorrect books.

The Disintegration of Charlemagne's Empire

Charlemagne's empire did not long survive his death. The Frankish custom of dividing an estate among all male heirs was bound to result in chaos and civil war when that estate was the kingdom itself. Only one of Charlemagne's sons survived to rule, so that the problem of division was avoided temporarily, but his three grandchildren fought bitterly until they settled their differences in 843 by dividing the empire.

A series of new invasions further destroyed all active central government. Vikings from the north, Moslems from the south, and Magyars from the east all inflicted great suffering on the population of western Europe. As the central governments proved helpless to provide security and impose order, real power fell into the hands of the local nobility, who alone were in a position to organize an army and maintain a semblance of government. Localized authority took the place of central authority.

Our sources for this chaotic century are sparse. One of the best is a history kept in the monastery at Xanten, which was in the area of Cologne.

(845)   Twice in the canton of Worms there was an earthquake, the first in the night following Palm Sunday, the second in the holy night of Christ's Resurrection. In the same year the heathen broke in upon the Christians at many points, but more than twelve thousand of them were killed by the Frisians. Another party of invaders devastated Gaul; of these more than six hundred men perished. Yet owing to his indulgence, Charles * agreed to give them many thousand pounds of gold and silver if they would leave Gaul; and this they did. Nevertheless, the cloisters of most of the saints were destroyed and many of the Christians were led away captive. . . .

* **Charles** and **Louis** were two of Charlemagne's grandsons. Each ruled a portion of Charlemagne's empire.

Source: James Harvey Robinson, editor, *Readings in European History*, Boston: Ginn & Company, 1904, Vol. I, pp. 158–63.

(846) According to their custom the Northmen plundered Eastern and Western Frisia and burned the town of Dordrecht, with two other villages, before the eyes of Lothaire, who was then in the castle of Nimwegen but could not punish the crime. The Northmen, with their boats filled with immense booty including both men and goods, returned to their own country. . . .

At this same time, as no one can mention or hear without great sadness, the Mother of all churches, the Basilica of the Apostle Peter, was taken and plundered by the Moors, or Saracens, who had already occupied the region of Beneventum. The Saracens, moreover, slaughtered all the Christians whom they found outside the walls of Rome, either within or without this church. They also carried men and women away prisoners. They tore down, among many others, the altar of the blessed Peter, and their crimes from day to day bring sorrow to Christians. Pope Sergius departed life this year.

(847) The Northmen here and there plundered the Christians and engaged in a battle with the counts Sigir and Liuthar. They continued up the Rhine as far as Dordrecht and nine miles farther to Meginhard, when they turned back, having taken their booty. . . .

(849) While King Louis was ill his army of Bavaria took its way against the Bohemians. Many of these were killed and the remainder withdrew, much humiliated, into their own country. The heathen from the north wrought havoc in Christendom as usual and grew greater in strength; but it is revolting to say more of this matter.

(850) On January 1 of that season, . . . toward evening, a great deal of thunder was heard and a mighty flash of lightning seen; and an overflow of water afflicted the human race during this winter. In the following summer an all too great heat of the sun burned the earth. Leo, Pope of the Apostolic See, an extraordinary man, built a fortification round the Church of St. Peter the Apostle. The Moors, however, devastated here and there the coast towns of Italy. . . .

(851) The Normans inflicted much harm in Frisia and about the Rhine. A mighty army of them collected by the river Elbe against the Saxons, and some of the Saxon towns were besieged, others burned, and most terribly did they oppress the Christians. A meeting of our kings took place on the Maas [the river Meuse].

(852) The steel of the heathen glistened; excessive heat; a famine followed. There was not fodder enough for the animals. The pasturage for the swine was more than sufficient.

(853) A great famine in Saxony so that many were forced to live on horsemeat. . . .

(882) The Northmen in ·the month of October entrenched themselves at Condé and horribly devastated the kingdom of Carloman, while King Charles with his army took his stand on the Somme at Barleux. . . .

They destroyed houses, and razed monasteries and churches to the ground, and brought to their death the servants of our holy religion by famine and sword, or sold them beyond the sea. They killed the dwellers in the land and none could resist them.

Abbot Hugo, when he heard of these calamities, gathered an army and came to aid the King. When the Northmen came back from a plundering expedition . . . he, in company with the King, gave them chase. They, however, betook themselves to a wood, and scattered hither and yon, and finally returned to their ships with little loss. . . .

(883) In the spring the Northmen left Condé and sought the country along the sea. Here they dwelt through the summer; they forced the Flemings to flee from their lands and raged everywhere, laying waste the country with fire and sword.

Feudal Society

The life of the feudal lord, the splendor of his castle, the gallantry of chivalry, and the fighting ability of the knight have all been somewhat romanticized by later generations. Modern scholars have attempted to give a more accurate picture of feudal life. In the first and second selections, Sidney Painter, an American medievalist, discusses the feudal castle and knightly chivalry; in the third, C. W. C. Oman, a British scholar, describes the nature of feudal warfare.

·

Life in a Medieval Castle

On the material side the life of the feudal class was rough and uncomfortable. The castles were cold and drafty. If a castle was of

LIFE IN A MEDIEVAL CASTLE. Source: Sidney Painter, *Medieval Society*, Ithaca, New York: Cornell University Press, 1951, pp. 30–31. Reprinted by permission of the publishers.

wood, you had no fire, and if a stone castle allowed you to have one, you smothered in the smoke. Until the thirteenth century no one except a few great feudal princes had a castle providing more than two rooms. In the hall the lord . . . received his officials and vassals, held his court, and entertained ordinary guests. There the family and retainers ate on trestle tables that at night served as beds for the servants and guests. The chamber was the private abode of the lord and his family. The lord and lady slept in a great bed, their children had smaller beds, and their personal servants slept on the floor. Distinguished visitors were entertained in the chamber. When the lord of the castle wanted a private talk with a guest, they [both] sat on the bed. The lord and his family could have all the food they could eat, but it was limited in variety. Great platters of game, both birds and beasts, were the chief standby, reinforced with bread and vast quantities of wine. They also had plenty of clothing, but the quality was largely limited by the capacity of the servant girls who made it. In short, in the tenth and eleventh centuries the noble had two resources, land and labor. But the labor was magnificently inefficient and by our standards the land was badly tilled. Not until the revival of trade could the feudal class begin to live in anything approaching luxury.

Chivalry

During the eleventh and twelfth centuries there grew out of the environment and way of life of the feudal class a system of ethical ideas that we call chivalry: virtues appropriate to the knight or chevalier. . . .

The German warriors had brought with them into the Roman Empire an admiration for the warrior virtues, courage and prowess in battle. They also valued the sound judgment that the feudal age was to call wisdom and fidelity to one's . . . word, later known as loyalty. Respect for these virtues was not a recent acquisition of the Frankish nobles. Their importance among the Germanic peoples can be clearly seen by a reader of the Norse sagas and Anglo-Saxon literature. But they were peculiarly applicable to feudal society. A man whose chief function was fighting had to be brave and effective in battle. Wisdom was a

CHIVALRY. Source: *Ibid.*, pp. 32–34.

necessary attribute of the successful captain. The whole structure of the feudal system depended on respect for one's oath of homage and fidelity. These were the basic feudal virtues and formed the core of feudal chivalry.

The earliest ethical ideas of the feudal class concerned their chief occupation and were designed to make war more pleasant for its participants. Armor was heavy and extremely hot under the blazing sun. No knight wanted to wear his armor when he was simply riding about, yet no knight was ever entirely safe from sudden attack by an enemy. Hence the idea developed that it was highly improper to attack an unarmed knight. You could ambush your foe, but you did not attack him until he had had time to put on his armor and prepare for battle. Then the chief purpose of feudal warfare was to take prisoners who could be ransomed. In the early days you put your prisoner in chains and dumped him in an unused storage bin under your hall. But this was highly unpleasant for the prisoner — and he was likely to be the captor next time. Soon it was the custom to treat a knightly prisoner as an honored guest. The next step was to accept a son or nephew as a hostage while the captive collected his ransom. By the thirteenth century it was usual to release a captured knight on his pledge to return if he could not raise his ransom. The early tournaments were, as has been suggested, merely arranged battles. But the knights who fought in them felt it necessary to rationalize their activity. Hence they soon believed that they fought in tournaments not for amusement or to profit by ransoms but to win glory. As time went on the tournaments were carried over into actual warfare. To Froissart * the Hundred Years' War was just a vast series of pleasant and amusing jousts between noble knights whose only purpose was the desire for glory. Perhaps the high point of chivalric behavior was the return of King John of France to prison in England when he found he could not raise his ransom, unless it be the action of a noble lord who hanged one of his infantrymen because he had had the bad taste to kill a knight in battle.

One more virtue of feudal chivalry requires mention: generosity. In most societies men have admired the giver of lavish gifts, and this was a marked trait among the Germans. But this virtue assumed an unusually important place in the feudal code of chivalry. Although the concepts of feudal chivalry sprang from the feudal environment, they

* **Froissart:** a medieval writer.

were popularized and made universally known by professional story-
tellers. The evenings dragged heavily in the gloomy castles, and knights
and ladies were avid for entertainment. This was supplied by various
types of wanderers. There were the tellers of . . . stories, the dancing
bears, and dancing girls. But there were also *trouvères,* who composed
and recited long tales in verse, and minstrels who sang the composi-
tions of others. It was through these stories that the ideas of chivalry
were spread. The livelihood of the singers and composers depended on
the generosity of their patrons. Hence in their stories generosity was
inclined to become the chief of all knightly virtues.

The Knight in Battle

The feudal organization of society made every person of gentle
blood a fighting man, but it cannot be said that it made him a soldier.
If he could sit his charger steadily and handle lance and sword with
skill, the horseman of the twelfth or thirteenth century was regarded
as a model of military efficiency. That discipline or tactical skill may
be as important to an army as mere courage he had no conception. Assembled with difficulty, insubordinate, unable to maneuver, ready to
melt away from its standard the moment that its short period of service was over, a feudal force presented an assemblage of unsoldierlike
qualities such as have seldom been known to coexist. Primarily intended to defend its own borders from the Magyar, the Northman, or
the Saracen, the foes who in the tenth century had been a real danger
to Christendom, the institution [of feudalism] was utterly unadapted to
take the offensive. When a number of tenants-in-chief had come together, each blindly jealous of his fellows and recognizing no superior
but the king — and often even the king was powerless to control his
nobles — it would require a leader of uncommon skill to persuade them
to institute that hierarchy of command which must be established in
every army that is to be something more than an undisciplined
mob. . . . The radical vice of insubordination continued to exist. It was
always possible that at some critical moment a battle might be pre-
cipitated, a formation broken, a plan [upset], by the rashness of some

THE KNIGHT IN BATTLE. Source: C. W. C. Oman, *The Art of War in the
Middle Ages,* revised and edited by John W. Beeler, Ithaca, New York: Cornell University Press, 1953, pp. 57–64. Reprinted by permission of the publishers.

petty baron . . . who could listen to nothing but the promptings of his own heady valor. When the hierarchy of command was based on social status rather than on professional experience, the noble who led the largest contingent or held the highest rank felt himself entitled to assume the direction of the battle. The veteran who brought only a few lances to the array could seldom aspire to influencing the movements of his superiors.

When mere courage takes the place of skill and experience, tactics and strategy alike disappear. Arrogance and stupidity combine to give a certain definite color to the proceedings of the average feudal host. . . . When the enemy came into sight, nothing could restrain the western knights; the shield was shifted into position, the lance dropped into rest, the spur touched the charger, and the mailclad line thundered on, regardless of what might be before it. As often as not its career ended in being dashed against a stone wall or tumbled into a canal, in painful flounderings in a bog or futile surgings around a palisade. The enemy who possessed even a rudimentary system of tactics could hardly fail to be successful against such armies. The fight of El Mansûra (A.D. 1250) may be taken as a fair specimen of the military customs of the thirteenth century. When the French vanguard saw a fair field before them and the lances of the infidel gleaming among the palm groves, they could not restrain their eagerness. With the Count of Artois at their head, they started off in a headlong charge, in spite of St. Louis' (Louis IX) strict prohibition of an engagement. The Mamelukes * retreated, allowed their pursuers to entangle themselves in the streets of a town, and then turned fiercely on them from all sides at once. In a short time the whole "battle" of the Count of Artois was dispersed and cut to pieces. Meanwhile the main body, hearing of the danger of their companions, had ridden off hastily to their aid. However, as each commander took his own route and made what speed he could, the French army arrived upon the field in dozens of small, scattered bodies. These were attacked in detail, and in many cases routed by the Mamelukes. No general battle was fought, but a number of detached and incoherent cavalry combats had all the results of a great defeat. A skirmish and a street fight could overthrow the chivalry of the West, even when it went forth in great strength and was inspired by all the enthusiasm of a Crusade. . . .

* **Mamelukes:** a warlike group of people living in Egypt.

Great battles were, on the whole, infrequent, a fact which appears strange when the long-continued wars of the period are taken into consideration. Whole years of hostilities produced only a few partial skirmishes; compared with modern campaigns, the general engagements were incredibly few. Frederick the Great or Napoleon I fought more battles in one year than a medieval commander in ten. The fact would appear to be that the opposing armies, being guided by no very definite aims and invariably neglecting to keep in touch with each other by means of outposts . . . might often miss each other altogether. . . .

Infantry was in the twelfth and thirteenth centuries absolutely insignificant: foot soldiers accompanied the army for no better purpose than to perform the menial duties of the camp or to assist in the numerous sieges of the period. Occasionally they were employed as light troops, to open the battle by their ineffective demonstrations. There was, however, no really important part for them to play. Indeed, their lords were sometimes affronted if they presumed to delay too long the opening of the cavalry charges, and ended the skirmishing by riding into and over their wretched followers.

The Life of a Peasant

Manorialism was the economic system which fed and sustained feudalism. Manorial institutions go back at least to the third century A.D. when small farmers, oppressed by the taxes of the Roman Empire, gave their land to a powerful lord in return for security. For more than a thousand years the manor and the institution of serfdom dominated European agricultural life. During this period, agricultural labor was not an honorable profession, and a lord never indulged in it.

The serf was not a slave. He had certain rights, hallowed by custom; and even if these rights were sometimes disregarded by the lord they offered a measure of protection. The life of the serf, however, was far from pleasant. Hunger and starvation were never far away. Feudal wars destroyed his home and his crops. Much of his working time belonged to the lord, and taxes were a great burden. Grim though this existence was, it was punctuated by communal festivals and religious holidays. As the centuries passed, conditions for the peasant improved considerably.

In the following selection, the daily life of a peasant on the manor in fourteenth-century England is vividly reconstructed by H. S. Bennett.

Sunday

The sun rose early, for it was late June, but not much earlier than the peasants of the little village of Belcombe, in the year 1320. As the light strengthened, bit by bit the village became visible. . . . In the center of it all, the stone-built church loomed up high and very new looking above everything about it, and made the peasants' houses appear small and insignificant. On closer view, the village was seen to radiate from the church, and down each of the winding ways that led up to it the peasants had built their homes. There they stood, some neat and trim, with their thatched roofs and roughly finished walls in good repair, while others were dilapidated and showed evident signs of neglect and decay. The larger houses stood a little back from the lane, so that the ground in front of each of them was roughly enclosed and set with young cabbage, onions, and parsley, and here and there a few herbs were growing along the sides of the pathway to the house. Most of them had a rudely constructed shed or lean-to at the back of the house, and running away from this stretched another enclosed piece of ground. This was mainly broken up and planted with vegetables, and both here and in the rough grass beyond there were a few apple and cherry trees. At the bottom of the garden where it ran down to the stream the pigs had their sties, and any villager fortunate enough to own a cow tethered it there. . . .

Within most of these houses men were stirring, and before long began to appear at their cottage doors, taking a look at the sky before they ate a brief meal (if such it might be called) of a lump of bread and a draught of ale. Then they came out again, fetched their scythes and rakes from the sheds, and started off down the street, so that for a few minutes the noisy chatter and greetings of neighbors broke the silence. They soon passed by the church and came out into open country, for no hedges or fences were to be seen. One large tract, however, had clearly been cultivated recently, for as they passed they saw how it was

Source: H. S. Bennett, *Life on an English Manor: A Study of Peasant Conditions, 1150–1400*, New York: Cambridge University Press, 1937, pp. 4–7; 14–18. Reprinted by permission of the publishers.

divided into narrow plots, each with grassy raised strips dividing it from its neighbors. Now, however, this field was fallow, and early as it was, one of their fellows was there before them, and was guarding the sheep, which were quietly feeding on such sparse vegetation as was to be found, for the first plowing had already taken place, and next month any weeds the sheep might leave would all be plowed in.

A little farther on they passed a stone cross. Almost unconsciously . . . they crossed themselves, and a moment later turned from the main path to follow a track which led to a piece of meadowland. This, unlike the fallow, was enclosed on three sides with a hedge, while a little stream formed its other boundary. On entering the field the peasants broke up in little groups, some going to one and some to another part of the meadow, for among the long grass there were little pegs and twigs marking off one portion of the field from another. By this time the sun was well up and the dew was drying rapidly as they prepared for work. The wide blade of the scythe was sharpened with the whetstone, and then they turned and with rhythmic movements began to mow the grass in wide sweeping swathes.

In one corner of the field John Wilde and his two sons, Richard and Roger, kept to their tasks for some time without pause. The younger son moved steadily across the strip, turning the hay which had been cut on the previous morning, while his brother Richard worked side by side with his father at the mowing. Save for a pause when the scythes were resharpened, they worked without resting and with but little to say, for there was much to do and time was short, since this was Sunday, and ere long they would have to leave their work for Mass. Indeed, they were fortunate to be on the field at all on such a day, but Sir William, their vicar, had always been lenient in times of harvest; and although he looked with concern at such work, he did not absolutely forbid it, so long as the Mass itself were not neglected. So all three continued until the sun was getting well up in the heavens, when they stopped their work and left the field together with many others. As they passed the church John glanced at the Mass clock on its wall near the door, and saw by the shadow . . . that they had good time before the service, as it was not yet eight.

During their absence the house had not been untended, and after a while the good wife Agnes and her daughter Alice appeared from a room which led out of the main living room. Alice ran out in the garden close and soon the clucking of the hens was heard, and a little later she returned and set down on the wooden bench inside the door a rough earthenware jar of milk which she had just taken from the cow. Meanwhile, her mother had brushed up the embers and had piled together the kindling and a few logs, and already a fire was burning cleanly, and over it hung a large metal pot of water. Then she and her daughter went into the small inner room, which was cleaner and less sooty than its neighbor, and pulled back the thick coverlets and remade the only two beds that stood there. Once this was done, the rough earthen floors of both rooms were swept out with a brush of large twigs, and then the trestle table was put in its place near the side of the room. Some bread and a little ale satisfied Agnes' hunger, while Alice took a drink of the milk she had just brought in. All being done, they turned to prepare for Mass. A large wooden tub on the trestle table served for a washbowl, and after a little washing they occupied themselves for some time in plaiting and arranging their hair, before they drew out of a wooden chest that stood at the foot of the bed the bright-colored dresses which they wore only on Sundays and festivals.

Monday

The next morning saw another early start, for John knew well that Lord Prior's officers would be on the lookout for latecomers; and indeed, it was only a few years since they had tried to insist on everyone appearing at dawn. Though that had been declared contrary to the custom of the manor when it had been discussed at the Manor Court, and therefore had been quietly dropped, nevertheless it was still unwise to appear much later than the neighbors. So John roused up the two boys, and Alice as well, for on these days everyone save the housewife had to appear and help with the lord's hay. As they started they soon met many neighbors: it was a far larger party than that of yesterday, all making their way to the lord's great meadow (for on this manor all the Prior's pasture was in one immense field) which lay in the little valley to the west of the village, and through the midst of which the streamlet flowed so sweetly. Soon after they arrived they had been divided up into groups and placed in different parts of the field by the reeve * and the hayward,* who bustled about from place to place to see that all was well and that work was beginning in good earnest.

* **reeve** and **hayward:** administrators on the manor.

So to the music of whetstone striking on scythe the work began, and the mowers bent to their task, sweeping down the grass in wide swathes as they slowly moved from side to side of the piece allotted to them. John was glad to see old William Honiset already in the field. He could no longer use a scythe, but he was very crafty in the straightening and sharpening of obstinate blades, and the whole day long sat under a great beech tree in one corner of the field with hammer and stone and put a new edge on many a scythe before nightfall. As the sun rose higher and higher the blades swung to and fro, while up and down the field moved a man with a stave in his hand, whose duty it was to oversee the workers. John looked at him as he passed, recalling his own early days, and how often he and the father of this man who now stood over him had worked together in this very meadow, for they had been partners, or "marrows," as the country people termed it, and so did whatever was possible to help one another. But, in his old age, his friend had bought his freedom at a great price, for he had paid to the Lord Prior six marks of silver, the savings of a lifetime, and as much as the yearly income of Sir William, the vicar, himself. Now, therefore, his son was free of everything except a few small services from time to time, of which this was one. . . .

Steadily the work went on till well-nigh noon, when at last the hayward's horn was heard. John straightened himself, and made for the shade with his companions. There they threw themselves down, and soon the manor servants appeared, some carrying great loaves and cheeses, while others brought the ever-welcome barrels of ale. John and his family were given four of the loaves for themselves, and as they cut them open they saw that these were the good wheaten loaves, which so seldom came their way. They ate ravenously of these and of the cheese after their six hours in the open air, and called again and again for ale, of which there was no stint, for this was one of the few days of the year on which the custumal specified that they were to "drink at discretion."

After this meal there was a short, welcome rest, and then they went back to the field once more. Steadily the work went on, and from time to time the now tiring mowers looked at the sky and watched the slow course of the sun over the big trees which bordered the field. The girls and women busied themselves in raking and turning the first cut hay, while the officials were moving busily from place to place trying to keep the workers at their tasks. At last the long-awaited sound of the hayward's horn was heard, and in a few minutes the field was deserted and old and young were making their way and chattering together as they went toward the manor house. The toil of the day was over, and all that remained was the good evening meal that the Lord Prior always gave them as a reward for their labors. . . . Soon the manorial servants brought in the cauldrons, and a mess of thick pease pottage [porridge] was served out to which had been added a little meat for flavoring. This, and a draught of ale, took the sharp edge off their hunger, and they awaited with pleasurable anticipation the next course. The winter had been a hard one, and few of them had been able to buy flesh or to expect more than a bit of boiled bacon from time to time. Some could afford to keep but few chickens or geese, and had to exist as best they might on their scanty produce and on cheese and curds, with oatmeal cake or thick oatmeal pottage to satisfy their ever-hungry children. This and a sour bread of peas and beans had been the lot of many for several months, so that the entry of the servants with great dishes of roast meat caused a hum of satisfaction to go up around the room. Each group tackled the portion set down before them with eagerness, and with many a call to a friend here and a joke with a neighbor at another table, the meal wore on. Ale flowed liberally, and there was "cheese at call" for those who were still hungry.

The Excommunication
of Three Assassins

In a troubled world where life was often short and bitter, the Church provided meaning to man's existence. The bliss of heaven and the horrors of hell were both very real and very close by in the mind of medieval man. The purpose of life on earth was to achieve salvation. Questions of faith and observance, therefore, were of crucial importance.

To each individual the Church offered a means of receiving divine grace through the system of sacraments. Since the Church claimed to hold the keys to the Kingdom of Heaven, it could enforce its will by denying individuals or a whole area the right to receive the sacraments. These forms of punishment *were known respectively as excommunication and interdict. The following is a decree of excommunication from the tenth century against the assassins of a church official.*

In the name of God, and by the power of the Holy Ghost, and the authority divinely granted to bishops by Peter, chief of the Apostles, we separate them from the bosom of holy Mother Church, and condemn them with the anathema of the eternal curse, that they may have no help of man nor any converse with Christians. Let them be accursed in the city and accursed in the country. Accursed be their barns and accursed their bones; accursed be the . . . seed of their lands, their flocks of sheep, and their herds of cattle. Accursed be they in their entering and in their outgoing. Be they accursed at home and homeless elsewhere. . . . Upon their heads fall all the curses with which God through His servant Moses threatened the transgressors of the Divine Law. Let them be *anathema maranatha* [terribly accursed], and let them perish in the second coming of the Lord; and let them moreover endure whatever of evil is provided in the sacred canons and the apostolic decrees for murder and sacrilege. Let the righteous sentence of Divine Condemnation consign them to eternal death. Let no Christian salute them. Let no priest say Mass for them, nor in sickness receive their confession, nor, unless they repent, grant them the sacrosanct communion even on their deathbed. But let them be buried in the grave of an ass, . . . that their shame and malediction may be a warning to present and future generations. And, as these lights which we now cast from our hands are extinguished, so may their light be quenched in eternal darkness.

Source: Henry C. Lea, editor, *Studies in Church History*, Philadelphia: Henry C. Lea, pp. 333–34.

Justice by Ordeal

If innocence or guilt could not be determined by witnesses and evidence, the judgment of God would be invoked. The ordeal was administered by the clergy, though the custom itself goes back to early Germanic tradition.

Of all the ordeals, trial by battle was the most common among the nobility. Women and clergymen, who could not participate, were represented by sturdy champions. Ordeal by hot water and hot iron, usually limited to the servile classes, involved the examination of the wound by the clergy after several days. If the wound were healing properly, the innocence of the individual was established. The clergy, by making the final judgment, would thereby be deciding the case. By the thirteenth century the Church had turned against the. use of ordeal, and it had been generally discontinued by secular authorities as well.

Let the priest go to the church with the prosecutors and with him who is about to be tried. And while the rest wait in the vestibule of the church let the priest enter and put on the sacred garments except the chasuble * and, taking the Gospel and the chrismarium † and the relics of the saints and the chalice, let him go to the altar and speak thus to all the people standing near: "Behold, brethren, the offices of the Christian religion. Behold the law in which are hope and remission of sins, . . . the consecration of the body and blood of our Lord. . . ."

Then let him thus address the one who is to undertake the ordeal: "I command thee, N., in the presence of all, by the Father, the Son, and the Holy Ghost, by the tremendous day of judgment, by the ministry of baptism, by thy veneration for the saints, that if thou art guilty of this matter charged against thee, if thou hast done it or consented to it or hast knowingly seen the perpetrators of this crime, thou enter not into the church nor mingle in the company of Christians unless thou wilt confess and admit thy guilt before thou art examined in public judgment."

Then he shall designate a spot in the vestibule where the fire is to be made for the water, and shall first sprinkle the place with holy water, and shall also sprinkle the kettle when it is ready to be hung and the water in it, to guard against the illusions of the Devil. Then, entering the church with the others, he shall celebrate the Ordeal Mass. After the celebration let the priest go with the people to the place of the ordeal, the Gospel in his left hand, the cross, censer, and relics of

* **chasuble:** an outer ecclesiastical vestment similar to a cloak.
† **chrismarium:** a cruet or vessel for holding consecrated oil.

Source: *Translations and Reprints from the Original Sources in European History,* Philadelphia: University of Pennsylvania Press, 1898, Vol. IV, No. 4, pp. 7–9.

the saints being carried ahead, and let him chant seven penitential psalms. . . .

Then let the man who is to be tried, as well as the kettle or pot in which is the boiling water, be fumed with the incense of myrrh. . . .

Then let the hand that is to be placed in the water be washed with soap, and let it be carefully examined whether it be sound; and before it is thrust in let the priest say: "I adjure thee, O vessel, by the Father, and the Son, and the Holy Ghost, and by the Holy Resurrection, and by the tremendous day of judgment, and by the four Evangelists, that if this man be guilty of this crime either by deed or by consent, let the water boil violently, and do thou, O vessel, turn and swing."

After this let the man who is to be tried plunge in his hand, and afterward let it be immediately sealed up. After the ordeal let him take a drink of holy water. Up to the time of the decision regarding the ordeal * it is a good thing to mix salt and holy water with all his food and drink.

* A period of three days was allowed to elapse before the hand was examined.

St. Benedict's Rules for Monastic Life

In almost every religion, certain individuals have renounced the pleasures of the world and have gone off by themselves or in groups to seek religious perfection and to worship God. Monastic life, which predates Christianity, attracted many pious souls in the Middle Ages. Not all, however, were suited for this particular form of religious life. To counteract the tendencies toward extreme idleness or asceticism which grew up in some places, it was necessary to establish a practical rule of monastic life. The Rule of St. Basil (c. 329–379) became the standard code of monasteries in the East, and the Rule of St. Benedict (c. 480–543) of monasteries in the West.

St. Benedict was born into a wealthy family but chose the austere life of a hermit. Though he shunned the world, his piety attracted many followers. In about 520 he and his disciples established the famous monastery at Monte Cassino. There Benedict drew up a set of rules which became the model of thousands of monasteries. Benedict emphasized labor along with prayer. He also provided for a trial period before the individual took the binding vows of poverty, chastity, and obedience. The followers of Benedict made great contributions to the improvement of agriculture and were responsible for the copying and preservation of thousands of ancient manuscripts.

The instruments of good works — First, to love the Lord God with all the heart, and with all the soul, and with all the strength, and then his neighbor as himself. Then not to kill, not to commit adultery, not to steal, not to covet, not to bear false witness, to honor all men, and not to do to another what he would not have another do to him. To deny himself that he may follow Christ, to chasten the body, to renounce luxuries, to love fasting. To feed the poor, to clothe the naked, to visit the sick, to bury the dead, to offer help in trouble, to comfort the sorrowing. To separate himself from the things of the world, to prefer nothing above the love of Christ, not to give way to anger, not to bear any grudge, not to harbor deceit in the heart, . . . not to be wanting in charity. Not to swear, lest he perjure himself; to speak the truth from the heart. Not to return evil for evil. Not to injure others, but to suffer injuries patiently. To love his enemies. Not to return curse for curse, but rather to bless; to suffer persecution for righteousness' sake. Not to be proud, nor drunken, nor a glutton, nor given to much sleeping, nor slothful, nor complaining, nor slanderous. To put his hope in God; when he sees anything good in himself to ascribe it to God, and when he does any evil, to ascribe it to himself. . . .

Obedience — The first grade of humility is obedience without delay, which is becoming to those who hold nothing dearer than Christ. So, when one of the monks receives a command from a superior, he should obey it immediately, as if it came from God himself. . . .

Monks should not have personal property — The sin of owning private property should be entirely eradicated from the monastery. No one shall presume to give or receive anything except by the order of the abbot; no one shall possess anything of his own, books, paper, pens, or anything else; for monks are not to own even their own bodies and wills

Source: Oliver J. Thatcher and Edgar H. McNeal, editors, A *Source Book for Medieval History*, New York: Charles Scribner's Sons, 1905, pp. 438–74.

to be used at their own desire, but are to look to the father [abbot] of the monastery for everything. So they shall have nothing that has not been given or allowed to them by the abbot. . . .

The amount of food — Two cooked dishes, served either at the sixth or the ninth hour, should be sufficient for the daily sustenance. We allow two because of differences in taste, so that those who do not eat one may satisfy their hunger with the other, but two shall suffice for all the brothers, unless it is possible to obtain fruit or fresh vegetables, which may be served as a third. One pound of bread shall suffice for the day, whether there be one meal or two. . . . In the case of those who engage in heavy labor, the abbot may at his discretion increase the allowance of food, but he should not allow the monks to indulge their appetites by eating or drinking too much. . . .

The daily labor of the monks — Idleness is the great enemy of the soul, therefore the monks should always be occupied, either in manual labor or in holy reading. . . .

The reception of guests — All guests who come to the monastery are to be received in the name of Christ, who said: "I was a stranger and ye took me in" [Matt. 25:35]. Honor and respect shall be shown to all, but especially to Christians and strangers. When a guest is announced, the superior and the brothers shall hasten to meet him and shall give him the kindest welcome. . . .

Monks are not to receive letters or anything — No monk shall receive letters or gifts or anything from his family or from any persons on the outside, nor shall he send anything, except by the command of the abbot. . . .

Artisans of the monastery — If there are any skilled artisans in the monastery, the abbot may permit them to work at their chosen trade, if they will do so humbly. . . .

The way in which new members are to be received — Entrance into the monastery should not be made too easy. . . . So when anyone applies at the monastery, asking to be accepted as a monk, he should first be proved by every test. He shall be made to wait outside four or five days, continually knocking at the door and begging to be admitted; and then he shall be taken in as a guest and allowed to stay in the guest chamber a few days. If he satisfies these preliminary tests, he shall then be made to serve a novitiate of at least one year, during which he shall be placed under the charge of one of the older and wiser brothers, who shall examine him and prove by every possible means his sincerity, his zeal, his obedience, and his ability to endure shame. And he shall be told in the plainest manner all the hardships and difficulties of the life which he has chosen. . . . He shall have been given every chance for mature deliberation and every opportunity to refuse the yoke of service. But if he still persists in asserting his eagerness to enter and his willingness to obey the rule and the commands of his superiors, he shall then be received into the congregation, with the understanding that from that day forth he shall never be permitted to draw back from the service or to leave the monastery.

St. Francis Counsels
His Followers

Not all who desired to devote their lives to the service of God were content to live in secluded monasteries. Poverty, suffering, and lack of piety were everywhere to be seen. In the busy new towns especially, there was a danger that men would forget or neglect their salvation. The Franciscan and Dominican orders of friars, both established in the early thirteenth century, were dedicated to the ideal of service of God by working in the world among men.

St. Francis of Assisi (c. 1182–1226) was a pleasure-loving, wealthy young man until he underwent a dramatic religious conversion in his twenties. He rejected all worldly goods, his sole aim being to emulate the life of Jesus. He ministered to the sick and the poor and he preached to the masses. He inspired many to follow his example.

I counsel, warn, and exhort my brothers in the Lord Jesus Christ that when they go out into the world they shall not be quarrelsome or contentious, nor judge others. But they shall be gentle, peaceable and kind, mild and humble, and virtuous in speech, as is becoming to all. They shall not ride on horseback unless compelled by manifest necessity or infirmity to do so. When they enter a house they shall say,

Source: Oliver J. Thatcher and Edgar H. McNeal, editors, A *Source Book for Medieval History*, New York: Charles Scribner's Sons, 1905, pp. 500–04.

"Peace be to this house." According to the Holy Gospel, they may eat of whatever food is set before them.

I strictly forbid all the brothers to accept money or property either in person or through another. Nevertheless, for the needs of the sick and for clothing the other brothers, the ministers and guardians may, as they see that necessity requires, provide through spiritual friends according to the locality, season, and the degree of cold which may be expected in the region where they live. But, as has been said, they shall never receive money or property.

Those brothers to whom the Lord has given the ability to work shall work faithfully and devotedly, so that idleness, which is the enemy of the soul, may be excluded and not extinguish the spirit of prayer and devotion. . . . As the price of their labors they may receive things that are necessary for themselves and the brothers, but not money or property. And they shall humbly receive what is given them, as is becoming to the servants of God and to those who practice the most holy poverty.

The brothers shall have nothing of their own, neither house, nor land, nor anything, but as pilgrims and strangers in this world, serving the Lord in poverty and humility, let them confidently go asking alms. Nor let them be ashamed of this, for the Lord made himself poor for us in this world. This is that highest pitch of poverty which has made you, my dearest brothers, heirs and kings of the kingdom of heaven, which has made you poor in goods, and exalted you in virtues. . . .

All the brothers must have one of their number as their general minister and servant of the whole brotherhood, and they must obey him. . . .

If any of the brothers shall be divinely inspired to go among Saracens and other infidels, they must get the permission to go from their provincial minister, who shall give his consent only to those who he sees are suitable to be sent.

The Revival of Commerce

Urban commerce and industry declined in the late Roman Empire and practically disappeared during the turbulent early Middle Ages. From about A.D. 1000, town life and trade began to revive. *Land routes and sea routes were opened up as European power expanded in all directions. The Crusades added great stimulus to the already growing commercial traffic.*

Townspeople and traders did not quite fit into the existing categories of clergy, nobility, and peasant. The rise of the town created a new class called burghers or bourgeoisie which tended to disrupt the prevailing class structure. Townsmen could make great fortunes and live like nobles or better. They had wealth enough to be able to buy from the lord of the region the right to govern themselves or, if necessary, to take up arms against him. The energetic and ambitious peasant, or serf, on the manor could now find a haven and freedom by running away to a town.

The first selection is a description of the thriving city of London at the end of the twelfth century by a contemporary, William Fitz-Stephen. The second is the story of St. Godric, who lived in the twelfth century, written by one who knew him. Godric's career was unusual in that he gave up his business and became a monk.

London in the Twelfth Century

Among the noble cities of the world that fame celebrates, the City of London, of the Kingdom of the English, is the one seat that pours out its fame more widely, sends to farther lands its wealth and trade, lifts its head higher than the rest. It is happy in the healthiness of its air, in the Christian religion, in the strength of its defenses, the nature of its site, the honor of its citizens, the modesty of its matrons, pleasant in sports, fruitful of noble men. . . .

Those engaged in the several kinds of business, sellers of several things, contractors for several kinds of work, are distributed every morning into their several localities and shops. Besides, there is in London on the riverbank, among the wines sold by the vintners in shops and cellars, a public cook shop; there eatables are to be found every day, according to the season: dishes of meat, roast, fried, and boiled; great and small fish; coarser meats for the poor, more delicate for the rich, of game, fowls, and small birds. . . . Outside one of the gates, . . .

LONDON IN THE TWELFTH CENTURY. Source: R. B. Morgan, editor, *Readings in English Social History*, Cambridge, England: Cambridge University Press, 1923, pp. 80, 83–85. Reprinted by permission of Cambridge University Press, New York.

immediately in the suburb, is a . . . smooth . . . field. Every Friday, unless it be a higher day of appointed solemnity, there is in it a famous show of noble horses for sale. Earls, barons, knights, and many citizens who are in town come to see or buy. . . . In another part of the field stand by themselves the goods proper to rustics; implements of husbandry, swine with long flanks, cows with full udders, oxen of bulk immense, and woolly flocks. . . . To this city from every nation under heaven merchants delight to bring their trade by sea. . . .

This city . . . is divided into wards, . . . has senatorial and lower magistrates, sewers and aqueducts in its streets, its proper places, and separate courts for cases of each kind. . . . I do not think there is a city with more commendable customs of church attendance, honor to God's ordinances, keeping sacred festivals, almsgiving, hospitality, confirming betrothals, contracting marriages, celebration of nuptials, preparing feasts, cheering the guests, and also in care for funerals and the interment of the dead. The only pests of London are the immoderate drinking of fools and the frequency of fires. . . .

Let us now come to the sports and pastimes, seeing it is fit that a city should not only be commodious and serious but also merry and sportful. . . . The ancient and wealthy men of the city come forth on horseback to see the sport of the young men, and to take part of the pleasure in beholding their agility. Every Friday in Lent a fresh company of young men comes into the field on horseback, and the best horseman conducteth the rest. Then march forth the citizens' sons and other young men with disarmed lances and shields, and there they practice feats of war. Many courtiers likewise, when the king lieth near, and attendants of noblemen do repair to these exercises, and while the hope of victory doth inflame their minds, do show good proof how serviceable they would be in martial affairs.

In Easter holidays they fight battles on the water. A shield is hung upon a pole fixed in the midst of a stream, a boat is prepared without oars to be carried by [the current] of the water, and in the forepart thereof standeth a young man, ready to give charge upon the shield with his lance. If so be he breaketh his lance against the shield and doth not fall, he is thought to have performed a worthy deed; if so be, without breaking his lance, he runneth strongly against the shield, down he falleth into the water, for the boat is violently forced with the tide, but on each side of the shield ride two boats, furnished with young men, which recover him that falleth as soon as they may. Upon the

121

bridge, wharfs, and houses, by the river's side, stand great numbers to see and laugh thereat.

In the holidays, all the summer the youths are exercised in leaping, dancing, shooting, wrestling, casting the stone, and practicing their shields; the maidens . . . dance as long as they can well see. In winter, every holiday before dinner, the boars . . . are set to fight, or else bulls and bears are baited.

The Story of St. Godric

The boy had passed his childish years quietly at home; then, as he began to grow to manhood, he began to follow more prudent ways of life, and to learn carefully and persistently the teachings of worldly forethought [wisdom]. . . . Aspiring to the merchant's trade, he began to follow the chapman's [merchant's] way of life, first learning how to gain in small bargains and things of insignificant price; and thence, while yet a youth, his mind advanced little by little to buy and sell and gain from things of greater expense. In his beginnings, he was wont to wander with small wares around the villages and farmsteads of his own neighborhood; but, in process of time, he gradually associated himself by compact [agreement] with city merchants. Hence, within a brief space of time, the youth who had trudged for many weary hours from village to village, from farm to farm, did so profit by his increase of age and wisdom as to travel with associates of his own age through towns and boroughs, fortresses and cities, to fairs, and to all the various booths of the marketplace. . . .

Seeing that he then dwelt by the seashore, he went down one day to the strand [beach] to seek for some means of livelihood. . . . The place is called Wellstream, hard by [near] the town of Spalding; there, when the tide was out, the countryfolk were wont to scour and explore the stretches of sand, discovering and converting to their own use whatever wreckage or drift the sea might have brought to shore; . . . hence they sometimes get wealth, since they are free to seize there upon whatsoever goods or commodities they may find by the shore. The

THE STORY OF ST. GODRIC. Source: G. G. Coulton, editor, *Social Life in Britain from the Conquest to the Reformation,* Cambridge, England: Cambridge University Press, 1918, pp. 415–20. Reprinted by permission of Cambridge University Press, New York.

Saint, then, inspired by such hopes, roamed one day over these stretches of shore; and, finding nothing at first, he followed on and on to a distance of three miles, where he found three porpoises lying high and dry, either cast upon the sands by the waves or left there by the ebb tide. Two were still alive and struggling: the third, in the midst, was dead or dying. Moved with pity, he left the living untouched, cut a portion from the dead fish, and began carrying this away upon his back.* But the tide soon began to flow, and Godric, halting under his burden, was overtaken by the waves; first they wet his feet, then his legs, then his upper body was compassed about by the deep; † at length the waters went even over his head; yet Godric, strong in faith, bare his burden onwards even under the waves, until, by God's help, he struggled out upon the very shore from which he had gone forth. Then, bringing the fish to his parents, he told them the whole tale, and exhorted them to declare the glory of God. . . .

At first, he lived as a chapman for four years in Lincolnshire, going on foot and carrying the smallest wares; then he traveled abroad, first to St. Andrews in Scotland and then for the first time to Rome. On his return, having formed a familiar friendship with certain other young men who were eager for merchandise, he began to launch upon bolder courses, and to coast frequently by sea to the foreign lands that lay around him. Thus, sailing often to and fro between Scotland and Britain, he traded in many divers [different] wares and, amid these occupations, learned much worldly wisdom. . . . Thus aspiring ever higher and higher, and yearning upward with his whole heart, at length his great labors and cares bore much fruit of worldly gain. For he labored not only as a merchant but also as a shipman . . . to Denmark and Flanders and Scotland; in which lands he found certain rare, and therefore more precious, wares, which he carried to other parts wherein he knew them to be least familiar and coveted by the inhabitants beyond the price of gold itself; wherefore he exchanged these wares for others coveted by men of other lands. . . . Hence he made great profit in all his bargains, and gathered much wealth in the sweat of his brow; for he sold dear in one place the wares which he had bought elsewhere at a small price.

Then he purchased half of a merchant ship with certain of his

* Fats were rare and costly in the Middle Ages; therefore, porpoise was highly esteemed and always brought a considerable price.

† That is, surrounded by water.

partners in the trade; and again by his prudence he bought the fourth part of another ship. At length, by his skill in navigation, wherein he excelled all his fellows, he earned promotion to the post of steersman. . . .

And now he had lived sixteen years as a merchant, and began to think of spending on charity, to God's honor and service, the goods which he had so laboriously acquired. He therefore took the cross as a pilgrim to Jerusalem, and having visited the Holy Sepulcher, came back to England by way of St. James [of Compostella]. Not long afterward he became steward to a certain rich man of his own country, with the care of his whole house and household. But certain of the younger household were men of iniquity [evil], who stole their neighbors' cattle and thus held luxurious feasts, whereat Godric, in his ignorance, was sometimes present. Afterward, discovering the truth, he rebuked and admonished them to cease; but they made no account of his warnings; wherefore he concealed not their iniquity, but disclosed it to the lord of the household, who, however, slighted his advice. Wherefore he begged to be dismissed and went on a pilgrimage . . . to Rome, the abode of the Apostles, that thus he might knowingly pay the penalty for those misdeeds wherein he had ignorantly partaken. I have often seen him, even in his old age, weeping for this unknowing transgression. . . .

In order that he might follow Christ the more freely, he sold all his possessions and distributed them among the poor. Then, telling his parents of this purpose and receiving their blessing, he went forth to no certain abode, but withersoever the Lord should deign to lead him; for above all things he coveted the life of a hermit.

The Regulation of a Craft Guild

Both merchants and craftsmen in the new towns formed associations, or guilds. The merchant guilds, which preceded the craft guilds, sometimes doubled as the government of the town. Guilds often regulated trade, protected their members against unfair competition and ill-treatment by foreigners, established prices that would be fair to the buyer as well as to the seller, and provided a social and religious center for their members.

The admission of apprentices and their training was entirely in the hands of the masters of a particular guild. Although the system worked well for some time, toward the end of the Middle Ages the masters began to make it increasingly difficult for all but close relatives to enter their ranks. This created hard feelings and friction.

The following selection is from the Ordinances of the White-Tawyers. The white-tawyers were artisans engaged in dressing leather "with salt, alum, and other substances, giving it a white surface."

In the first place, they have ordained that they will find a wax candle to burn before our Lady in the Church of Allhallows, near London wall.

Also, that each person of the said trade shall put in the box such sum as he shall think fit, in aid of maintaining the said candle.

Also, if by chance anyone of the said trade shall fall into poverty, whether through old age or because he cannot labor or work, and have nothing with which to keep himself, he shall have every week from the said box 7d. for his support, if he be a man of good repute. And after his decease, if he have a wife, a woman of good repute, she shall have weekly for her support 7d. from the said box, so long as she shall . . . keep single.

And that no stranger shall work in the said trade, or keep house for the same in the city, if he be not an apprentice, or a man admitted to the franchise of the said city.

And that no one shall take the servingman of another to work with him, during his term, unless it be with the permission of his master.

And if anyone of the said trade shall have work in his house that he cannot complete, or if for want of assistance such work shall be in danger of being lost, those of the said trade shall aid him so that the said work be not lost.

And if anyone of the said trade shall depart this life, and have not wherewithal to be buried, he shall be buried at the expense of their common box. . . .

Source: *Translations and Reprints from the Original Sources of European History*, Philadelphia: University of Pennsylvania Press, 1897, Vol. II, No. 1, pp. 23–25.

And if any servingman shall conduct himself in any other manner than properly toward his master and act rebelliously toward him, no one of the said trade shall set him to work until he shall have made amends before the mayor and aldermen. . . .

Also, that the good folks of the same trade shall once in the year be assembled in a certain place, convenient thereto, there to choose two men of the most loyal and benefiting of the said trade to be overseers of work and all other things touching the trade for that year; which persons shall be presented to the mayor and aldermen for the time being, and sworn before them diligently to inquire and make search and loyally to present to the said mayor and aldermen such defaults as they shall find touching the said trade without sparing anyone for friendship or for hatred, or in any other manner. And if anyone of the said trade shall be found rebellious against the said overseers, so as not to let them properly make their search and assay as they ought to do, or if he shall absent himself from the meeting aforesaid without reasonable cause, after due warning by the said overseers, he shall pay to the Chamber, upon the first default, 40d.; and on the second like default, half a mark; and on the third, one mark; and on the fourth, 20s., and shall forswear the trade forever.

Also, that if the overseers shall be found lax and negligent about their duty, or partial to any person for gift or for friendship, maintaining him or voluntarily permitting him to continue in his default, and shall not present him to the mayor and aldermen, as before stated, they are to incur the penalty aforesaid. . . .

Also, that no one who has not been an apprentice and has not finished his term of apprenticeship in the said trade shall be made free of the same trade, unless it be attested by the overseers for the time being, or by four persons of the said trade, that such person is able and sufficiently skilled to be made free of the same.

Also, that no one of the said trade shall induce the servant of another to work with him in the said trade until he has made a proper fine with his first master, at the discretion of the said overseers, or of four reputable men of the said trade. And if anyone shall do to the contrary thereof, or receive the serving workman of another to work with him during his term without leave of the trade, he is to incur the said penalty.

Also, that no one shall take for working in the said trade more than they were wont heretofore [accustomed to previously].

126

The Spirit of the Crusades

The Crusades were part of a great religious revival that gripped Europe in the eleventh century. The influence of the Church both in religion and in secular affairs had been growing. In responding to the appeals of the Byzantine Emperor for help against the fanatical Turks, Pope Urban II may have seen an opportunity of restoring unity between the Eastern and Western churches, as well as an opportunity to regain the Holy Land from the Moslems.

One of the most successful and dramatic orations ever delivered was the call for a crusade by Pope Urban in 1095. Thousands of nobles, moved by a mixture of sincere piety, love of adventure, guarantees of absolution from sin, and the dream of immense riches, took the cross and prepared to travel to the Holy Land.

The first selection includes extracts from two contemporary versions of Urban's speech. The second selection illustrates how a twelfth-century Moslem poet looked upon the crusaders.

A Call for a Crusade

The Council of Clermont, 1095. Fulcher of Chartres

Although, O sons of God, you have promised more firmly than ever to keep the peace among yourselves and to preserve the rights of the Church, there remains still an important work for you to do. Freshly quickened by the divine correction, you must apply the strength of your righteousness to another matter which concerns you as well as God. For your brethren who live in the East are in urgent need of your help, and you must hasten to give them the aid which has often been promised them. For, as the most of you have heard, the Turks and Arabs have attacked them and have conquered the territory of Romania [the Byzantine Empire] as far west as the shore of the Mediterranean and the Hellespont, which is called the Arm of St. George. They have occupied more and more of the lands of those Christians, and have

A CALL FOR A CRUSADE. Source: Oliver J. Thatcher and Edgar H. McNeal, editors, A Source Book for Medieval History, New York: Charles Scribner's Sons, 1905, pp. 516–17; 520–21.

overcome them in seven battles. They have killed and captured many, and have destroyed the churches and devastated the Empire. If you permit them to continue thus for a while with impunity, the faithful of God will be much more widely attacked by them. On this account I . . . beseech you as Christ's heralds to publish this everywhere and to persuade all people of whatever rank, foot soldiers and knights, poor and rich, to carry aid promptly to those Christians and to destroy that vile race from the lands of our friends. I say this to those who are present; it is meant also for those who are absent. Moreover, Christ commands it.

All who die by the way, whether by land or by sea, or in battle against the pagans, shall have immediate remission of sins. This I grant them through the power of God with which I am invested. O what a disgrace if such a despised and base race, which worships demons, should conquer a people which has the faith of omnipotent God and is made glorious with the name of Christ! With what reproaches will the Lord overwhelm us if you do not aid those who, with us, profess the Christian religion! Let those who have been accustomed unjustly to wage private warfare against the faithful now go against the infidels and end with victory this war which should have been begun long ago. Let those who for a long time have been robbers now become knights. Let those who have been fighting against their brothers and relatives now fight in a proper way against the barbarians. Let those who have been serving as mercenaries for small pay now obtain the eternal reward. Let those who have been wearing themselves out in both body and soul now work for a double honor. Behold! On this side will be the sorrowful and poor, on that, the rich; on this side, the enemies of the Lord, on that, His friends. Let those who go not put off the journey, but rent their lands and collect money for their expenses; and as soon as winter is over and spring comes, let them eagerly set out on the way with God as their guide.

The Council of Clermont, 1095. Robert the Monk

When Pope Urban had said this and much more of the same sort, all who were present were moved to cry out with one accord, "It is the will of God. It is the will of God." When the Pope heard this he raised his eyes to heaven and gave thanks to God, and commanding silence with a gesture of his hand he said: "My dear brethren, today there is fulfilled in you that which the Lord says in the Gospel, 'Where two or three are gathered together in My name, there am I in the midst' [Matt.

18:20]. For unless the Lord God had been in your minds you would not all have said the same thing. For although you spoke with many voices, nevertheless it was one and the same thing that made you speak. So I say unto you, God who put those words into your hearts has caused you to utter them. Therefore, let these words be your battle cry, because God caused you to speak them. Whenever you meet the enemy in battle, you shall all cry out, 'It is the will of God. It is the will of God.' And we do not command the old or weak to go, or those who cannot bear arms. No women shall go without their husbands, or brothers, or proper companions, for such would be a hindrance rather than a help, a burden rather than an advantage. Let the rich aid the poor and equip them for fighting and take them with them. Clergymen shall not go without the consent of their bishop, for otherwise the journey would be of no value to them. Nor will this pilgrimage be of any benefit to a layman if he goes without the blessing of his priest. Whoever therefore shall determine to make this journey and shall make a vow to God [and shall] offer himself as 'a living sacrifice, holy, acceptable to God' [Rom. 12:1], shall wear a cross on his brow or on his breast. And when he returns after having fulfilled this vow, he shall wear the cross on his back. In this way he will obey the command of the Lord, 'Whosoever doth not bear his cross and come after Me is not worthy of Me' " [Luke 14:27]. When these things had been done, while all prostrated themselves on the earth and beat their breasts, one of the cardinals, named Gregory, made confession for them, and they were given absolution for all their sins. After the absolution, they received the benediction and the permission to go home.

A Moslem View of the Crusaders

Mysterious are the works of the Creator, the author of all things! When one comes to recount cases regarding the Franks, he cannot but glorify Allah (exalted is he!) and sanctify him, for he sees them as animals possessing the virtues of courage, but nothing else; just as animals have only the virtues of strength and carrying loads. . . .

A MOSLEM VIEW OF THE CRUSADERS. Source: *An Arab-Syrian Gentleman and Warrior in the Period of the Crusades: Memoirs of Usamah ibn-Munqidh,* translated by Philip K. Hitti, New York: Columbia University Press, 1929, pp. 161–63. Reprinted by permission of the publishers.

A case illustrating their curious medicine is the following:

The lord of al-Munaytirah wrote to my uncle asking him to dispatch a physician to treat certain sick persons among his people. My uncle sent him a Christian physician named Thabit. Thabit was absent but ten days when he returned. So we said to him, "How quickly hast thou healed thy patients!" He said:

"They brought before me a knight in whose leg an abscess had grown, and a woman afflicted with imbecility. To the knight I applied a small poultice until the abscess opened and became well; and the woman I put on diet. . . . Then a Frankish physician came to them and said, 'This man knows nothing about treating them.' He then said to the knight, 'Which wouldst thou prefer, living with one leg or dying with two?' The latter replied, 'Living with one leg.' The physician said, 'Bring me a strong knight and sharp ax.' A knight came with the ax. And I was standing by. Then the physician laid the leg of the patient on a block of wood and bade the knight strike his leg with the ax and chop it off at one blow. . . . The patient died on the spot. He then examined the woman and said, 'This is a woman in whose head there is a devil which has possessed her. Shave off her hair.' Accordingly they shaved it off and the woman began once more to eat their ordinary diet — garlic and mustard. Her imbecility took a turn for the worse. The physician then said, 'The devil has penetrated through her head.' He therefore took a razor, [and] made a deep cruciform incision on it. . . . The woman also expired instantly. Thereupon I asked them whether my services were needed any longer, and when they replied in the negative I returned home, having learned of their medicine what I knew not before."

I have, however, witnessed a case of their medicine which was quite different from that.

The king of the Franks had for treasurer a knight named Bernard, who (may Allah's curse be upon him!) was one of the most accursed and wicked among the Franks. A horse kicked him in the leg, which was subsequently infected and which opened in fourteen different places. Every time one of these cuts would close in one place, another would open in another place. All this happened while I was praying for his perdition. Then came to him a Frankish physician and removed from the leg all the ointments which were on it and began to wash it with very strong vinegar. By this treatment all the cuts were healed and the man became well again. He was up again like a devil. . . .

Everyone who is a fresh emigrant from the Frankish lands is ruder in character than those who have become acclimatized and have held long association with the Moslems.

John and His Barons

Magna Carta (1215) is the most hallowed monument of the long struggle for liberty and constitutional government in England. Whatever personal interest the great barons might have had when they forced the Charter of Liberties on King John in 1215 they were, nevertheless, securing in writing what hitherto had been custom — the principle that the king could not put himself above the law of the land. In future generations Englishmen on many occasions turned to the Charter as a guarantee of their liberties.

Few rulers have emerged with so evil a reputation as King John. Traditionally, he has been viewed as a cruel tyrant, sinking to the depths of immorality, suspicious to the point of madness, and caring nothing for the rights of his subjects. Even his most favorable biographers do not deny some of these charges. They insist, however, that the evils of his rule have been exaggerated. One of the difficulties of gaining a balanced estimate of John is that he became a symbol of tyranny just as the Charter became the symbol of liberty.

Roger of Wendover's Contemporary Account

In the year 1215, which was the seventeenth year of his reign, King John held his Christmas court at Winchester for one day; after that he hurried up to London and took up his quarters at the New Temple, where the . . . nobles came to him in martial array and demanded the confirmation of the liberties and laws of King Edward, with other liberties granted to them and to the kingdom and Church of England, as were contained in the charter and laws of Henry I; they also asserted that

ROGER OF WENDOVER'S CONTEMPORARY ACCOUNT. Source: Norman L. Frazer, editor, *English History Illustrated from Original Sources*, London: A. & C. Black, Ltd., 1912, pp. 192–98. Reprinted by permission of the publishers.

. . . he had promised to restore those laws and ancient liberties, and was bound by his own oath to observe them. The King, hearing the bold tone of the barons in making this demand, much feared an attack from them, as he saw that they were prepared for battle; however, he replied that their demands were a matter of importance and difficulty, and he therefore asked a truce till the end of Easter, that he might, after due consideration, be able to satisfy them as well as the dignity of his crown. . . . Thereupon the nobles returned to their homes. The King, however, wishing to take precautions for the future, made all the nobles throughout England to swear fealty to him alone against all men, and to renew their homage to him. . . .

In Easter week of this same year, the above-mentioned nobles assembled at Stamford, with horses and arms; for they had now induced almost all the nobility of the whole kingdom to join them, and constituted a very large army; for in their army there were reckoned to be 2,000 knights, besides horse soldiers, attendants, and foot soldiers. . . .

When the King learned this, he sent to them . . . to inquire what the laws and liberties were which they demanded. The barons then delivered to the messengers a paper containing in great measure the laws and ancient customs of the kingdom, and declared that unless the King immediately granted them, and confirmed them under his seal, they would, by taking possession of his fortresses, compel him to give them satisfaction in the matter of their demands. . . . When he heard [this], . . . the King said in derision and indignation: "Why, among these unjust demands, did not the barons ask for my kingdom also?" . . . And at length he angrily declared with an oath that he would never grant them such liberties as would make him their slave. . . .

When the nobles heard what John said, they . . . sent letters throughout England to those earls, barons, and knights who appeared to be still faithful to the King . . . and advised them with threats, if they regarded the safety of all their property and possessions, to abandon a King who was perjured and who warred against his barons, and together with them to stand firm and fight against the King for their rights and for peace; and that, if they refused to do this, they, the barons, would make war against them all, as against open enemies, and would destroy their castles, burn their houses and other buildings, and destroy their warrens, parks, and orchards.

King John, when he saw that he was deserted by almost all, so that out of his [many] royal . . . followers he scarcely retained seven knights, was much alarmed lest the barons should attack his castles and reduce them without difficulty, . . . and sent to them William Marshal, Earl of Pembroke, with other trustworthy messengers, and told them that for the sake of peace, and for the . . . honor of the kingdom, he would willingly grant them the laws and liberties they required; he also sent word to the barons by these same messengers to appoint a fitting day and place to meet and carry all these matters into effect. . . . The barons . . . appointed June 15 for the King to meet them, in a field lying between Staines and Windsor. So, at the time and place agreed upon, the King and nobles came to the appointed conference; and when each party had taken up its position apart from the other, they began a long discussion about terms of peace and the aforesaid liberties. . . . At length, after various points on both sides had been discussed, King John, seeing that he was inferior in strength to the barons, without raising any difficulty, granted the underwritten laws and liberties, and confirmed them by his charter.

The Great Charter

1. [We agree] that the English Church shall be free, and shall have her rights entire and her liberties inviolate [unimpaired]; and it is our will that it be thus observed. . . . We have also granted to all free-men of our kingdom, for us and for our heirs forever, all the liberties written below, to be had and held by them and their heirs . . . forever.

13. The city of London shall have all its ancient liberties and free customs by land as well as by water. Furthermore, we grant that all other cities, boroughs, towns, and ports shall have all their liberties and free customs. . . .

15. We will not in future grant anyone the right to take an aid [tax] from his own freemen, except for ransoming his person, for making his eldest son a knight, and for once marrying his eldest daughter; and for these only a reasonable aid shall be levied. . . .

21. Earls and barons shall not be [fined] except by their peers, and only in accordance with the degree of the offense. . . .

28. No constable or other bailiff of ours shall take anyone's corn or

THE GREAT CHARTER. Source: Harry Rothwell, editor and translator, *English Historical Documents*, Vol. III. Reprinted by permission of Eyre & Spottiswoode (Publishers) Ltd., London, and Oxford University Press, New York.

other chattels unless he pays spot cash for them or can delay payment by arrangement with the seller. . . .

30. No sheriff or bailiff of ours, or anyone else, . . . shall take the horses or carts of any freeman for transport work save with the agreement of that freeman.

31. Neither we nor our bailiffs will take other people's timber for castles or other works of ours except with the agreement of him whose timber it is.

32. We will not hold for more than a year and a day the lands of those convicted of felony, and then the lands shall be handed over to the lords of the fiefs. . . .

38. No bailiff shall in future put anyone to trial upon his own unsupported testimony, without reliable witnesses brought for this purpose.

39. No freeman shall be arrested or imprisoned or [dispossessed] or outlawed or exiled or in any way destroyed, neither will we set forth against him or send against him, except by the lawful judgment of his peers and . . . by the law of the land.

40. To no one will we sell, to no one will we refuse or delay, right or justice.

41. All merchants shall have safe and secure exit from, and entry into, England, and dwelling and travel in England as well by land as by water, for buying and selling by the ancient and right customs, free of all evil tolls. . . .

42. Without prejudicing the allegiance due to us, it shall be lawful in future for anyone to leave our kingdom and return safely and securely by land and water, save, in the public interest, for a short period in time of war. . . .

52. If anyone has been dispossessed or removed by us without the legal judgment of his peers from his lands, castles, franchises, or his right, we will immediately restore them to him. . . .

61. We give and grant them the under-written security, namely, that the barons shall choose any twenty-five barons of the kingdom they wish, who must with all their might observe . . . the peace and liberties which we have granted, . . . so that if we . . . or any one of our servants offend in any way against anyone, or transgress any of the articles of the peace or the security, and the offense be notified to four of the aforesaid twenty-five barons, those four barons shall come to us, . . . and, laying the transgression before us, shall petition us to have that transgression corrected without delay. And if we do not correct the

transgression . . . within forty days, . . . the aforesaid four barons shall refer that case to the rest of the twenty-five barons and those twenty-five barons, together with the community [the Council of Great Barons] of the whole land, shall [compel] us in every way they can; namely, by seizing castles, lands, possessions, and in such other ways as they can, saving our person and the persons of our queen and our children, until, in their opinion, amends have been made. . . . Given by our hand in the meadow which is called Runnymede . . . on the fifteenth day of June, in the seventeenth year of our reign.

Louis IX—the Ideal Medieval King

Louis IX (1226–1270) approximated the ideals of medieval monarchy more closely than any other king. He was renowned for his deep piety and his crusading zeal. His sense of justice was respected throughout Europe. His charity, his integrity, his simple and honest way of life, and his sincere love of peace helped to make him a legendary figure in his own day. Shortly after his death he was declared a saint by the Church.

Louis was also a very strong ruler. He did not wish to engage in unjust wars, but he was jealous of his power and he labored throughout his long reign to strengthen the position of the monarchy in France. He left the monarchy with more prestige and power than it had ever had.

Jean de Joinville, who wrote his chronicle at the beginning of the fourteenth century, was a French noble who knew Louis well and accompanied him on his first crusade in 1248.

In the name of God Almighty, I, Jean, Lord of Joinville, . . . dictate the life of our holy King Louis; that which I saw and heard by the space of six years that I was in his company on pilgrimage oversea, and

Source: Geoffroi de Villehardouin and Jean de Joinville, *Memoirs of the Crusades*, translated by Sir Frank T. Marzials, New York: Dutton Paperback Edition, 1958, pp. 139–41, 149–50. Reprinted by permission of E. P. Dutton & Co., Inc., and J. M. Dent & Sons, Ltd., London.

135

that which I saw and heard after we returned. And before I tell you of his great deeds and of his prowess, I will tell you what I saw and heard of his good teachings and of his holy words, so that these may be found here set in order for the edifying of those who shall hear thereof.

This holy man loved God with all his heart and followed Him in His acts; and this appeared in that, as God died for the love He bore His people, so did the King put his body in peril, and that several times, for the love he bore to his people. . . .

The great love that he bore to his people appeared in what he said during a very sore sickness that he had at Fontainebleau, unto my Lord Louis, his eldest son. "Fair son," he said, "I pray thee to make thyself beloved of the people of thy kingdom; for truly I would rather that a Scot should come out of Scotland and govern the people of the kingdom well and equitably than that thou shouldest govern it ill in the sight of all men." The holy King so loved truth, that, as you shall hear hereafter, he would never consent to lie to the Saracens as to any covenant that he had made with them.

Of his mouth he was so sober that on no day of my life did I ever hear him order special meats, as many rich men are wont to do; but he ate patiently whatever his cooks had made ready and was set before him. In his words he was temperate; for on no day of my life did I ever hear him speak evil of anyone; nor did I ever hear him name the Devil — which name is very commonly spoken throughout the kingdom, whereby God, as I believe, is not well pleased.

He put water into his wine by measure, according as he saw that the strength of the wine would suffer it. At Cyprus he asked me why I put no water into my wine, and I said this was by order of the physicians, who told me I had a large head and a cold stomach so that I could not get drunk. And he answered that they deceived me; for if I did not learn to put water into my wine in my youth and wished to do so in my old age, gout and diseases of the stomach would take hold upon me and I should never be in health; and if I drank pure wine in my old age, I should get drunk every night, and that it was too foul a thing for a brave man to get drunk.

He asked me if I wished to be honored in this world, and to go into paradise at my death. And I said, "Yes." And he said, "Keep yourself then from knowingly doing or saying anything which, if the whole world heard thereof, you would be ashamed to acknowledge.". . .

He asked me if I washed the feet of the poor on Holy Thursday.

"Sire," said I, "it would make me sick! The feet of these villains will I not wash." "In truth," said he, "that was ill said; for you should never disdain what God did for our teaching. So I pray you, for the love of God first, and then for the love of me, that you accustom yourself to wash the feet of the poor.". . .

Ofttimes it happened that he would go, after his Mass, and seat himself in the wood of Vincennes and lean against an oak, and make us sit round him. And all those who had any cause in hand came and spoke to him without hindrance. . . . Then would he ask, out of his own mouth, "Is there anyone who has a cause in hand?" And those who had a cause in hand stood up. Then would he say, "Keep silence all, and you shall be heard in turn, one after the other." Then he would call my Lord Peter of Fontaines and my Lord Geoffrey of Villette, and say to one of them, "Settle me this cause."

And when he saw that there was anything to amend in the words of those who spoke on his behalf, or in the words of those who spoke on behalf of any other person, he would himself, out of his own mouth, amend what they had said. Sometimes have I seen him in summer go to do justice among his people in the garden of Paris, clothed in a tunic of camlet,* a surcoat of tartan without sleeves, and a mantle of black taffeta about his neck, his hair well combed, no cap, and a hat of white peacock's feathers upon his head. And he would cause a carpet to be laid down, so that we might sit round him, and all the people who had any cause to bring before him stood around. And then would he have their causes settled, as I have told you afore he was wont to do in the wood of Vincennes.

* **camlet:** a fabric made of camel's hair or Angora wool.

The Controversy Between the Empire and the Papacy

One of the most frequent sources of conflict in the Middle Ages was the division of authority between monarch and pope. A particular problem was the selection and installation of bishops. Bishops were powerful feudal lords who owed allegiance to the king for the lands they held, and thus it was imperative to monarchs to be able to exercise control over them. It was the papacy's view, however, that bishops were ecclesiastical officials whose first duty was to the Church. For centuries, the weakness of the Church and the need of the papacy to rely on secular rulers for protection had left the Church at the mercy of the state. During the religious revival of the eleventh century, the Church struggled to free itself from secular control, and even to assert its supremacy. The most effective reformer in this movement was the pious and determined Hildebrand, first as papal assistant and then as Pope Gregory VII (1073–1085). When he issued a decree forbidding secular rulers to invest bishops with the symbols of office (the ring and the staff), he encountered heavy royal opposition.

Most affected by this decree was the Holy Roman Emperor, whose authority was founded on the support of his powerful ecclesiastical vassals. A bitter quarrel developed in 1075 between Gregory and the young Holy Roman Emperor Henry IV (1056–1106), in which both sides made extravagant claims. The Emperor and his bishops deposed Gregory, who in turn excommunicated the Emperor. The German nobles, who could only gain in strength from such a quarrel, sided with the Pope and threatened Henry's crown. Henry, at this juncture, journeyed to Canossa where the Pope was staying, and begged forgiveness as a penitent. After keeping the Holy Roman Emperor waiting for three days, Gregory finally absolved him. The investiture controversy was finally settled in 1122 by a compromise in the Concordat of Worms between Pope Calixtus II and Henry V.

The Deposition of Pope Gregory VII

Henry, king not by usurpation, but by the holy ordination of God, to Hildebrand, not pope, but false monk.

This is the salutation which you deserve, for you have never held any office in the Church without making it a source of confusion and a curse to Christian men instead of an honor and a blessing. To mention only the most obvious cases out of many, you have not only dared to

Source: Oliver J. Thatcher and Edgar H. McNeal, editors, *A Source Book for Medieval History*, New York: Charles Scribner's Sons, 1905, pp. 151–52; 155–56; 157–59; 165; 166.

touch the Lord's anointed, the archbishops, bishops, and priests; but you have scorned them and abused them, as if they were ignorant servants not fit to know what their master was doing. This you have done to gain favor with the vulgar crowd. You have declared that the bishops know nothing and that you know everything; but if you have such great wisdom you have used it not to build but to destroy. Therefore we believe that St. Gregory, whose name you have presumed to take, had you in mind when he said: "The heart of the prelate is puffed up by the abundance of subjects, and he thinks himself more powerful than all others." All this we have endured because of our respect for the papal office, but you have mistaken our humility for fear, and have dared to make an attack upon the royal and imperial authority which we received from God. You have even threatened to take it away, as if we had received it from you, and as if the Empire and kingdom were in your disposal and not in the disposal of God. Our Lord Jesus Christ has called us to the government of the Empire, but he never called you to the rule of the Church. This is the way you have gained advancement in the Church: through craft you have obtained wealth; through wealth you have obtained favor; through favor, the power of the sword; and through the power of the sword, the papal seat, which is the seat of peace; and then from the seat of peace you have expelled peace. . . . Come down, then, from that apostolic seat which you have obtained by violence; for you have been declared accursed by St. Paul for your false doctrines and have been condemned by us and our bishops for your evil rule. Let another ascend the throne of St. Peter, one who will not use religion as a cloak of violence, but will teach the life-giving doctrine of that Prince of the Apostles. I, Henry, king by the grace of God, with all my bishops, say unto you: "Come down, come down, and be accursed through all the ages."

The First Deposition and Excommunication of the Emperor Henry IV

St. Peter, Prince of the Apostles, incline thine ear unto me, I beseech thee, and hear me, thy servant, whom thou hast nourished from mine infancy and hast delivered from mine enemies that hate me for my fidelity to thee. Thou art my witness, as are also my mistress, the Mother of God, and St. Paul thy brother, and all the other saints, that thy Holy Roman Church called me to its government against my own will, and that I did not gain thy throne by violence; that I would rather have ended my days in exile than have obtained thy place by fraud or for worldly ambition. It is not by my efforts, but by thy grace, that I am set to rule over the Christian world which was specially intrusted to thee by Christ. . . . Confident of my integrity and authority, I now declare in the name of omnipotent God, the Father, Son, and Holy Spirit, that Henry, son of the Emperor Henry, is deprived of his kingdom of Germany and Italy; I do this by thy authority and in defense of the honor of thy Church, because he has rebelled against it. . . . He has refused to obey as a Christian should; he has not returned to God from whom he has wandered; he has had dealings with excommunicated persons; he has done many iniquities; he has despised the warnings which, as thou art witness, I sent to him for his salvation; he has cut himself off from thy Church, and has attempted to rend it asunder; therefore, by thy authority, I place him under the curse. It is in thy name that I curse him, that all people may know that thou art Peter, and upon thy rock the Son of the living God has built his Church, and the gates of hell shall not prevail against it.

Pope Gregory VII to the German Princes

In the meantime we learned that the King was approaching. Now before he entered Italy he had sent to us and had offered to make complete satisfaction for his fault, promising to reform and henceforth to obey us in all things, provided we would give him our absolution and blessing. We hesitated for some time, taking occasion in the course of the negotiations to reprove him sharply for his former sins. Finally he came in person to Canossa, where we were staying, bringing with him only a small retinue and manifesting no hostile intentions. Once arrived, he presented himself at the gate of the castle, barefoot and clad only in wretched woolen garments, beseeching us with tears to grant him absolution and forgiveness. This he continued to do for three days, until all those about us were moved to compassion at his plight and interceded for him with tears and prayers. . . . At length his persistent declarations of repentance and the supplications of all who were there with us overcame our reluctance, and we removed the excommunication from him and received him again into the bosom of the Holy Mother Church.

The Promise of Pope Calixtus II

We hereby grant that in Germany the elections of the bishops and abbots who hold [land] directly from the crown shall be held in your [the Emperor's] presence. . . . In the case of disputed elections you shall have the right to decide between the parties, after consulting with the archbishop of the province and his fellow bishops. You shall confer the regalia [symbols] of the office upon the bishop or abbot-elect by giving him the scepter, and this shall be done freely without exacting any payment from him; the bishop or abbot-elect on his part shall perform all the duties that go with the holding of the regalia. . . .

Finally, I hereby make a true and lasting peace with you and with all of your followers, including those who supported you in the recent controversy.

The Promise of the Emperor Henry V

I agree that elections and consecrations shall be conducted canonically [according to church laws] and shall be free from all interference. I surrender also the possessions and regalia of St. Peter which have been seized by me during this quarrel, or by my father in his lifetime, and which are now in my possession, and I promise to aid the Church to recover such as are held by any other persons. I restore also the possessions of all other churches and princes, clerical or secular, which have been taken away during the course of this quarrel, which I have, and promise to aid them to recover such as are held by any other persons.

Finally, I make true and lasting peace with Pope Calixtus and with the Holy Roman Church and with all who are or have ever been of his party.

The Misfortunes and Follies of Frederick II, Holy Roman Emperor

Frederick II (1211–1250) was the most versatile and imaginative of the medieval monarchs. His interest in philosophy and science, his extraordinary administrative ability, and his devotion to literature and education led his admirers to proclaim him "wonder of the world." His reforms, it should be noted, were confined mainly to Sicily, where he had grown up. The German part of the empire he tended to neglect, and because of his absentee rule the nobles increased their powers.

His attempt to subdue all Italy brought him into conflict with the independent Italian cities and with the papacy. On more than one occasion Frederick was excommunicated. After his death his heirs were pursued until his line was destroyed.

Those who favored the papacy in this struggle could not find much to admire in Frederick. Salimbene, the author of the following selection, was a thirteenth-century Franciscan monk who saw Frederick as a monster and a heretic. His description of Frederick's reign, nevertheless, provides us with an insight into the Emperor's remarkable personality.

Frederick II, formerly Emperor, although he was great and rich and a mighty Emperor, had nevertheless many misfortunes. Concerning these something should be said. The first of all his misfortunes was that his first-born son Henry, who should have ruled after him, went over to the Lombards against his will, and so Frederick captured him, bound him, and put him in prison. Thus the Emperor could say with Job, "They whom I loved are turned against me."

His second misfortune was that he wished to subjugate the Church, so that the Pope and the cardinals and other prelates should be poor, and should go on foot. . . .

Source: James Bruce Ross and Mary Martin McLaughlin, editors, *The Portable Medieval Reader*, New York: Copyright 1949 by The Viking Press, Inc., pp. 362–68. Reprinted by permission of the publishers.

The third of his misfortunes was that he wanted to conquer the Lombards and could not, because when he had them on one side, he lost them on the other. . . .

His fourth misfortune was that Pope Innocent IV deposed him from the Empire in the Plenary Council of Lyons, and made public there all his wickedness and iniquities. . . .

The seventh misfortune [occurred] when the men of Parma took his city Vittoria, which he had built near Parma, and burned, razed, and completely destroyed it, and filled up the holes so that no vestige of it remained; according to the Apocalypse, "A city which was and is no more." Also, they put Frederick and his army shamefully to flight, and killed many of them, and led many captive to their city of Parma. . . . Also they despoiled him and took his whole treasury. . . . The cry of Frederick could be that of Job: "He hath stripped me of my glory, and taken the crown from my head." This can be taken to mean Pope Innocent IV, who deposed him from the Empire, or the city of Parma, which literally stripped him and took his crown from his head. . . .

Frederick's eighth misfortune was that his princes and barons rebelled against him. . . .

His ninth misfortune was that his son, King Enzio, was captured by the Bolognese, which was right and just, for he had captured at sea prelates who were going to the Council of Pope Gregory IX. . . .

To these . . . misfortunes of the Emperor Frederick we can add two more: . . . first, that he was excommunicated by Pope Gregory IX; and second, that the Church tried to take away from him the kingdom of Sicily. And he was not without blame in this, for when the Church sent him across the sea to recover the Holy Land, he made a peace with the Saracens without advantage for the Christians. Moreover, he had the name of Mohammed publicly chanted in the church of God, as we have set down in another chronicle, where we described the twelve crimes of Frederick. . . .

But now I have something to say about the follies of Frederick. His first folly was that he had the thumb of a notary cut off because he spelled his name in a different way from what he wished. Frederick desired that the first syllable of his name be written i, like this, Fridericus, and that notary had written it with an e, Fredericus.

His second folly was that he wanted to find out what kind of speech and what manner of speech children would have when they grew up if they spoke to no one beforehand. So he bade foster mothers and nurses to suckle the children, to bathe and wash them, but in no way to prattle with them or to speak to them, for he wanted to learn whether they would speak the Hebrew language which was the oldest, or Greek, or Latin, or Arabic, or perhaps the language of their parents, of whom they had been born. But he labored in vain, because the children all died, for they could not live without the petting and the joyful faces and loving words of their foster mothers. . . .

His third folly was that when he saw the land across the sea, the Holy Land, which God had so often praised, in that He called it "the land flowing with milk and honey" and the most excellent of all lands, it displeased him, and he said that the God of the Jews had not seen his own lands, namely, the Terra di Lavoro, Calabria, Sicily, and Apulia. Otherwise, He would not so often have praised the land that He promised and gave to the Jews. . . .

His fourth folly was that he often sent a certain Nicholas, against his will, to the bottom of the Faro, and many times he returned. But Frederick wanted to discover whether or not he had really gone to the bottom and returned, so he threw his golden cup in the sea, where he thought it was the deepest. And Nicholas plunged in, found the cup, and brought it to him, which astonished the Emperor. But when Frederick wanted to send him back once again, Nicholas said, "Do not send me there again at any price, for the sea is so troubled in its depths that if you send me I shall never return." The Emperor sent him nevertheless, and he never returned. . . .

The seventh and last of his curiosities and follies was that . . . when he was in a certain palace on a certain day, he asked Michael Scot, his astrologer, how far he was from the sky, and the astrologer told him how far it seemed to him. Then the Emperor . . . ordered the architects or carpenters to lower the hall of the palace in such a way that no one could detect it. . . . When, after many days, the Emperor was staying in the same palace with his astrologer, . . . he asked him whether he was still as far from the sky as he had said the other time. After he had made his computation, the astrologer said that either the sky had been raised or certainly the earth had been lowered. And then the Emperor knew that the astrologer spoke truly. I know and I have heard many other follies of Frederick, which for the sake of brevity I do not mention, and because it bores me to relate so many of his follies, and also because I hasten to speak of other things.

144

The Claims of Pope Boniface VIII

Boniface VIII (1294–1303) made no new claims for the supremacy of the Church; but his boldness, his lack of tact, and his love of power brought the battle between popes and monarchs to a head. The issue was the right of the secular state to tax the clergy. The English and the French monarchs, at war with one another, were in need of money and made demands on the clergy, contending that they were citizens of the realm. Boniface denied that the clergy could be taxed without his consent, and in 1296 he issued the bull Clericis Laicos to make his point. The monarchs made life so difficult for the clergy that Boniface had to withdraw the bull.

The struggle flared up again within a few years when the French king, Philip IV, imprisoned a bishop for treason. The Pope denied that the clergy could be tried in a secular court. In response to more papal bulls, Philip made an unprecedented appeal to the people by calling together representatives of the Three Estates of France. Even the clergy gave him overwhelming support. Boniface then issued the bull Unam Sanctam (1302), which was an unqualified statement of the supremacy of "spiritual power" (the papacy) over "temporal authority" (the rulers of states). Philip, instead of backing down, called an assembly of lay and ecclesiastical lords which condemned Boniface for many crimes. The King then sent his minister to arrest the Pope. Boniface was captured, but was soon rescued by the enraged local populace. Shortly thereafter the aged pontiff died.

The following selections are from the two famous bulls of Pope Boniface.

Clericis Laicos

Antiquity shows us that the laity has always been exceedingly hostile to the clergy; and the experience of the present time clearly

Source: *Translations and Reprints from the Original Sources of European History*, Philadelphia: University of Pennsylvania Press, 1897, Vol. III, No. 6, pp. 23–24; 20–21.

demonstrates this since, not content with their limitations, the laity strive for forbidden things. . . .

They do not prudently observe that all control over the clergy, as well as over all ecclesiastical persons and their possessions, is denied them, but impose heavy burdens upon the prelates of the churches, upon the churches themselves, and upon ecclesiastical persons both regular and secular, exacting . . . contributions from them. From such persons they require and extort the payment of a half, a tenth, a twentieth, or some other quota of their property or income, and strive in many other ways to subject the churchmen to slavery and bring them under their control.

And (with grief do we declare it) certain prelates of the churches and ecclesiastical persons, fearing what they ought not to fear and seeking a temporary peace, dreading to offend a temporal more than the eternal majesty, do, without having received the permission or sanction of the Apostolic See, acquiesce in such abuses, not so much from recklessness as want of foresight. We, therefore, desiring to check these iniquitous practices, by the council of our brothers, do, of our apostolic authority, decree that whatever prelates and ecclesiastical persons, whether monastic or secular, whatever their order, condition, or status, shall pay or promise or agree to pay to laymen any contributions . . . in the form of an aid, loan, subvention, subsidy, or gift, or upon any other pretense or fiction whatsoever, without authority from this same Apostolic See, likewise emperors, kings and princes, dukes, counts, [and] barons who shall . . . exact or receive such payments . . . shall, by the very act, incur the sentence of excommunication. . . .

No one, moreover, shall be freed from the above-mentioned sentences . . . without the authority and special permission of the Apostolic See, since it is our intention to make no kind of compromise with such a horrible abuse of the secular power.

Unam Sanctam

That there is one Holy Catholic and Apostolic Church we are impelled by our faith to believe and to hold — this we do firmly believe and openly confess — and outside of this there is neither salvation nor remission of sins. . . .

146

In this Church and in its power are two swords, to wit, a spiritual and a temporal, and this we are taught by the words of the Gospel. . . . And surely he who claims that the temporal sword is not in the power of Peter has but ill understood the word of our Lord when he said, "Put up thy sword in its scabbard." Both, therefore, the spiritual and material swords, are in the power of the Church, the latter indeed to be used for the Church, the former by the Church; the one by the priest, the other by the hand of kings and soldiers, but by the will and sufferance of the priest. It is fitting, moreover, that one sword should be under the other, and the temporal authority subject to the spiritual power. . . .

Therefore, if the earthly power shall err, it shall be judged by the spiritual power; if the lesser spiritual power err, it shall be judged by the higher. But if the supreme power err, it can be judged by God alone and not by man. . . . We, moreover, proclaim, declare, and pronounce that it is altogether necessary to salvation for every human being to be subject to the Roman Pontiff.

The Black Death Strikes England

The Black Death which ravaged Europe in the middle of the fourteenth century was the most devastating plague in history. Originating in Asia, it spread to the Near East, then to southern Europe, then across the Alps to the north and west. Death followed within a few days or even hours after the appearance of small black spots on the body. Since there was no time for burial, corpses had to be thrown into rivers or dumped into pits.

The chaos that followed the deaths of thousands of people accelerated the transformation of European society. Some survivors became rich overnight when they took possession of the land and goods of the dead. Prices, after an initial decline, increased rapidly as food and other necessities became scarce. Serfs found themselves in an advantageous position to make better terms with their lords or to win their freedom altogether. Society was shaken to its foundations both psychologically and economically. The frantic efforts of rulers to control prices and wages by law met with only limited success.

Henry Knighton, from whose Chronicle the following se-
lection is taken, was a youth when the plague struck England.
He relies on contemporary sources as well as his own memory.

Then the grievous plague penetrated the seacoasts from South-
ampton and came to Bristol, and there almost the whole strength of
the town died, struck as it were by sudden death; for there were few
who kept their beds more than three days, or two days, or half a day;
and after this . . . death broke forth on every side with the course of
the sun. There died at Leicester in the small parish of St. Leonard more
than 380; in the parish of Holy Cross more than 400; in the parish of
St. Margaret of Leicester more than 700; and so in each parish a great
number. Then the bishop of Lincoln sent through the whole bishopric
and gave general power to all and every priest, both regular and secular,
to hear confessions, and absolve with full and entire episcopal authority
except in matters of debt, in which case the dying man, if he could,
should pay the debt while he lived, or others should certainly fulfill that
duty from his property after his death. Likewise, the Pope granted full
remission of all sins to whoever was absolved in peril of death, and
granted that this power should last till next Easter, and everyone could
choose a confessor at his will. In the same year there was a great plague
of sheep everywhere in the realm, so that in one place there died in one
pasturage more than 5,000 sheep and so rotted that neither beast nor
bird would touch them. And there were small prices for everything on
account of the fear of death, for there were very few who cared about
riches or anything else. A man could have a horse which before was
worth 40s. for 6s. 8d. . . . Sheep and cattle went wandering over fields
and through crops, and there was no one to go and drive or gather them,
so that the number cannot be reckoned which perished in the ditches
of every district for lack of herdsmen; for there was such a lack of
servants that no one knew what he ought to do. . . . Many crops
perished in the fields for want of someone to gather them. . . . The
Scots, hearing of the cruel pestilence of the English, believed it had
come to them from the avenging hand of God, and — as it was commonly reported in England — took for their oath when they wanted to
swear, "By the foul death of England." But when the Scots, believing

Source: W. J. Ashley, translator, *Edward III and His Wars, 1327–1360*, London: David Nutt, 1887, pp. 122–26.

the English were under the shadow of the dread vengeance of God, came together in the forest of Selkirk with purpose to invade the whole realm of England, [the plague] came upon them and the sudden and awful cruelty of death winnowed them, so that about 5,000 died in a short time. Then the rest, some feeble, some strong, determined to return home, but the English followed and overtook them and killed many of them. . . .

At the same time priests were in such poverty everywhere that many churches were . . . lacking the divine offices, masses, matins, vespers, sacraments, and other rites. . . . Within a short time a very great multitude of those whose wives had died in the pestilence flocked into orders, of whom many were illiterate and little more than laymen except so far as they knew how to read, although they could not understand.

Meanwhile the King sent proclamation into all the counties that reapers and other laborers should not take more than they had been accustomed to take, under the penalty appointed by statute. But the laborers were so . . . obstinate that they would not listen to the King's command, but if anyone wished to have them he had to give them what they wanted and either lose his fruit and crops, or satisfy the . . . wishes of the workmen. . . . Afterward, the King had many laborers arrested and sent to prison; many withdrew themselves and went into the forests and woods; and those who were taken were heavily fined. Their ringleaders were made to swear that they would not take daily wages beyond the ancient custom and then were freed from prison. . . . After the aforesaid pestilence many buildings, great and small, fell into ruins in every city, borough, and village for lack of inhabitants; likewise many villages and hamlets became desolate, not a house being left in them, all having died who dwelt there; and it was probable that many such villages would never be inhabited again.

The Trial of St. Joan of Arc

Joan of Arc (1412–1431) was responsible for reviving the fighting spirit of France in the bitter Hundred Years' War with England. The peasant girl from Domrémy, who had heard voices urging her to drive the English out of France, presented herself at the court of Charles VII in 1429 and obtained permission to lead his army against the English. With renewed vigor and confidence, the French, by what appeared to be a miracle, saved the city of Orléans from falling into English hands. Joan's great triumph was a turning point in the war, but soon thereafter she was captured by the Burgundians, who handed her over to their English allies in return for payment of ransom.

After months of imprisonment, she was brought before a local church court to be tried as a heretic and a witch. Amid French indifference she was condemned and burned at the stake, but the patriotism she aroused did not die with her. Her conviction was later reversed. In 1920 she was declared a saint by the Church.

The following selection is taken from the records of the trial of Joan of Arc (whose name in French is Jeanne d'Arc).

To all those who shall see these present letters, Pierre, by divine mercy bishop of Beauvais, greeting in Our Lord. A certain woman commonly called Jeanne the Maid has during the course of the present year been taken and captured within the boundaries and limits of our diocese. On behalf of the most illustrious prince our lord the King she has been delivered and restored to us, her ordinary judge, defamed as she was by common and public report, as scandalous and suspected of many spells, incantations, invocations, and conversations with evil spirits, and of many other matters concerning the faith, so that we could institute proceedings against her according to the legal form customary in matters of faith. . . .

[*February 22, 1431, Second Session. A professor of theology, Jean Baupere, questions Joan.*] And first he exhorted her to answer truly, as she had sworn, what he should ask her. To which she replied: "You may well ask me such things that to some I shall answer truly, and to others I shall not." And she added, "If you were well informed about me, you would wish me to be out of your hands. I have done nothing except by revelation."

Asked how old she was when she left her father's house, she said she could not vouch for her age.

Asked if in her youth she had learned any craft, she said yes, to

Source: W. P. Barrett, *The Trial of Jeanne d'Arc*, New York: Gotham House, 1932, pp. 20, 43–47. Reprinted by permission of the author and Routledge & Kegan Paul, Ltd., London.

sew and spin: and in sewing and spinning she feared no woman in Rouen. . . . She added too, that as long as she was at home with her father, she saw to the ordinary domestic tasks; and that she did not go to the fields to look after the sheep and other animals. . . .

Afterward she declared that at the age of thirteen she had a voice from God to help her and guide her. . . . The first time she was much afraid. . . . This voice came toward noon, in summer, in her father's garden; and the said Jeanne had [not] fasted on the preceding day. She heard the voice on her right, in the direction of the church; and she seldom heard it without a light. This light came from the same side as the voice, and generally there was a great light. When she came to France* she often heard the voice.

Asked how she could see the light of which she spoke, since it was at the side, she made no reply, and went on to other things. She said that if she was in a wood she easily heard the voice come to her. It seemed to her a worthy voice, and she believed it was sent from God; when she heard the voice a third time she knew that it was the voice of an angel. She said also that this voice always protected her well and that she understood it well.

Asked what instruction this voice gave her for the salvation of her soul, she said it taught her to be good and to go to church often; and it told her that she must come to France. . . . She further said that this voice told her once or twice a week that she should leave and come to France, and that her father knew nothing of her leaving. She said that the voice told her to come, and she could no longer stay where she was; and the voice told her again that she should raise the siege of the city of Orléans. She said, moreover, that the voice told her that she, Jeanne, should go to Robert de Baudricourt, in the town of Vaucouleurs of which he was captain, and he would provide an escort for her. And the said Jeanne answered that she was a poor maid, knowing nothing of riding or fighting. She said she went to an uncle of hers, and told him she wanted to stay with him for some time; and she stayed there about eight days. . . . She told her uncle she must go to the said town of Vaucouleurs, and so her uncle took her.

Then she said that when she reached Vaucouleurs she easily recognized Robert de Baudricourt, although she had never seen him before; and she knew him through her voice, for the voice had told her it was

* **France:** the area directly under the control of the King of France. Domrémy, Joan's home, which was in Lorraine, was not directly under his control.

151

he. And the said Jeanne told Robert she must come to France. The said Robert twice refused to hear her and repulsed her; the third time he listened to her and gave her an escort. And the voice had told her that it would be so.

Then she declared that the Duke of Lorraine ordered that she should be taken to him; and she went to him and told him she wished to go to France. . . .

She declared that on her departure from Vaucouleurs she wore the habit of a man and carried a sword which Robert de Baudricourt had given her but no other arms; and accompanied by a knight, a squire, and four servants, she reached the town of Saint Urbain, where she slept in an abbey. . . .

Required to say by what advice she took to man's dress, she several times refused to answer. . . .

She said also that it was altogether necessary to change her women's clothes for men's. . . .

She said that she sent to the English at Orléans letters telling them to depart. . . .

After this the said Jeanne told that she went without hindrance to him whom she calls her King. . . . She told him she wanted to make war on the English.

Then Jeanne said that her voice had promised her that as soon as she should come to the King he would receive her. She said also that those of her party knew well that the voice was sent to Jeanne from God, and they saw and knew this voice. She said further that her King and several others heard and saw the voice which came to the said Jeanne. . . .

Then Jeanne said that there is not a day when she does not hear this voice; and she has much need of it. She said she never asked of it any final reward but the salvation of her soul. The voice told her to remain at St.-Denis in France, and the said Jeanne wished to remain; but against her will the lords took her away. However, if she had not been wounded, she would not have left; she was wounded in the trenches before Paris, after she left St.-Denis, but recovered in five days. Further, she confessed that she caused an assault to be made before Paris. . . .

Asked if she thought it was a good thing to do, she answered: "Pass on [to the next question]." When this was over . . . it appeared to us sufficient for one day.

A Father Writes to His Sons

Medieval education and intellectual life were centered in the Church. Monasteries and cathedrals established and conducted schools, though only a very small portion of the male population could take advantage of them. For the lower classes, obtaining an education was extremely difficult; and among the nobility, learning was hardly considered as important as fighting.

The twelfth and thirteenth centuries witnessed a revival of learning. The availability of Arabic knowledge and the ancient classics which had been preserved by the Arabs provided considerable stimulus to European thought. A number of towns and cities became the homes of universities — guilds for the purpose of learning. The universities of southern Europe tended to follow the model of Bologna, where the students were in control of hiring and firing their teachers; those in the north followed the model of Paris, where the organization of teachers maintained its authority over the students.

Medieval students had to put up with many hardships, including hunger and cold. Student life, however, had its lighter side. Student revelries and battles with townsmen were not uncommon. Letters between students and their parents were very much the same then as they are now.

The following letter was written in 1315 by a doctor to his two sons at the University of Toulouse.

Beware of eating too much and too often, especially during the night. Avoid eating raw onions in the evening except rarely, because they dull the intellect and senses generally.

Avoid all very lacteal foods such as milk and fresh cheese except very rarely. Beware of eating milk and fish or milk and wine at the same meal, for milk and fish or milk and wine produce leprosy.

Don't have fresh pork too often. Salt pork is all right.

Don't eat many nuts except rarely and following fish. I say the same of meat and fruit, for they are bad and difficult to digest. . . .

Remember about the well water of Toulouse. Wherefore boil it,

Source: Lynn Thorndike, *University Records and Life in the Middle Ages*, New York: Columbia University Press, 1944, pp. 156–59. Reprinted by permission of the publishers.

and the same with water of the Garonne, because such waters are bad.

Also, after you have risen from table, wash out your mouth with wine. . . .

Avoid sleeping on your back except rarely, for it has many disadvantages; but sleep on your side or stomach, and first on the right side, then on the left.

Don't sleep in winter with cold feet; but first warm them at the fire or by walking about or some other method. And in summer don't sleep with bed slippers on your feet, because they generate vapors which are very bad for the brain and memory. . . .

Likewise in winter keep your room closed from all noxious wind, and have straw on the pavement lest you suffer cold. . . .

Also, be well clad and well shod, and outdoors wear pattens,* to keep your feet warm. . . .

And when you see other students wearing their caps, . . . you do likewise, and if need be, put on one of fur. . . .

And when you go to bed at night, have a white nightcap on your head and beneath your cheeks, and another colored one over it, for at night the head should be kept warmer than during the day.

Moreover, at the time of the great rains it is well to wear outdoors, over your cap, a bonnet or helmet of undressed skin; that is, a covering to keep the head from getting wet. . . .

Also, look after your stockings, and don't permit your feet to become dirty.

Also, wash the head, if you are accustomed to wash it, at least once a fortnight with hot lye and in a place sheltered from drafts, on the eve of a feast day toward nightfall. Then dry your hair with a brisk massage; afterward do it up; then put on a bonnet or cap.

Also, comb your hair daily if you will, morning and evening before eating or at least afterward, if you cannot do otherwise.

Also, look out that a draft does not strike you from window or crack while you study or sleep, or indeed at any time, for it strikes men without their noticing.

Also, in summer, in order not to have fleas or to have no more of them, sweep your room daily with a broom and not sprinkle it with water, for [fleas] are generated from damp dust. But you may spray it occasionally with strong vinegar, which comforts heart and brain.

* **pattens:** a type of overshoe with a high wooden sole.

If you will, walk daily somewhere morning and evening. And if the weather is cold, if you can run, run on empty stomach, or at least walk rapidly, that the natural heat may be revived. . . . However, it is not advisable to run on a full stomach but to saunter slowly in order to settle the food in the stomach.

If you cannot go outside your lodgings, either because the weather does not permit or it is raining, climb the stairs rapidly three or four times, and have in your room a big, heavy stick like a sword, and wield it now with one hand, now with the other, as if in a scrimmage, until you are almost winded. This is splendid exercise to warm one up. . . . Jumping is a similar exercise. Singing, too, exercises the chest. And if you will do this, you will have healthy limbs, a sound intellect and memory, and you will avoid rheum. The same way with playing ball. All these were invented not for sport but for exercise. Moreover, too much labor is to be avoided as a continual practice.

St. Thomas Aquinas Offers Proof of the Existence of God

What is the relationship between knowledge derived from human reason and knowledge derived from divine revelation? Medieval philosophers were vitally concerned with this question, especially after they became acquainted with the works of Aristotle. As Aristotle's influence increased, philosophers undertook the task of reconciling his writings with the sacred scriptures themselves. Scholasticism is the term used to describe these various attempts to reconcile reason and faith.

The greatest of the scholastic philosophers and the one whose works have been most influential was the thirteenth-century Dominican, St. Thomas Aquinas. He argued that there was no essential conflict between reason and faith. God had given man reason for his use in understanding the world; God had provided revelation for man's salvation. Each had its separate province and both were essential. Revelation, of course, could not err and sound reason would not arrive at conclusions that contradicted revelation. Therefore, in the event of a conflict be-

tween reason and faith, Aquinas insisted that the error must be sought in human logic.

Although Thomas Aquinas has become the most influential philosopher in the Catholic Church, he did not meet with universal approval in his day. His great reliance on reason and logic created considerable suspicion.

The following selection is from his Summa Theologica.

The existence of God can be proved in five ways.

The first and more manifest way is the argument from motion. It is certain, and evident to our senses, that in the world some things are in motion. Now whatever is moved is moved by another. . . . It is therefore impossible that in the same respect and in the same way a thing should be both mover and moved, i.e., that it should move itself. Therefore, whatever is moved must be moved by another. If that by which it is moved be itself moved, then this also must needs be moved by another, and that by another again. But this cannot go on to infinity, because then there would be no first mover. . . . Therefore it is necessary to arrive at a first mover, moved by no other; and this [first mover] everyone understands to be God.

The second way is from the nature of efficient cause [that force which brings about an effect or a change]. In the world of [nature] we find there is an order of efficient causes. There is no case known (neither is it, indeed, possible) in which a thing is found to be the efficient cause of itself; for so it would be prior to itself [it would have to precede itself], which is impossible. . . . Therefore it is necessary to admit a first efficient cause, to which everyone gives the name of God.

The third way is taken from possibility and necessity. . . . If at one time nothing was in existence, it would have been impossible for anything to have begun to exist; and thus now nothing would be in existence — which is absurd. Therefore, not all beings are merely possible, but there must exist something the existence of which is necessary. But every necessary thing either has its necessity caused by another, or not. Now it is impossible to go on to infinity in necessary things which have their necessity caused by another, as has been al-

Source: Anton C. Pegis, editor, *Basic Writings of St. Thomas Aquinas*, New York: Random House, Inc., 1945, Vol. I, pp. 22–23. Reprinted by permission of Random House, Inc., and Burns & Oates, Ltd., London.

ready proved in regard to efficient causes. Therefore we cannot but admit the existence of some being having of itself its own necessity, and not receiving it from another, but rather causing in others their necessity. This all men speak of as God.

The fourth way is taken from the gradation to be found in things. Among beings there are some more and some less good, true, noble, and the like. But *more* and *less* are predicated of [based on] different things according as they resemble in their different ways something which is the maximum, as a thing is said to be hotter according as it more nearly resembles that which is hottest; so that there is something which is truest, something best, something noblest, and, consequently, something which is most being, for those things that are greatest in truth are greatest in being. . . . Now the maximum in any genus is the cause of all in that genus, as fire, which is the maximum of heat, is the cause of all hot things. . . . Therefore there must also be something which is to all beings the cause of their being, goodness, and every other perfection; and this we call God.

The fifth way is taken from the governance of the world. We see that things which lack knowledge, such as natural bodies, act for an end, and this is evident from their acting always, or nearly always, in the same way, so as to obtain the best result. Hence it is plain that they achieve their end, not fortuitously [by chance], but designedly [by design]. Now whatever lacks knowledge cannot move toward an end, unless it be directed by some being endowed with knowledge and intelligence; as the arrow is directed by the archer. Therefore some intelligent being exists by whom all natural things are directed to their end; and this being we call God.

PART FOUR

The Emergence
of Modern Europe

The Renaissance Courtier

*Like the ancient Greeks and Romans they admired, the Italians of
the Renaissance were dedicated to living the good life on earth.
They devoted themselves to the cultivation of all the qualities
and talents of the individual. The ideal of the Renaissance was
the well-rounded personality. Among the many books dealing
with the education and training of the "universal man," the
most popular was Baldassare Castiglione's The Book of the
Courtier, published in Italian in 1528. Castiglione (1478–1529)
was himself a courtier and a successful diplomat. His book was
translated into many languages and went through numerous edi-
tions. Castiglione's portrait of the perfect courtier and his in-
structions for the development of both body and mind provided
a model for the training and the behavior of a gentleman for the
upper classes in Europe.*

I am of opinion that the principal and true profession of the
Courtier ought to be that of arms; which I would have him follow ac-
tively above all else, and be known among others as bold and strong, and
loyal to whomsoever he serves. And he will win a reputation for these
good qualities by exercising them at all times and in all places, since
one may never fail in this without severest censure. . . .

And . . . I would have him well built and shapely of limb, and
would have him show strength and lightness and suppleness, and know
all bodily exercises that befit a man of war: whereof I think the first
should be to handle every sort of weapon well on foot and on horse, to
understand the advantages of each, and especially to be familiar with
those weapons that are ordinarily used among gentlemen. . . .

[The Courtier should] avoid affectation to the uttermost; . . .
and, to use possibly a new word, to practice in everything a certain non-
chalance that shall conceal design and show that what is done and said
is done without effort and almost without thought. . . .

Source: Baldassare Castiglione, *The Book of the Courtier*, translated by Leonard E. Opdycke, New York: Charles Scribner's Sons, 1903, pp. 25 *passim*.

Our Courtier then will be esteemed excellent and will attain grace in everything, particularly in speaking, if he avoids affectation; into which fault many fall, and often more than others, some of us Lombards, who, if they have been a year away from home, on their return at once begin to speak Roman, sometimes Spanish or French, and God knows how. And all this comes from overzeal to appear widely informed. . . .

I think that what is chiefly important and necessary for the Courtier in order to speak and write well is knowledge. . . .

Nor would I have him speak always of grave matters, but of amusing things, of games, jests, and waggery, according to the occasion; but sensibly of everything, and with readiness and lucid fullness; and in no place let him show vanity or childish folly. . . .

I would have him more than passably accomplished in letters, at least in those studies that are called the humanities, and conversant not only with the Latin language but with the Greek, for the sake of the many different things that have been admirably written therein. Let him be well versed in the poets, and not less in the orators and historians, and also proficient in writing verse and prose, especially in this vulgar [vernacular] tongue of ours. . . .

You must know that I am not content with the Courtier unless he be also a musician and unless, besides understanding and being able to read notes, he can play upon divers instruments. For if we consider rightly, there is to be found no rest from toil or medicine for the troubled spirit more becoming and praiseworthy in time of leisure than this. . . .

I wish to discuss another matter, which I deem of great importance and therefore think our Courtier ought by no means to omit: and this is to know how to draw and to have acquaintance with the very art of painting.

And do not marvel that I desire this art, which today may seem to savor of the artisan and little to befit a gentleman; for I remember having read that the ancients, especially throughout Greece, had their boys of gentle birth study painting in school as an honorable and necessary thing. . . .

The game of tennis . . . is nearly always played in public, and is one of those sports to which a crowd lends much distinction. Therefore I would have our Courtier practice this, and all the others except the handling of arms, as something that is not his profession, and let him show that he does not seek or expect praise for it, nor let him seem to devote much care or time to it, although he may do it admirably. . . .

There are certain other exercises that can be practiced in public and in private, like dancing; and in this I think the Courtier ought to have a care, for when dancing in the presence of many and in a place full of people, it seems to me that he should preserve a certain dignity. . . .

Besides daily showing everyone that he possesses the worth we have already described, I would have the Courtier strive, with all the thoughts and forces of his mind, to love and almost to adore the prince whom he serves, above every other thing, and mold his wishes, habits, and all his ways to his prince's liking. . . .

Our Courtier . . . will not be a bearer of evil tidings; he will not be thoughtless in sometimes saying things that offend instead of pleasing as he intends. He will not be obstinate and disputatious, as some are who seem to delight in nothing but to be troublesome and disagreeable like flies, and who make a point of spitefully contradicting everyone. . . .

Let him above all take care not to weary his lord, and let him wait for favors to be offered him rather than angle for them so openly as many do, who are so greedy that it seems as if they must die if they do not get what they seek. . . .

I would that our Courtier . . . might love, honor, and respect others according to their worth and merits, and always contrive to consort [mingle] more with such as are in high esteem and noble and of known virtue, than with the ignoble and those of little worth; in such ways that he may be loved and honored by them also. And he will accomplish this if he be courteous, kind, generous, affable, and mild with others, zealous and active to serve and guard his friends' welfare and honor both absent and present, enduring such of their natural defects as are endurable, without breaking with them for slight cause, and correcting in himself those that are kindly pointed out. . . .

I do not care at present to go more into detail in speaking of things that are too well known, such as that our Courtier ought not to avow himself a great eater or drinker, or given to excess in any evil habit; . . . because a man of this kind not only may not hope to become a good Courtier, but can be set to no more fitting business than feeding sheep. . . .

If our Courtier excels in anything besides arms, I would have him get profit and esteem from it in fine fashion; and I would have him so discreet and sensible as to be able with skill and address to attract men to see and hear what wherein he thinks he excels, always appearing not to do it from ostentation, but by chance and at others' request rather than by his own wish. . . . Then, in that of which he knows he is wholly ignorant, I would never have him make any pretense or seek to win any fame; nay if need be, let him frankly confess his ignorance. . . .

I wish our Courtier to guard against getting the name of a liar or a boaster, which sometimes befalls even those who do not deserve it. . . .

Let it suffice to say, besides the things already said, that he should be of such sort as never to be without something to say that is good and well suited to those with whom he is speaking, and that he should know how to refresh the minds of his hearers with a certain sweetness, and by his amusing witticisms and pleasantries to move them cleverly to mirth and laughter.

The Conviction and Recantation of Galileo

The hypothesis of Copernicus that the sun and not the earth was the center of the universe won general acceptance only when it was verified by observation and formulated in terms of scientific law. The work of the versatile Galileo Galilei (1564–1642) furthered the acceptance of Copernican ideas, added a great deal of new knowledge, and demonstrated the erroneous nature of many accepted notions. Galileo made a telescope and used it to support his assertion that there was no distinction between heavenly bodies and the earth. Though some of his opponents refused to look through his telescope, he was able to demonstrate that the moon had a rough surface like that of the earth and that the surface of the sun was not perfect but was covered with "spots." He noticed that Jupiter had a number of satellite moons and looked like a miniature solar system. He proved that all bodies, in the absence of air friction, fall at the same speed regardless of weight, thus discrediting a long-accepted notion.

His ideas on the nature of the universe got him into trouble with the Inquisition, first in 1615, and again in 1633. On this latter occasion, Galileo, old and sick, was frightened by the threat of torture into signing a complete recantation. He was convicted of heresy and had to spend the remainder of his life confined to his home.

The Conviction

We, the undersigned, . . . by the grace of God, Cardinals of the Holy Roman Church, Inquisitors General throughout the whole Christian Republic, Special Deputies of the Holy Apostolic Chair against heretical depravity:

Whereas you, Galileo, son of the late Vincenzio Galilei of Florence, aged seventy years, were denounced . . . to this Holy Office for holding as true a false doctrine taught by many, namely, that the sun is immovable in the center of the world, and that the earth moves, and also with a diurnal * motion; also, for having pupils whom you instructed in the same opinions; also, for maintaining a correspondence on the same with some German mathematicians; also, for publishing certain letters on the sunspots, in which you developed the same doctrine as true. . . .

The proposition that the sun is in the center of the world and immovable from its place is absurd, philosophically false, and formally heretical, because it is expressly contrary to the Holy Scriptures.

The proposition that the earth is not the center of the world nor immovable, but that it moves and with a diurnal motion is also absurd, philosophically false, and, theologically considered, at least erroneous in faith. . . .

Therefore, by our order you have been cited to this Holy Office, where on your examination upon oath you have acknowledged the said book as written and printed by you. . . .

But whereas it appeared to us that you had not disclosed the whole truth with regard to your intention, we thought it necessary to proceed

* **diurnal:** the repeating twenty-four-hour rotation cycle of the earth.

Source: J. J. Fahie, *Galileo — His Life and Work*, New York: James Pott & Company, 1903, pp. 313–21.

to the rigorous examination of you, in which . . . you answered like a good Catholic.

Therefore, having seen and maturely considered the merits of your cause, with your said confessions and excuses and everything else which ought to be seen and considered, we have come to the underwritten final sentence against you:

Invoking, therefore, the most holy name of our Lord Jesus Christ, and of his most glorious Virgin Mother Mary, . . . we pronounce, judge, and declare that you, the said Galileo, by reason of these things which have been detailed in the course of this writing, and which as above you have confessed, have rendered yourself vehemently suspected by this Holy Office of heresy; that is, of having believed and held the doctrine . . . that the sun is the center of the world and that it does not move from east to west, and that the earth does move and is not the center of the world; also, that an opinion can be held and supported as probable after it has been declared and finally decreed contrary to the Holy Scripture, and consequently that you have incurred all the censures and penalties imposed . . . in the sacred canons . . . against delinquents of this description. From which it is our pleasure that you be absolved, provided that with a sincere heart and unfeigned faith, in our presence, you abjure, curse, and detest the said errors and heresies, and every other error and heresy contrary to the Catholic and Apostolic Church of Rome, in the form now shown to you.

But that your grievous and pernicious error and transgression may not go altogether unpunished, and that you may be made more cautious in the future and may be a warning to others to abstain from delinquencies of this sort, we decree that the book *Dialogues of Galileo Galilei* be prohibited by a public edict, and we condemn you to the formal prison of this Holy Office for a period determinable at our pleasure; and by way of salutary penance, we order you during the next three years to recite, once a week, the seven penitential psalms. . . .

So we, the subscribing Cardinals, pronounce.

The Recantation

I, Galileo Galilei, son of the late Vincenzio Galilei of Florence, aged seventy years, being brought personally to judgment and kneeling before you, Most Eminent and Most Reverend Lords Cardinals, General Inquisitors of the Universal Christian Republic against heretical depravity, having before my eyes the Holy Gospels which I touch with my own hands, swear that I have always believed and with the help of God will in future believe every article which the Holy Catholic and Apostolic Church of Rome holds, teaches, and preaches. But because I have been enjoined by this Holy Office altogether to abandon the false opinion which maintains that the sun is the center and immovable, and forbidden to hold, defend, or teach the said false doctrine in any manner; and because, after it had been signified to me that the said doctrine is repugnant to the Holy Scripture, I have written and printed a book in which I treat of the same condemned doctrine, and adduce reasons with great force in support of the same, . . . and therefore have been judged grievously suspected of heresy; that is to say, that I held and believed that the sun is the center of the world and immovable and that the earth is not the center and movable, I am willing to remove from the minds of your Eminences and of every Catholic Christian this vehement suspicion rightly entertained towards me; therefore, with a sincere heart and unfeigned faith, I abjure, curse, and detest the said errors and heresies, and generally every other error and sect contrary to the said Holy Church; and I swear that I will never more in future say or assert anything, verbally or in writing, which may give rise to a similar suspicion of me; but that if I shall know any heretic, or anyone suspected of heresy, I will denounce him to this Holy Office or to the Inquisitor and Ordinary of the place in which I may be. I swear, moreover, and promise that I will fulfill and observe fully all the penances which have been or shall be laid on me by this Holy Office. But if it shall happen that I violate any of my said promises, oaths, and protestations (which God avert!), I subject myself to all the pains and punishments which have been decreed and promulgated by the sacred canons and other general and particular constitutions against delinquents of this description. So, may God help me, and His Holy Gospels, which I touch with my own hands, I, the above named Galileo Galilei, have abjured, sworn, promised, and bound myself as above; and, in witness thereof, with my own hand have subscribed this present writing of my abjuration, which I have recited word for word.

At Rome, in the Convent of Minerva, June 22, 1633, I, Galileo Galilei, have abjured as above with my own hand.

Da Vinci's Advice
to Aspiring Artists

Of all the outstanding personalities of the Renaissance, the
most brilliant, the most versatile, and the one coming closest to
the ideal of the "universal man" was Leonardo da Vinci (1452–
1519). He had an insatiable curiosity and was gifted with a fertile imagination. His notebooks are filled with detailed scientific
observations as well as exciting sketches of proposed inventions
such as flying machines.

Though skilled as a mathematician and an engineer, he is
best remembered for his art, which included masterpieces in
architecture and sculpture as well as painting. For his paintings
and sculpture he took great pains to study nature and to acquire
an accurate knowledge of anatomy; yet his main purpose was
to capture the individual personality of his subject.

Among men who are powerful in strength, which muscles are of
greater thickness and more prominent? . . .

Which muscles are those which stand out as people grow old or in
the young when they become lean? . . .

The greatest thickness which the limbs acquire is in the part of the
muscle that is farthest away from their attachments.

The flesh never increases upon the parts of the bones which are
near the surface of the limbs.

The movements of the fingers are chiefly those of extension and
bending. Extension and bending are done in various ways, that is, sometimes by bending all in one piece at the first joint, at another time by
bending or straightening themselves halfway at the second joint, and at
another time by bending in their whole length and at the same time in
all the three joints. If the two first joints are prevented from bending,

Source: Edward MacCurdy, editor, *The Notebooks of Leonardo da Vinci*, New
York: Reynal and Hitchcock, 1938, Vol. I, pp. 190–204. Reprinted by permission of Harcourt, Brace & World, Inc.

the third joint will bend more readily than before, but it can never bend of itself alone if the other joints are free, but all the three joints must bend.

Observe how the shoulder changes with all the movements of the arm, moving up and down, inward and outward, backward and forward, and so also with turning movements or any other movements. And do the same with the neck, the hands and feet, and the chest above the hips.

O painter skilled in anatomy, beware lest the undue prominence of the bones, sinews, and muscles cause you to become a wooden painter from the desire to make your . . . figures reveal all their emotions. And if you wish to remedy this you should consider in what way the muscles of old or lean persons cover or clothe the bones, and furthermore note the principle on which these same muscles fill up the spaces of the surface which come between them, and which are the muscles that never lose their prominence in any degree of fatness whatsoever, and which those whereof the tendons become indistinguishable at the least suggestion of it.

The eyes of all animals have pupils which have power of increase or diminish of their own accord, according to the greater or less light of the sun or other luminary. In birds, however, the difference is greater, and especially with nocturnal birds of the owl species. . . . With these the pupil increases until it almost covers the whole eye or diminishes to the size of a grain of millet, preserving all the time its round shape. But in the lion species, such as panthers, leopards, lionesses, tigers, wolves, lynxes, Spanish cats, and others, the pupil as it diminishes changes from the perfect circle to an elliptical figure.

A Handbook for Princes

The city of Florence was ruled by the wealthy and brilliant Medici family throughout most of the fifteenth century. After a brief republican interlude from 1492 to 1512, the Medici des-

pots again gained control. One of those to suffer exile on the return of the Medici was Niccolò Machiavelli, who had worked in the Florentine diplomatic service. During his exile he wrote several books, the first of which, The Prince (1513), was a manual for rulers addressed to Lorenzo, the Medici prince. Written partially in the vain hope of regaining his official position, Machiavelli also pleaded with Lorenzo to put himself at the head of a "national" movement for the unification of the whole Italian peninsula and the expulsion of foreign armies.

Machiavelli had read deeply in the classics and, unlike so many of his predecessors who wrote about politics, had acquired a great deal of practical experience in government. Not concerned with ideal men and ideal societies or with religious principles, he confined himself to the realities of political life. His theories and recommendations were supported by examples which he drew from history. The Prince has influenced politicians and statesmen until our own day and Machiavelli's name has become (probably unjustly) a synonym for that which is unscrupulous.

Of the Things for Which Men, and Especially Princes, Are Praised or Blamed

It now remains to be seen what are the methods and rules for a prince as regards his subjects and friends. . . . A man who wishes to make a profession of goodness in everything must necessarily come to grief among so many who are not good. Therefore it is necessary for a prince who wishes to maintain himself to learn how not to be good, and to use this knowledge and not use it according to the necessity of the case.

Leaving on one side, then, those things which concern only an imaginary prince, and speaking of those that are real, I state that all men, and especially princes, who are placed at a greater height, are reputed for certain qualities which bring them either praise or blame. Thus one is considered liberal, another . . . miserly; . . . one cruel, another merciful; one a breaker of his word, another trustworthy; . . . one humane, another haughty; . . . one frank, another astute; one hard, another

Source: Niccolò Machiavelli, The Prince, translated by Luigi Ricci, New York: Random House, Inc., 1940, pp. 56–65. Reprinted by permission of Oxford University Press, London.

easy; one serious, another frivolous; one religious, another an unbeliever, and so on. I know that everyone will admit that it would be highly praiseworthy in a prince to possess all the above-named qualities that are reputed good, but as they cannot all be possessed or observed, human conditions not permitting of it, it is necessary that he should be prudent enough to avoid the scandal of those vices which would lose him the state. . . . And yet he must not mind incurring the scandal of those vices without which it would be difficult to save the state, for if one considers well, it will be found that some things which seem virtues would, if followed, lead to one's ruin, and some others which appear vices result in one's greater security and well-being.

Of Cruelty and Clemency, and Whether It Is Better to Be Loved or Feared

Proceeding to the other qualities before named, I say that every prince must desire to be considered merciful and not cruel. He must, however, take care not to misuse this mercifulness. . . .

Nevertheless, he must be cautious in believing and acting, and must not be afraid of his own shadow, and must proceed in a temperate manner with prudence and humanity, so that too much confidence does not render him incautious. . . .

From this arises the question whether it is better to be loved more than feared, or feared more than loved. The reply is that one ought to be both feared and loved, but as it is difficult for the two to go together, it is much safer to be feared than loved if one of the two has to be wanting. For it may be said of men in general that they are ungrateful, . . . anxious to avoid danger, and covetous of gain. . . . And the prince who has relied solely on their words, without making other preparations, is ruined; for the friendship which is gained by purchase and not through grandeur and nobility of spirit is bought but not secured. . . . And men have less scruple in offending one who makes himself loved than one who makes himself feared; for love is held by a chain of obligation which, men being selfish, is broken whenever it serves their purpose; but fear is maintained by a dread of punishment which never fails.

Still, a prince should make himself feared in such a way that if he does not gain love, he at any rate avoids hatred; for fear and the absence of hatred may well go together, and will be always attained by one who abstains from interfering with the property of his citizens and subjects. . . . And when he is obliged to take the life of anyone, let him do so when there is a proper justification and manifest reason for it; but above all he must abstain from taking the property of others, for men forget more easily the death of their father than the loss of their patrimony [inheritance]. . . .

But when the prince is with his army and has a large number of soldiers under his control, then it is extremely necessary that he should not mind being thought cruel; for without this reputation he could not keep an army united or disposed to any duty. . . .

I conclude, therefore, with regard to being feared and loved, that men love at their own free will, but fear at the will of the prince, and that a wise prince must rely on what is in his power and not on what is in the power of others, and he must only contrive to avoid incurring hatred, as has been explained.

In What Way Princes Must Keep Faith

How laudable it is for a prince to keep good faith and live with integrity, and not with astuteness, everyone knows. Still, the experience of our times shows those princes to have done great things who have had little regard for good faith, and have been able by astuteness to confuse men's brains, and who have ultimately overcome those who have made loyalty their foundation.

You must know then that there are two methods of fighting, the one by law, the other by force; the first method is that of men, the second of beasts; but as the first method is often insufficient, one must have recourse to the second. It is therefore necessary for a prince to know well how to use both the beast and the man. . . .

A prince being thus obliged to know well how to act as a beast must imitate the fox and the lion, for the lion cannot protect himself from traps, and the fox cannot defend himself from wolves. One must therefore be a fox to recognize traps and a lion to frighten wolves. Those that wish to be only lions do not understand this. Therefore, a prudent ruler ought not to keep faith when by so doing it would be against his interest, and when the reasons which made him bind himself no longer exist. If men were all good, this precept [rule] would not be a good one; but as they are bad and would not observe their faith with you, so you are not bound to keep faith with them. Nor have legitimate grounds ever failed a prince who wished to show . . . excuse for the nonfulfillment of his promise. Of this one could furnish an infinite number of modern examples and show how many times peace has been broken, and how many promises rendered worthless by the faithlessness of princes; and those that have been best able to imitate the fox have succeeded best. . . .

It is not, therefore, necessary for a prince to have all the above-named qualities, but it is very necessary to seem to have them. I would even be bold to say that to possess them and always to observe them is dangerous, but to appear to possess them is useful. Thus it is well to seem merciful, faithful, humane, sincere, religious, and also to be so; but you must have the mind so disposed that when it is needful to be otherwise you may be able to change to the opposite qualities. And it must be understood that a prince, and especially a new prince, cannot observe all those things which are considered good in men, being often obliged in order to maintain the state to act against faith, against charity, against humanity, and against religion. And therefore he must have a mind disposed to adapt itself according to the wind and as the variations of fortune dictate, and, as I said before, not deviate from what is good, if possible, but be able to do evil if constrained [compelled].

A prince must take great care that nothing goes out of his mouth which is not full of the above-named five qualities, and, to see and hear him, he should seem to be all mercy, faith, integrity, humanity, and religion.

The Brutality of the Conquerors in the New World

The rich, sparsely populated lands of the New World brought many adventurers and settlers from Europe where the population was comparatively dense and opportunity limited. Those ambitious adventurers who won an empire for Spain in the decades after the discovery of the New World are known as the conquistadores. The conquest of the native people was accomplished by superior weapons, treachery, and bloodshed. Whole civilizations were destroyed in Mexico and Peru. The territory was robbed of its precious metals, and the inhabitants were often subjected to extreme cruelty.

Among those who cried out in defense of the Indian was Bartholomew de Las Casas (1474–1566), who had come as a conqueror, but soon joined the Dominican Order of Friars. After spending years as Bishop of Chiapas in Mexico, he returned to Spain and published a devastating account of the treatment of Indians by the Spaniards. Though some scholars have argued that he told a one-sided story, and though his figures are exaggerated, his account is generally correct.

In the island of Hispañola — which was the first . . . to be invaded by the Christians — the immense massacres and destruction of [the Indians] began. It was the first to be destroyed and made into a desert. The Christians began by taking the women and children, to use and to abuse them, and to eat of the substance of their toil and labor, instead of contenting themselves with what the Indians gave them spontaneously, according to the means of each. Such stores are always small, because they keep no more than they ordinarily need, which they acquire with little labor; but what is enough for three households of ten persons each for a month, a Christian eats and destroys in one day. From their using force, violence, and other kinds of vexations the Indians began to perceive that these men could not have come from heaven. . . .

The Christians, with their horses and swords and lances, began to slaughter and practice strange cruelty among them. They penetrated into the country and spared neither children nor the aged, nor . . . women, . . . all of whom they ran through the body and lacerated, as though they were assaulting so many lambs herded in their sheepfold.

They made a gallows just high enough for the feet to nearly touch the ground, and by thirteens, . . . they put wood underneath and, with fire, they burned the Indians. . . .

They generally killed the lords and nobles in the following way: they made wooden gridirons of stakes, bound them upon them, and made a slow fire beneath; thus the victims gave up the spirit by degrees, emitting cries of despair in their torture. . . .

And because all the people who could flee hid among the moun-

Source: Francis A. MacNutt, *Bartholomew de Las Casas: His Life, His Apostate, and His Writings*, New York: G. P. Putnam's Sons, 1909, pp. 318–21. Reprinted by permission of the publishers.

173

tains and climbed the crags to escape from men so deprived of humanity, so wicked, such wild beasts, exterminators and capital enemies of all the human race, the Spaniards taught and trained the fiercest boarhounds to tear an Indian to pieces as soon as they saw him, so that they more willingly attacked and ate one than if he had been a boar. These hounds made great havoc and slaughter.

And because sometimes, though rarely, the Indians killed a few Christians for just cause, they made a law among themselves that for one Christian whom the Indians killed, the Christians should kill a hundred Indians.

Luther Refuses to Submit to the Diet of Worms

When Martin Luther posted his ninety-five theses on the door of the court church at Wittenberg on October 31, 1517, he expected to initiate a scholarly debate. Instead he found himself at the head of a great revolution. Within a few years it became clear that he differed with the Church not only on the matter of abuses but also on fundamental religious doctrines.

By 1520 Luther had set forth views on religion (such as justification by faith alone) that undermined the basis of the Catholic priesthood. When the Pope issued a bull threatening him with excommunication, Luther in defiance publicly burned the papal bull. In 1521 he was summoned by the Holy Roman Emperor, Charles V, to defend his position before the Imperial Diet at Worms. There, in a dramatic encounter with his opponents, Luther again refused to retract his opinions. The Diet thereupon condemned him and declared him an outlaw. To his protection came his prince, Frederick the Wise, Elector of Saxony, who took him to his castle. Luther's stand before the Diet made him a popular hero in many parts of Germany.

The Dr. Eck mentioned in the selection debated with Luther in 1519 and was instrumental in having Luther's doctrines condemned by the Pope.

[Eck, Official of the Archbishop of Trier, asked Luther:] Do you wish to defend the books which are recognized as your work? Or to retract anything contained in them? . . .

[Luther replied:] Most serene Lord Emperor, most illustrious Princes, most gracious Lords: . . . I beseech you to grant a gracious hearing to my plea, which I trust will be a plea of justice and truth; and if through my inexperience I neglect to give to any their proper titles or in any way offend against the etiquette of the court in my manners or behavior, be kind enough to forgive me, I beg, since I am a man who has spent his life not in courts but in the cells of a monastery; a man who can say of himself only this, that to this day I have thought and written in simplicity of heart, solely with a view to the glory of God and the pure instruction of Christ's faithful people. . . .

Your Imperial Majesty and your Lordships: I ask you to observe that my books are not all of the same kind.

There are some in which I have dealt with piety in faith and morals with such simplicity and so agreeably with the Gospels that my adversaries themselves are compelled to admit them useful, harmless, and clearly worth reading by a Christian. . . .

The second kind consists in those writings leveled against the papacy and the doctrine of the papists, as against those who by their wicked doctrines and precedents have laid waste Christendom by doing harm to the souls and the bodies of men. No one can either deny or conceal this, for universal experience and worldwide grievances are witnesses to the fact that through the Pope's laws and through manmade teachings the consciences of the faithful have been most pitifully ensnared, troubled, and racked in torment, and also that their goods and possessions have been devoured (especially amongst this famous German nation) by unbelievable tyranny, and are to this day being devoured without end in shameful fashion. . . .

The third kind consists of those books which I have written against private individuals, so-called; against those, that is, who have exerted themselves in defense of the Roman tyranny and to the overthrow of that piety which I have taught. . . .

However, since I am a man and not God, I cannot provide my

Source: Henry Bettenson, editor, *Documents of the Christian Church*, London: Oxford University Press, 1947, pp. 283–85; and from *Documents of the Continental Reformation*, edited by the Reverend B. J. Kidd, Oxford: The Clarendon Press, 1911. Reprinted by permission of the publishers.

writings with any other defense than that which my Lord Jesus Christ provided for his teaching. When he had been interrogated concerning his teaching . . . and had received a buffet from a servant, he said: "If I have spoken evil, bear witness of the evil." If the Lord himself, who knew that he could not err, did not refuse to listen to witness against his teaching, even from a worthless slave, how much more ought I, scum that I am, capable of naught but error, to seek and to wait for any who may wish to bear witness against my teaching.

And so, through the mercy of God, I ask your Imperial Majesty, and your illustrious Lordships, or anyone of any degree to bear witness, to overthrow my errors, to defeat them by the writings of the Prophets or by the Gospels; for I shall be most ready, if I be better instructed, to recant any error, and I shall be the first in casting my writings into the fire. . . .

Thereupon the Orator of the Empire, in a tone of upbraiding, said that [Luther's] answer was not to the point. . . . He was being asked for a plain reply . . . to this question: Was he prepared to recant, or no?

Luther then replied: Your Imperial Majesty and your Lordships demand a simple answer. Here it is, plain and unvarnished. Unless I am convicted of error by the testimony of Scripture or (since I put no trust in the unsupported authority of Pope or of councils, since it is plain that they have often erred and often contradicted themselves) by manifest reasoning I stand convicted by the Scriptures to which I have appealed, and my conscience is taken captive by God's word, I cannot and will not recant anything, for to act against our conscience is neither safe for us, nor open to us.

On this I take my stand. I can do no other. God help me. Amen.

The Doctrines of Calvin

John Calvin (1509–1564) was a very powerful force in the spread of Protestantism. In 1534 he left the Catholic Church and fled from France, his homeland, to Switzerland. Two years later he wrote his Institutes of the Christian Religion, which became one of the most influential works among Protestants. In Geneva he established and, in effect, governed a theocratic, or church, state which became the center of international Protestantism. Whereas Lutheranism tended ultimately to appeal to the established powers in various German and Scandinavian states, Calvinism was for the most part the faith of a determined minority igniting religious and political disorder in many parts of Europe.

Calvin put great stress on the doctrine of predestination. According to this belief, some were chosen by God for salvation and others selected for damnation. "The elect" were few, and the ways of God in choosing them utterly mysterious. Calvin also emphasized the dignity of human labor. Each man, called by God to perform a task, must religiously devote himself to his vocation. Work as such became a means of serving God.

The Idea of the Elect

No one who wishes to be thought religious dares simply deny predestination, by which God adopts some to hope of life and sentences others to eternal death. But our opponents, especially those who make foreknowledge its cause, envelop it in numerous petty objections. We indeed place both doctrines in God, but we say that subjecting one to the other is absurd.

When we attribute foreknowledge to God, we mean that all things always were, and perpetually remain, under his eyes, so that to his knowledge there is nothing future or past but all things are present. . . . And this foreknowledge is extended throughout the universe to every creature. We call predestination God's eternal decree, by which he determined with himself what he willed to become of each man. For all are not created in equal condition; rather, eternal life is foreordained for some, eternal damnation for others. Therefore, as any man has been created to one or the other of these ends, we speak of him as predestined to life or to death.

On Vocations

Finally, this point is to be noted: the Lord bids each one of us in all life's actions to look to his calling. For he knows with what great restlessness human nature flames, with what fickleness it is borne hither

Source: John Calvin, *Institutes of the Christian Religion*, edited by John T. McNeill, translated by F. L. Battles, Philadelphia: The Westminster Press, 1960, Vol. II, p. 926; Vol. I, pp. 724–25. © 1960 by W. L. Jenkins. Reprinted by permission of The Westminster Press.

and thither, how its ambition longs to embrace various things at once. Therefore, lest through our stupidity and rashness everything be turned topsy-turvy, he has appointed duties for every man in his particular way of life. And that no one may thoughtlessly transgress his limits, he has named these various kinds of living "callings." Therefore each individual has his own kind of living assigned to him by the Lord as a sort of sentry post, so that he may not heedlessly wander about throughout life. . . .

But I will not delay to list examples. It is enough if we know that the Lord's calling is in everything the beginning and foundation of well-doing. And if there is anyone who will not direct himself to it, he will never hold to the straight path in his duties. . . . Accordingly, your life will then be best ordered when it is directed to this goal. For no one, impelled by his own rashness, will attempt more than his calling will permit, because he will know that it is not lawful to exceed its bounds. A man of obscure station will lead a private life ungrudgingly so as not to leave the rank in which he has been placed by God. Again, it will be no slight relief from cares, labors, troubles, and other burdens for a man to know that God is his guide in all these things. The magistrate will discharge his functions more willingly; the head of the household will confine himself to his duty; each man will bear and swallow the discomforts, vexations, weariness, and anxieties in his way of life, when he has been persuaded that the burden was laid upon him by God. From this will arise also a singular consolation: that no task will be so sordid and base, provided you obey your calling in it, that it will not shine and be reckoned very precious in God's sight.

The Council of Trent Reforms the Church

The reform of the Catholic Church began in some regions even before the Protestant Reformation. As the Protestant revolt gathered momentum, the cries for reform within the Church grew louder. Some demanded that a council of the Church be called together. The popes, fearing a threat to their own authority, long resisted. Pope Paul III, in 1545, finally convened the Council of Trent, which met intermittently until 1563.

After many battles between those who wanted a rigid adherence to established beliefs and those who sought a compromise with the Protestants, the Council issued a statement of doctrine which confirmed and clarified the Catholic position and did not give an inch to the Protestants. At the same time, the Council made a determined stand against all abuses within the Church. Papal powers were left intact when the Council gave the papacy the right to make the final decision on carrying out its reforming decrees. The reanimated Catholic Church was able to prevent the extension of the Reformation and to regain some lost ground as well.

The following are some of the decrees enacted by the Council of Trent.

This holy Council enjoins on all bishops and others who are charged with teaching that they instruct the faithful diligently concerning the intercession and invocation of saints, the honor paid to relics, and the legitimate use of images. Let them teach that the saints, who reign together with Christ, offer up their own prayers to God for men; that it is good and useful . . . to invoke them, . . . and that those persons think impiously who deny that the saints, who enjoy eternal happiness in heaven, are to be invoked; or who assert that the saints do not pray for men, or that the invocation of them to pray for each of us individually is idolatry, . . . or that it is foolish to supplicate, orally or mentally, those who reign in heaven.

They shall likewise teach that the holy bodies of martyrs and of others now living with Christ . . . are to be venerated by the faithful, through which relics many benefits are bestowed by God on men. Consequently, they who affirm that veneration and honor are not due to the relics of saints, or that these and other sacred memorials are uselessly honored by the faithful . . . are wholly to be condemned. . . .

Moreover, they shall teach that the images of Christ, of the Virgin Mother of God, and of the other saints are to be placed and retained particularly in churches, and that due honor and veneration are to be given them; not that any divinity or virtue is believed to be in them on account of which they are to be worshiped, or that anything is to be

Source: James Harvey Robinson, editor, *Readings in European History*, Boston: Ginn & Company, 1906, Vol. II, pp. 157–61.

179

asked of them, or that trust is to be reposed in images as was of old done by the heathen who placed their hope in idols, but because the honor which is shown them is referred to Christ and the saints which those images represent. . . .

If anyone saith that the New Testament does not provide for a distinct, visible priesthood, or that this priesthood has not any power of consecrating and offering up the true body and blood of the Lord and of forgiving and retaining sins, but is only an office and bare ministry of preaching the gospel, or that those who do not preach are not priests at all, let him be anathema [accursed]. . . .

If anyone saith that in the Catholic Church there is not a hierarchy instituted by divine ordination, consisting of bishops, priests, and ministers, let him be anathema.

If anyone saith that the sacraments of the new law were not all instituted by Jesus Christ our Lord, or that they are more or less than seven; . . . let him be anathema.

. . . This Council not only orders that bishops be content with modest furniture and a frugal table and diet, but that they also give heed that in the rest of their manner of living, and in their whole house, there be nothing seen which is alien to this holy institution and which does not manifest simplicity, zeal toward God, and a contempt of vanities.

It strictly forbids them, moreover, to strive to enrich their own kindred or domestics out of the revenues of the Church. . . . And what has been said of bishops, the same is to be observed by all who hold ecclesiastical benefices, whether secular or regular, each according to the nature of his rank.

The Defeat of the Spanish Armada

The cause of Protestantism in England was considerably advanced during the short reign of Henry VIII's young son, Edward VI (1547–1553). Edward's successor was Mary (1553–1558), the daughter of Catherine of Aragon, Henry's first wife.

A devout Catholic, Mary was determined to re-establish the old faith. Her marriage to Philip II of Spain and her willingness to be dominated by his policies did not endear her to her subjects. Her persecution of Protestants earned her the title "Bloody Mary." When she died, England was not unwilling to return to Protestantism.

Under the shrewd and tactful leadership of Elizabeth I (1558–1603), England left the Catholic Church for the last time. When Philip II of Spain became involved in a war to subdue his rebellious subjects in the Netherlands, Queen Elizabeth, after years of hesitation, sent an army in 1585 to the assistance of the hard-pressed Protestants. Philip was now more determined to destroy English power, and to bring this about, he began the construction of a great Armada.

In July 1588 Philip's fleet set sail for the invasion of England. The English ships, more maneuverable, more skillfully manned, and superior in firing power, inflicted heavy losses on the Armada in the English Channel. After the battle, as the Armada was sailing homeward around Scotland, a great storm sent many more Spanish ships to their destruction.

In the following selection, Garrett Mattingly, an American historian, discusses the significance of the battle.

Historians agree that the defeat of the Spanish Armada was a decisive battle, in fact one of the decisive battles of the world, but there is much less agreement as to what it decided. It certainly did not decide the issue of the war between England and Spain. . . . The war dragged itself out for nearly fourteen years more, as long, in fact, as Queen Elizabeth lived, and ended in no better than a draw. Some historians say that the defeat of the Armada "marked the decline of the Spanish colonial empire and the rise of the British." It is hard to see why they think so. By 1603 Spain had not lost to the English a single overseas outpost, while the English colonization of Virginia had been postponed for the duration. Nor did the Armada campaign "transfer the command of the sea from Spain to England." English sea power in the Atlantic had usually been superior to the combined strengths of Castile and Portugal, and so it continued to be, but after 1588 the margin of superiority di-

Source: Garrett Mattingly, *The Armada*, Boston: Houghton Mifflin Company, 1959, pp. 397–402. Reprinted by permission of the publishers.

minished. The defeat of the Armada was not so much the end as the beginning of the Spanish navy. The English could raid the Spanish coast, but they were not able to blockade it. Drake and Hawkins had dreamed of bringing Philip to his knees by cutting off his revenues from the New World, but, in fact, more American treasure reached Spain in the years between 1588 and 1603 than in any other fifteen years in Spanish history. In the War of Elizabeth, nobody commanded the seas. . . .

The older historians . . . who said that the defeat of the Armada decided that the Counter Reformation was not to triumph throughout Europe have a much better case. Perhaps there was nothing that Medina Sidonia * could have done to win the naval battle, but Howard † could certainly have lost it. Had he done so, perhaps some way could have been found to get Parma's ‡ army across to England. Had Parma landed and taken Rochester, as he meant to do, and then marched to London, supported by a victorious Spanish fleet in the Thames, the course of history in England, and on the Continent, might have been altered in any one of a number of ways. Even had Parma failed to conquer England, or to dethrone the Queen, just a limited Spanish success might have dealt the cause of Protestantism a serious, possibly even a fatal blow.

It seems more likely, however, that even had the Spaniards snatched a victory at sea, the final picture of Europe, when peace came, would not have been much different. Philip and his militant advisers dreamed of a great crusade which should wipe out heresy and impose on Christendom the king of Spain's Catholic peace. Drake and his fellow Puritans dreamed of spreading the religious revolution throughout Europe until . . . [the Pope] was hurled from his throne. Both dreams were wide of reality. Neither the Catholic nor the Protestant coalition had the necessary unity, or could dispose of the necessary force. . . .

Nevertheless, the defeat of the Spanish Armada was in one sense a decisive event, less for the combatants than for the onlookers. For the experts on both sides, the outcome at Gravelines [site of the Spanish defeat] was surprising chiefly because the Armada had done as well as it had. But the landsmen, English and Spanish, were less certain which way the scales of victory would incline, and other people were less cer-

* **Medina Sidonia:** admiral of the Armada.
† **Howard:** admiral of the English fleet.
‡ **Duke of Parma:** the Spanish commander in the Netherlands.

tain still. France and Germany and Italy had seen the Spanish . . . advance from victory to victory. . . .

For the spectators of both parties, the outcome, reinforced, as everyone believed, by an extraordinary tempest, was indeed decisive. The Protestants of France, the Netherlands, Germany, and Scandinavia saw with relief that God was, in truth, as they had always supposed, on their side. The Catholics of France and Italy and Germany saw with almost equal relief that Spain was not, after all, God's chosen champion. From that time forward, though Spain's preponderance was to last for more than another generation, the peak of her prestige had passed. . . .

So, in spite of the long, indecisive war which followed, the defeat of the Spanish Armada really was decisive. It decided that religious unity was not to be reimposed by force on the heirs of medieval Christendom. . . . The pattern of territorial, ultimately "national" states which was to characterize modern Europe was beginning to emerge, and after 1588 each major state was not only to be free, but increasingly to feel free to develop its own individual potentialities without conforming to any externally imposed system of beliefs. . . .

Meanwhile, as the episode of the Armada receded into the past, it influenced history in another way. Its story, magnified and distorted by a golden mist, became a heroic [tale] of the defense of freedom against tyranny, an eternal myth of the victory of the weak over the strong, of the triumph of David over Goliath. It raised men's hearts in dark hours, and led them to say to one another, "What we have done once, we can do again." Insofar as it did this, the legend of the defeat of the Spanish Armada became as important as the actual event — perhaps even more important.

A Day at the Court of Louis XIV

Louis XIV (1643–1715) dominated the Europe of his age. Known as the Sun King and the Grand Monarch, he was envied and emulated by the other rulers of Europe. He was only a boy of five when he inherited the crown; by the time he took the reins of power into his own hands in 1661, French absolutism was already firmly established and secure.

Louis was blessed with an imposing appearance and a majestic manner that went well with his view of his own sublime position. As an appropriate home for himself and his entourage, the Sun King constructed at Versailles an enormous and sumptuous palace, which took years to complete and involved a vast expenditure of money. There he invited the great nobles of the realm so that he could keep an eye on their activities and in order to provide himself with a suitable retinue. The most ordinary events of his day, such as getting up and going to bed, were dignified with elaborate ceremony. Royal princes considered it an honor to assist or even be present at these occasions.

The court of Versailles is described by the Duke of Saint-Simon, a sharp observer who was born at Versailles and spent many years there.

At eight o'clock the chief *valet de chambre* on duty, who alone had slept in the royal chamber and who had dressed himself, awoke the King. The chief physician, the chief surgeon, and the nurse (as long as she lived) entered at the same time. The last kissed the King; the others rubbed and often changed his shirt, because he was in the habit of sweating a great deal. At the quarter, the grand chamberlain was called (or, in his absence, the first gentleman of the chamber), and those who had what was called the *grandes entrées*. The chamberlain (or chief gentleman) drew back the curtains, which had been closed again, and presented the holy water from the vase at the head of the bed. These gentlemen stayed but a moment, and that was the time to speak to the King if anyone had anything to ask of him, in which case the rest stood aside. When, contrary to custom, nobody had aught to say, they were there but for a few moments. He who had opened the curtains and presented the holy water presented also a prayerbook. Then all passed into the cabinet of the council. A very short religious service being over, the King called [and] they re-entered. The same officer gave him his dressing gown; immediately after, other privileged courtiers entered, and then

Source: *Memoirs of the Duke of Saint-Simon on the Reign of Louis XIV and the Regency*, translated by Bayle St. John, London: Bickers & Son, 1880, Vol. III, pp. 21–27.

everybody, in time to find the King putting on his shoes and stockings, for he did almost everything himself, and with address and grace. . . .

As soon as he was dressed, he prayed to God at the side of his bed, where all the clergy persent knelt, the cardinals without cushions, all the laity remaining standing; and the captain of the guards came to the balustrade during the prayer, after which the King passed into his cabinet.

He found there, or was followed by all who had the *entrée*, a very numerous company, for it included everybody in any office. He gave orders to each for the day; thus within a half [or] a quarter of an hour it was known what he meant to do; and then all this crowd left directly. . . . It was then a good opportunity for talking with the King, for example, about plans of gardens and buildings. . . .

The King gave audiences when he wished to accord any, spoke with whomever he might wish to speak secretly to, and gave secret interviews to foreign ministers. . . .

The King went to Mass, where his musicians always sang an anthem. While he was going to and returning from Mass, everybody spoke to him who wished, after apprising the captain of the guard if they were not distinguished. The King, upon returning from Mass, asked almost immediately for the council. Then the morning was finished.

On Sunday, and often on Monday, there was a council of state; on Tuesday a finance council; on Wednesday council of state; on Saturday finance council. Rarely were two held in one day or any on Thursday or Friday. . . .

Thursday morning was almost always blank. It was the day for audiences that the King wished to give — often unknown to any — backstair audiences. . . .

The dinner was always *au petit couvert*; that is, the King ate by himself in his chamber, upon a square table in front of the middle window. It was more or less abundant, for he ordered in the morning whether it was to be "a little" or "very little" service. But even at this last, there were always many dishes and three courses without counting the fruit. . . .

Grand dinners were very rare and only took place on grand occasions, and then ladies were present. . . .

The King was fond of air, and when deprived of it his health suffered; he had headaches . . . caused by the undue use he had formerly made of perfumes, so that for many years he could not endure any ex-

cept the odor of orange flowers; therefore if you had to approach anywhere near him you did well not to carry them.

As he was but little sensitive to heat or cold or even to rain, the
weather was seldom sufficiently bad to prevent his going abroad. He
went out for three objects: stag hunting, once or more each week;
shooting in his parks (and no man handled a gun with more grace or
skill), once or twice each week; and walking in his gardens for exercise
and to see his workmen. . . .

At ten o'clock his supper was served. . . . This supper was always
on a grand scale, the royal household (that is, the sons and daughters
of France) at table, and a large number of courtiers and ladies present,
sitting or standing.

After supper the King stood some moments, his back to the balustrade of the foot of his bed, encircled by all his Court; then, with bows
to the ladies, passed into his cabinet, where on arriving he gave his orders. He passed a little less than an hour there, seated in an armchair,
with his children and his grandchildren, and their husbands or wives.

The King, wishing to retire, went and fed his dogs; then said good
night, passed into his chamber, . . . where he said his prayers as in the
morning, then undressed. He said good night with an inclination of the
head, and while everybody was leaving the room stood at the corner of
the mantelpiece, where he gave the order to the colonel of the guards
alone. Then commenced what was called the *petit coucher*, at which
only the specially privileged remained. That was short. They did not
leave until he got into bed. It was a moment to speak to him. Then
all left.

Colbert Directs
the French Economy

*The administrative and financial genius of Jean Baptiste Colbert,
Louis XIV's Controller-General of Finances (1662–1683), enabled the King to indulge his extravagant whims at home and
to carry on costly wars abroad. Colbert's economic policies fall
under the general category of mercantilism, which is sometimes
called Colbertism. State interference in all economic affairs was*

an essential part of his program. He labored to cut down on wasteful expenditure, eliminate internal trade barriers, encourage industry by subsidies, build a navy, establish colonies, and set up tariff walls against rival nations. France was to be entirely self-sufficient. Although Colbert was not altogether successful in his endeavors, he did increase the revenues and manage to advance the economic unity of France.

Colbert's economic policies are illustrated in a letter from Louis XIV to his officials at Marseilles.

Very dear and well beloved:

Considering how advantageous it would be to this realm to re-establish its foreign and domestic commerce, . . . we have resolved to establish a council particularly devoted to commerce, to be held every fortnight in our presence, in which all the interests of merchants and the means conducive to the revival of commerce shall be considered and determined upon, as well as all that which concerns manufactures.

We also inform you that we are setting apart, in the expenses of our state, a million livres each year for the encouragement of manufactures and the increase of navigation, to say nothing of the considerable sums which we cause to be raised to supply the companies of the East and West Indies;

That we are working constantly to abolish all the tolls which are collected on the navigable rivers;

That there has already been expended more than a million livres for the repair of the public highways, to which we shall also devote our constant attention;

That we will assist by money from our royal treasury all those who wish to reestablish old manufactures or to undertake new ones;

That we are giving orders to all our ambassadors or residents at the courts of the princes, our allies, to make, in our name, all proper efforts to cause justice to be rendered in all cases involving our merchants, and to assure for them entire commercial freedom;

That we will comfortably lodge at our court each and every merchant who has business there during all the time that he shall be obliged to remain there, having given orders to the grand marshal of our

Source: James Harvey Robinson, editor, *Readings in European History*, Boston: Ginn & Company, 1906, Vol. II, pp. 279–80.

187

palace to indicate a proper place for that purpose, which shall be called the House of Commerce. . . .

That all the merchants and traders by sea who purchase vessels or who build new ones for traffic or commerce shall receive from us subsidies for each ton of merchandise which they export or import on the said voyages.

We desire in this present letter not only to inform you concerning all these things, but to require you, as soon as you have received it, to cause to be assembled all the merchants and traders of your town of Marseilles, and explain to them very particularly our intentions in all matters mentioned above, in order that, being informed of the favorable treatment which we desire to give them, they may be the more desirous of applying themselves to commerce. Let them understand that for everything that concerns the welfare and advantage of the same they are to address themselves to Sieur Colbert.

Charles I Quarrels with Parliament

No king, however able, would have found it easy to be the successor of the esteemed Queen Elizabeth. James I (1603–1625), her Scottish cousin and heir, while thoroughly learned, lacked the popular appeal and tact which had enabled both Elizabeth and her father to lead the nation through many troubled years. Neither James I nor his son Charles I (1625–1649) was able to come to terms with Parliament. When James made extravagant claims for royal power based on the theory of the Divine Right of Kings, Parliament responded with equally extravagant claims based on tradition. Had it not been for their constant need of money, the Stuart kings might have been happy enough to rule without Parliament altogether. Rising prices, lavish expenditures, and costly foreign involvements, however, made it impossible for them to manage without Parliament's grants. When Charles I met Parliament in 1629, he had already enraged the people by breaking some of the provisions of the

Petition of Right which he had signed the year before. After the incident described in the following selection, Charles ruled without Parliament for eleven years.

Upon Monday the second of March, as soon as prayers were ended, the Speaker went into the chair and delivered the King's command for the adjournment of the House until Tuesday . . . following, the tenth of March.

The House [replied] that it was not the office of a Speaker to deliver any such command to them, but for the adjournment of the House it did properly belong to themselves, and after they had uttered some things they thought fit to be spoken of, they would satisfy the King.

The Speaker told them he had an express command from his Majesty that as soon as he had delivered his message he should rise; and upon that left the chair, but was by force drawn to it again by Mr. Densill Holles, son to the Earl of Clare, Mr. Valentine, and others. . . .

Here Sir John Elliott began in a rhetorical oration to inveigh against the Lord Treasurer and the Bishop of Winchester, saying he could prove the Lord Treasurer to be a great instrument in the innovation of religion,* and invasion of the liberties of the House and offered a remonstrance [complaint] to the House, wherein he said he could prove him to be the great enemy of the Commonwealth, saying "This is the Lord Treasurer, in whose person is contracted all the evil. . . . I find him the head of all that great party [of Catholics]. In this great question of Tonnage and Poundage,† instruments moved at his command and pleasure, he dismays our merchants and he invites strangers to come in to drive our trade and to serve their own ends."

The remonstrance which he offered was put to a question, but the

---

* **innovation of religion:** the Puritans in the House of Commons were objecting to religious practices which they felt bordered on Catholicism.
† **Tonnage and Poundage:** customs duties which Parliament granted to a monarch for his entire reign. When Charles I came to the throne in 1625, however, Parliament voted to allow him this tax for only one year. Charles continued to impose it after the year was over, and Parliament complained bitterly.

Source: Edward P. Cheyney, editor, *Readings in English History*, Boston: Ginn & Company, 1908, pp. 460–63. Reprinted by permission of the publishers.

Speaker refused to do it, and said he was otherwise commanded from the King. . . . The Speaker made a humble supplicatory speech to the House with extremity of weeping, showing what command he had received from his Majesty, and withal [besides] desiring them not to command his ruin; yet notwithstanding the Speaker's extremity of weeping and supplicatory oration, Sir Peter Hayman (a gentleman of his own country) bitterly inveighed against him, and told him he was sorry he was a Kentishman, and that he was a disgrace to his country and a blot to a noble family. . . .

Mr. Strowd spoke much to the same effect, and told the Speaker that he was the instrument to cut off the liberty of the subject by the root, and that if he would not be persuaded to put the same question to [vote], they must all return as scattered sheep, and a scorn put upon them as it was the last session. . . .

The King, hearing that the House continued to sit (notwithstanding his command for the adjournment thereof), sent a messenger for the Sergeant with his mace,* which being taken from the table there can be no further proceeding; but the key of the door was taken from the Sergeant and delivered to Sir Miles Hubert to keep, who, after he had received the same, put the Sergeant out of the House leaving his mace behind him, and then locked the door. After this, the King sent Mr. Maxell . . . for the dissolution of the Parliament; but being informed that neither he nor his message would be received by the House, the King grew into much rage and passion, and sent for the Captain of the Pensioners and Guard to force the door; but the rising [adjournment] of the House prevented the danger and ill-consequence that might have followed.

[The following are the three resolutions finally adopted at the violent session just described:]

1. Whosoever shall bring in innovation of religion . . . shall be reputed a capital enemy to this Kingdom and Commonwealth.

2. Whosoever shall counsel or advise the taking and levying of the subsidies of Tonnage and Poundage, not being granted by Parliament, or shall be an actor or instrument therein, shall be likewise reputed an innovator in the government and a capital enemy to the Kingdom and Commonwealth.

3. If any merchant or person whatsoever shall voluntarily yield or

---

* mace: a staff used as a symbol of authority.

190

pay the said subsidies of Tonnage or Poundage, not being granted by Parliament, he shall likewise be reputed a betrayer of the liberties of England and an enemy to the same.

An Assessment
of Oliver Cromwell

*In 1640, after eleven years of absolute rule, Charles I, in desper-
ate financial straits, was forced to call a meeting of Parliament.
By 1642 the quarrel between Charles and Parliament had
reached such proportions that civil war broke out. The country
was soon divided between the Cavaliers, who were royalists, and
the Roundheads, who were parliamentarians.*

*The most outstanding figure among the rebels was Oliver
Cromwell. A passionately religious Puritan and a fine soldier,
he organized an unbeatable army of religious zealots. Cromwell was able to defeat the King and to execute him, but proved
no more successful than Charles when it came to getting along
with elected bodies of representatives. Cromwell did not want
to be a despot; yet he never found a solution to the problems of
government by representative institutions. Though troubled by
his position, he ruled as a dictator in his last years. After his
death in 1658, he was succeeded by his son Richard, who was
soon induced to resign. Charles II, the son of Charles I, returned
to England in 1660 as King, amid great public rejoicing.*

*C. V. Wedgwood, a British historian, describes the char-
acter of Cromwell and his dismissal of the remnant of the Long
Parliament which had originally met in 1640.*

There is room for legitimate doubt of Cromwell's genius. His
military triumphs were too much the result of special circumstances to
place him among the great soldiers of the world, although his influence
with his men, his tenacity and his imaginative handling . . . of . . .

Source: C. V. Wedgwood, *Oliver Cromwell*, New York: The Macmillan
Company, 1956, pp. 56–60, 92–93. Reprinted by permission of The Macmillan
Company and Gerald Duckworth & Co., Ltd., London. First printed in the United
States in 1956.

problems would have distinguished him anywhere. His subsequent achievements as a statesman will always be the subject of controversy. But of his profound sincerity there can be no serious question. . . .

He had guided his conduct through the wars always by that conviction of God's will working with him which he then acquired. His men went into battle singing religious songs, and each soldier carried with him a little pocket edition of the Psalms done into English verse, . . . and used to this day in Scotland. It had served Cromwell's turn to imbue his troops with this practical religious feeling, to choose godly captains, and impress upon his men that they were indeed fighting the battles of the Lord. But it served his turn so well only because he himself believed in what he preached. Louder and more confident grew Cromwell's trumpet call of faith, resounding through his letters. "With this handful it pleased God to cast the scale," he had written after the fight at Grantham in 1643. At Marston Moor came the triumphant "God made them as stubble to our swords." At Naseby a wondering, almost awestriken joy in his victory: "This is none other but the hand of God."

By the end of the war Cromwell's religious confidence had swollen to gigantic proportions. "I advised you formerly to bear with men of different minds from yourself," he had written once angrily, . . . advice which he frequently gave to others but rarely followed himself. He was patient only with opinions which could be reconciled with his own, and he met direct opposition by instantly and sincerely invoking the Almighty. . . .

On April 20, 1653, Cromwell went down to Westminster with a small troop of musketeers. Leaving them outside, he entered the House of Commons as though nothing were amiss, sat quietly down, and listened to a speech from Sir Henry Vane. When Vane had finished, he rose himself to speak. After placid and even courteous opening words, he gradually warmed into an impassioned attack on the slothful and dishonest methods of the Commons. Carried forward by the flood of his own oratory, he left his place and began to stamp up and down the floor of the House, glaring and gesticulating. "The Lord has done with you!" he thundered out at the embarrassed assembly. As he came to his climax, twenty or thirty musketeers filed into the House. Cromwell shouted to the Speaker to come down. Lenthall did not move and Harrison stepped forward with a grimly courteous offer to assist him. Lenthall then gathered up his robes and made as dignified an exit as he

192

could. The rest of the members followed him out, leaving Cromwell stamping up and down in possession of the empty room. Swinging the mace off the table, "Take away this bauble," he shouted. And then, seeing the defeated Vane moving toward the door, burst out with vituperative scorn, "Sir Harry Vane! Sir Harry Vane! . . . May the Lord deliver me from Sir Harry Vane!" He had already delivered himself.

The forcible expulsion of the Long Parliament left Cromwell sole master of the situation. . . .

Much though not all of Cromwell's work died with him. His immediate service had been to stop the civil strife of England and give her back unity and self-respect. His more permanent service was to strengthen and develop the spirit of religious inquiry, of individualism, and of resistance to mental authority among the English, which flowered into the ineradicable, indestructible, harsh, fertile, stubborn growth of Nonconformity [Protestants other than members of the Church of England]. . . .

His body, buried with great pomp in the Abbey, was disinterred two years later and hanged at Tyburn; the last fate of his bones has never been conclusively proved. . . .

Many different estimates of his moral character and his aspirations have been made. In his last years he had often spoken bitterly, calling the people "a many-headed beast, incapable of reason," and declaring that the sword alone was the best argument. Yet, casting up such statements against others of a more generous kind, it is easy to see that even to the end he hoped for some better foundation for his government than mere force. Intensely, tragically, he loved the people and felt his responsibility toward them, nor did he ever wholly lose touch with them. To them his last thoughts turned: for them he prayed.

The Great Plague
and the Great Fire

No one ever accused Charles II of playing the fiddle while London burned, but a number of Puritans were convinced that the indifference of the monarch to morality helped bring down the wrath of God on the nation. In 1665 England was paralyzed by the last great outbreak of the bubonic plague, which killed many thousands. Then, in September 1666 London was struck by fire, and for six days the wind swept the blaze through the city, destroying numerous homes and public buildings. Vivid accounts of these terrible events are found in the diaries of Samuel Pepys and John Evelyn.

The Plague, 1665

July 12. A solemn fast day for the plague growing upon us. . . .

July 13. Above 700 died of the plague this week. . . .

July 20. So walked to Redriffe, where I hear the sickness is, and indeed is scattered almost everywhere, there dying 1,089 of the plague this week. . . .

July 30 (Lord's day). It was a sad noise to hear our bell toll and ring so often today, either for deaths or burials. . . .

August 3. A maidservant of Mr. John Wright's . . . falling sick of the plague, she was removed to an outhouse and a nurse appointed to look to her; who, being once absent, the [maid] got out of the house at the window and ran away. The nurse coming and knocking and having no answer, believed she was dead, and went and told Mr. Wright so; who and his lady were in great straits what to do to get her buried. At last resolved to go to Burntwood hard by, being in the parish, and there get people to do it. But they would not; so he went home full of trouble, and in the way met the [maid] walking over the common, which frighted him worse than before; and was forced to send people to take her, which he did; and they got one of the pest coaches and put her into it to carry her to a pesthouse. And passing in a narrow lane, Sir Anthony Browne, with his brother and some friends in the coach, met this coach with the curtains drawn close. The brother being a young man and believing there might be some lady in it that would not be seen, and the way being narrow, he thrust his head out of his own into her coach . . . to look, and there saw somebody look very ill, and in a sick dress, and stunk mightily; which the coachman also cried out upon. And presently they came up to some people that stood looking after it,

THE PLAGUE, 1665. Source: *The Diary of Samuel Pepys*, edited by Henry B. Wheatley, London: George Bell & Sons, Ltd., 1895, Vol. V, pp. 11–111.

and told our gallants that it was a [maid] of Mr. Wright's carried away sick of the plague; which put the young gentleman into a fright that almost cost him his life, but is now well again. . . .

August 31. This month ends with great sadness upon the public, through the greatness of the plague everywhere through the kingdom almost. Every day sadder and sadder news of its increase. In the city died this week 7,496, and of them 6,102 of the plague. But it is feared that the true number of the dead this week is near 10,000. . . .

October 16. Lord! how empty the streets are and melancholy, so many poor sick people in the streets full of sores; and so many sad stories overheard as I walk, everybody talking of this [one] dead and that man sick, and so many in this place and so many in that. And they tell me that in Westminster there is never a physician and but one apothecary left, all being dead; but that there are great hopes of a great decrease this week: God send it!

The Fire, 1666

September 2. This fatal night about ten began the deplorable fire, near Fish street, in London.

September 3. The fire having continued all this night (if I may call that night which was light as day for ten miles about, after a dreadful manner), when conspiring with a fierce eastern wind in a very dry season, I went on foot to the same place; and saw the whole south part of the city burning from Cheapside to the Thames, and all along Cornhill (for it likewise kindled back against the wind as well as forward). . . . The conflagration was so universal and the people so astonished that from the beginning, I know not by what despondency or fate, they hardly stirred to quench it; so that there was nothing heard or seen but crying out and lamentation, running about like distracted creatures, without at all attempting to save even their goods; such a strange consternation there was upon them, so [that] it burned both in breadth and length the churches, public halls, Exchange, hospitals, monuments, and ornaments; leaping after a prodigious manner from house to house and street to street, at great distances one from the

THE FIRE, 1666. Source: *The Diary of John Evelyn*, edited by William Bray, Akron, Ohio, St. Dunstan Society, 1901, Vol. II, pp. 20–25.

other. For the heat, with a long set of fair and warm weather, had even ignited the air and prepared the materials to conceive the fire, which devoured, after an incredible manner, houses, furniture, and everything. Here we saw the Thames covered with goods floating, all the barges and boats laden with what some had time and courage to save, as on the other side the carts, etc., carrying out to the fields, which for many miles were strewn with movables of all sorts, and erecting tents to shelter both people and what goods they could get away. Oh, the miserable and calamitous spectacle, such as haply the world had not seen since the foundation of it, nor can be outdone till the universal conflagration thereof. All the sky was of a fiery aspect, like the top of a burning oven, and the light seen above forty miles round about for many nights. God grant mine eyes may never behold the like, who now saw above 10,000 houses all in one flame! The noise and cracking and thunder of the impetuous flames, the shrieking of women and children, the hurry of people, the fall of towers, houses, and churches was like a hideous storm; and the air all about so hot and inflamed that at the least one was not able to approach it, so that they were forced to stand still and let the flames burn on, which they did, for near two miles in length and one in breadth. The clouds also of smoke were dismal, and reached, upon computation, near fifty miles in length. . . . London was, but is no more! . . .

September 5. It now pleased God, by abating the wind, and by the industry of the people, when almost all was lost, infusing a new spirit into them, that the fury began to abate about noon, so as it came no far- ther than the Temple westward nor than the entrance of Smithfield north: but continued all this day and night so impetuous toward Crip- plegate and the Tower as made us all despair. It also broke out again in the Temple, but the courage of the multitude persisting, and many houses being blown up, such gaps and desolations were soon made, as with the former three days' consumption, the back fire did not so vehe- mently urge upon the rest as formerly. There was yet no standing near the burning and glowing ruins by near a furlong's space. . . .

September 7. I went this morning on foot, . . . with extraordinary difficulty, clambering over heaps of yet smoking rubbish, and frequently mistaking where I was; the ground under my feet so hot that it even burnt the soles of my shoes. . . .

The people who now walked about the ruins appeared like men in some dismal desert, or rather, in some great city laid waste by a cruel enemy; to which was added the stench that came from some poor creatures' bodies, beds, and other combustible goods. . . .

I then went toward Islington and Highgate, where one might have seen 200,000 people of all ranks and degrees dispersed, and lying along by their heaps of what they could save from the fire, deploring their loss; and though ready to perish for hunger and destitution, yet not asking one penny for relief, which to me appeared a stranger sight than any I had yet beheld. His Majesty and Council indeed took all imaginable care for their relief by proclamation for the country to come in and refresh them with provisions.

The Revolutionary Settlement of 1689

The constitutional issues over which the Civil War had been fought remained unresolved on the death of Charles II in 1685. His successor, James II, was a devout Catholic. Lacking the political wisdom of his brother, James managed to infuriate even his friends. He tried to suspend the laws which restricted the rights of Catholics, and he went on to appoint them to positions of power and influence in the army and the universities. James might have lived out his life as King had not his wife given birth to a son in 1688, thus assuring a Catholic succession. At this point, opposing political factions united and offered the throne to Mary, the Protestant daughter of James, and her husband, William of Orange. When William landed in England in November 1688, James fled to France without offering resistance.

Parliament at once drew up legislation to clarify the position of the monarch. The Bill of Rights was passed by Parliament and signed by William and Mary in December 1689. Like Magna Carta, it came to be considered a milestone in the evolution of constitutional limited monarchy.

. . . Whereas the said late King James II having abdicated the government, and the throne being thereby vacant, his Highness the Prince of Orange (whom it hath pleased Almighty God to make the glorious instrument of delivering this kingdom from popery and arbitrary power) did (by the advice of the Lords . . . and divers [various] principal persons of the Commons) cause letters to be written to the Lords Spiritual and Temporal, being Protestants, . . . for the choosing of such persons to represent them as were of right to be sent to Parliament, to meet and sit at Westminster upon the two-and-twentieth day of January, in this year One Thousand Six Hundred Eighty and Eight, in order to such an establishment as that their religion, laws, and liberties might not again be in danger of being subverted; upon which letters elections have been accordingly made.

And thereupon the said Lords Spiritual and Temporal, and Commons, . . . being now assembled in a full and free representation of this nation, . . . do in the first place, . . . for the vindicating and asserting their ancient rights and liberties, declare:

1. That the pretended power of suspending of laws, or the execution of laws, by regal authority without consent of Parliament, is illegal.

2. That the pretended power of dispensing with laws, or the execution of laws, by regal authority as it hath been assumed and exercised of late, is illegal. . . .

3. [That the King is prohibited from commissioning special courts to avoid going through the normal channels of law.]

4. That levying money for or to the use of the Crown . . . without grant of Parliament . . . is illegal.

5. That it is the right of the subjects to petition the King, and all . . . prosecutions for such petitioning are illegal.

6. That the raising or keeping a standing army within the kingdom in time of peace, unless it be with consent of Parliament, is against law.

7. That the subjects who are Protestants may have arms for their defense suitable to their conditions and as allowed by law.

8. That election of members of Parliament ought to be free.

9. That the freedom of speech and debates or proceedings in Parliament ought not to be impeached or questioned in any court or place out of Parliament.

Source: *Translations and Reprints from the Original Sources of European History*, Philadelphia: University of Pennsylvania Press, 1897, Vol. I, No. 6, pp. 33–34.

10. That excessive bail ought not to be required, nor excessive fines imposed, nor cruel and unusual punishments inflicted.

11. That jurors ought to be duly impaneled and returned, and jurors who pass upon men in trials for high treason ought to be freeholders.

12. That all grants and promises of fines and forfeitures of particular persons before conviction are illegal and void.

13. And that for redress of all grievances, and for the amending, strengthening, and preserving of the laws, Parliament ought to be held frequently.

And they do claim, demand, and insist upon all [of these] as their undoubted rights and liberties; and that no declarations, judgments, doings or proceedings to the prejudice of the people in any of the said premises ought in any wise to be drawn hereafter into consequence or example.

PART FIVE

Enlightenment, Revolution, and Reaction

The Inalienable Rights of Man

*John Locke was the apostle of liberty and constitutional govern-
ment against tyranny and arbitrary rule.*

*After spending years in exile, Locke came back to England
during the Glorious Revolution. It is not surprising, therefore,
that he upheld the principles of the Revolution in his writings.
By imagining primitive man in a happy state of nature, Locke
argued that the right of life, liberty, and property preceded any
government whatsoever. According to Locke, government came
into existence by means of a social contract which was made by
men of their own free will to protect these rights. The rulers of
society received their authority solely from the people and thus
could not exercise unlimited power. In the event that a ruler
failed in his trust or infringed upon the basic inalienable rights
of man, he could legitimately be overthrown. Locke inspired
revolutionary thinking in both America and France in the
eighteenth century.*

*Locke published his Two Treatises of Government in 1690.
The following selection is from the Second Treatise.*

The State of Nature

To understand political power aright, and derive it from its original, we must consider what state all men are naturally in, and that is
a state of perfect freedom to order their actions and dispose of their possessions and persons as they think fit, within the bounds of the law of
nature, without asking leave or depending upon the will of any other
man. . . .

The state of nature has a law of nature to govern it, which obliges
everyone; and reason, which is that law, teaches all mankind who will
but consult it that, being all equal and independent, no one ought to
harm another in his life, health, liberty, or possessions. . . .

And that all men may be restrained from invading others' rights,

Source: John Locke, *Second Treatise of Civil Government* . . . , edited by
Charles L. Sherman, New York: Appleton-Century-Crofts, 1937, pp. 5 *passim*. Reprinted by permission of the publishers.

and from doing hurt to one another, and the law of nature be observed, which willeth the peace and preservation of all mankind, the execution of the law of nature is in that state put into every man's hand, whereby everyone has a right to punish the transgressors of that law to such a degree as may hinder its violation. . . .

To this strange doctrine — viz., That in the state of nature everyone has the executive power of the law of nature — I doubt not but it will be objected that it is unreasonable for men to be judges in their own cases, that self-love will make men partial to themselves and their friends. And on the other side, that ill nature, passion, and revenge will carry them too far in punishing others; and hence nothing but confusion and disorder will follow; and that therefore God hath certainly appointed government to restrain the partiality and violence of men. I easily grant that civil government is the proper remedy for the inconveniences of the state of nature, which must certainly be great where men may be judges in their own case, since 'tis easy to be imagined that he who was so unjust as to do his brother an injury, will scarce be so just as to condemn himself for it. But I shall desire those who make this objection to remember that absolute monarchs are but men, and if government is to be the remedy of those evils which necessarily follow from men's being judges in their own cases, and the state of nature is therefore not to be endured, I desire to know what kind of government that is, and how much better it is than the state of nature.

Property

God, who hath given the world to men in common, hath also given them reason to make use of it to the best advantage of life and convenience. . . .

Though the earth and all inferior creatures be common to all men, yet every man has a property in his own person; this nobody has any right to but himself. The labor of his body and the work of his hands we may say are properly his. Whatsoever, then, he removes out of the state that nature hath provided and left it in, he hath mixed his labor with and joined to it something that is his own, and thereby makes it his property. . . . For this labor being the unquestionable property of the laborer, no man but he can have a right to what that is once joined to, at least where there is enough, and as good left in common for others. . . .

And as different degrees of industry were apt to give men possessions in different proportions, so [the] invention of money gave them the opportunity to continue and enlarge them.

The Beginning of Political Societies

Men being, as has been said, by nature all free, equal, and independent, no one can be put out of this estate and subjected to the political power of another without his own consent, which is done by agreeing with other men to join and unite into a community for their comfortable, safe, and peaceable living one amongst another in a secure enjoyment of their properties, and a greater security against any that are not of it.

The Ends of Political Society and Government

The great and chief end, therefore, of men's uniting into commonwealths, and putting themselves under government, is the preservation of their property; to which in the state of nature there are many things wanting [lacking].

First, there wants an established, settled, known law, received and allowed by common consent to be the standard of right and wrong, and the common measure to decide all controversies between them. . . .

Secondly, in the state of nature there wants a known and indifferent [impartial] judge, with authority to determine all differences according to the established law. . . .

Thirdly, in the state of nature there often wants power to back and support the sentence when right, and to give it due execution. . . .

Thus mankind, notwithstanding all the privileges of the state of nature, being but in an ill condition, while they remain in it, are quickly driven into society.

The Extent of the Legislative Power

The great end of men's entering into society being the enjoyment of their properties in peace and safety, and the great instrument and means of that being the laws established in that society: the first and fundamental positive law of all commonwealths is the establishing of the legislative power. . . .

Though the legislative . . . be the supreme power in every commonwealth, yet . . . it is not, nor can possibly be, absolutely arbitrary over the lives and fortunes of the people. For it being but the joint power of every member of the society given up to that person, or assembly, which is legislator, it can be no more than those persons had in a state of nature before they entered into society, and gave it up to the community. . . .

The supreme power cannot take from any man any part of his property without his own consent. . . .

These are the bounds [limits] which . . . society, and the law of God and Nature, have set to the legislative power of every commonwealth, in all forms of government:

First, they are to govern by . . . established laws, not to be varied in particular cases, but to have one rule for rich and poor, for the favorite at court and the countryman at plow.

Secondly, these laws also ought to be designed for no other end ultimately but the good of the people.

Thirdly, they must not raise taxes on the property of the people without the consent of the people.

The Dissolution of Government

[Governments are dissolved] when . . . a single person or prince sets up his own arbitrary will in place of the laws which are the will of the society. . . .

There is . . . another way whereby governments are dissolved, and that is when the legislative or the prince, either of them, act contrary to their trust. . . .

The legislative acts against the trust reposed in them when they endeavor to invade the property of the subject and to make themselves or any part of the community masters or arbitrary disposers of the lives, liberties, or fortunes of the people. . . .

Whenever the legislators endeavor to take away and destroy the property of the people, or to reduce them to slavery under arbitrary power, they put themselves into a state of war with the people, who are thereupon absolved from any further obedience and are left to the common refuge which God hath provided for all men against force and violence.

Voltaire—Critic of Society

Few of the "philosophes" in the eighteenth century were really philosophers. For the most part they were ardent publicists of the gospel of reason and reformers dedicated to the eradication of intolerance, persecution, superstition, and ignorance. The leading voice of this movement was the witty and satirical François Marie Arouet de Voltaire — poet, essayist, playwright, historian, and, above all, critic of society. He was a great crusader for liberty, and was twice imprisoned in the Bastille for his writings. As his fame spread, he was sought out by kings and princes; and for a while he resided at the court of Frederick II of Prussia. In his life and in his works Voltaire represented the spirit of the Enlightenment.

Law and Government

That government would be an insult both to God and man in which the citizens might say, "The state has given us all we possess; and we owe it nothing but prayers. . . ."

Superstition is the most dreadful enemy of the human race. When it rules the prince, it hinders him from consulting the good of his people; when it rules the people, it makes them rebel against their prince. . . .

Liberty consists in depending upon the laws only. In this view, every man is free in Sweden, England, Holland, Switzerland, Geneva, and Hamburg. The case is the same in Venice and Genoa; though in these two places whoever does not belong to the body of the nobles is despised and condemned. But there are still many provinces and large Christian kingdoms where the greater part of the people are slaves. . . .

This equality does not destroy subordination. As men, we are all equal; as members of society we are not. . . . Thus in things essential all men are equal, though they play different parts in the theater of the world.

People are always asking what is the best form of government. Put

Source: *The Works of Voltaire*, translated by William Fleming, New York: The St. Hubert Guild, 1901, Vol. XXXVII, pp. 227, 230–32, 236–37; Vol. XI, pp. 131–33.

this question to a minister or to his deputy; they will doubtless be for absolute power. Put it to a baron; he would have the baronies have a share in the legislative power. The bishops will say the same. The citizen would have you consult reason, and the peasant would not wish to be forgotten. The best government seems to be that in which all ranks of men are equally protected by the laws. . . .

Despotism is the abuse of monarchy, as anarchy is the abuse of a republican form of government. . . .

A republic is not founded on virtue; it is founded on the ambition of every citizen, which checks the ambition of others; on pride restraining pride; and on the desire of ruling, which will not suffer another to rule. Hence are formed laws which preserve as great an equality as possible. It is a society where the guests eat at the same table with an equal appetite.

Censorship of Books

In general, we have as natural a right to make use of our pens as our language, at our peril, risk, and fortune. I know many books which fatigue, but I know of none which have done real evil. Theologians or pretended politicians cry: "Religion is destroyed, the government is lost, if you print certain truths or certain paradoxes. Never attempt to think till you have demanded permission. . . . It is against good order for a man to think for himself. . . ."

But if there appears among you any new book, the ideas of which shock your own — supposing you have any — or of which the author may be a party contrary to yours — or what is worse, of which the author may not be of any party at all — then you cry out "Fire!" and let all be noise, scandal, and uproar in your small corner of the earth. There is an abominable man who has printed that if we had no hands we could not make shoes nor stockings. Devotees cry out, furred doctors assemble, alarms multiply from college to college, from house to house, and why? For five or six pages, about which there no longer will be a question at the end of three months. Does a book displease you? Refuse it. Does it tire you? Read it not.

The Sovereignty of the People

Jean Jacques Rousseau (1712–1778) was one of the most perceptive, influential, and controversial figures of his age. He was
born in Geneva, Switzerland, and led a poor, unhappy, and un-
settled existence. He was erratic, socially awkward, and suspicious. Sooner or later he quarreled with everybody, including
the philosophes.

Rousseau believed that man's natural virtues had been corrupted by society and civilization. Realizing that a return to
primitive existence was impossible, he yearned to establish a
form of society in which natural freedom could be most nearly
approximated. He put great emphasis on the authority of a community of equals willed into existence by all its members, and he
believed that only such a community could provide liberty,
good laws, and the happiness that come from the respect of
citizens for each other.

As the eloquent spokesman of the sovereignty of the people,
he was revered more than any other writer by the revolutionaries
in France. The Social Contract, his most famous work, was
written in 1762.

Man is born free; and everywhere he is in chains. One thinks
himself the master of others, and still remains a greater slave than they.
How did this change come about? I do not know. What can make it
legitimate? That question I think I can answer.

If I took into account only force and the effects derived from it, I
should say: "As long as a people is compelled to obey, and obeys, it does
well; as soon as it can shake off the yoke, and shakes it off, it does still
better; for, regaining its liberty by the same right as took it away, either
it is justified in resuming it, or there was no justification for those who
took it away." But the social order is a sacred right which is the basis of
all other rights. Nevertheless, this right does not come from nature, and
must therefore be founded on conventions. Before coming to that, I
have to prove what I have just asserted.

Source: Jean Jacques Rousseau, *The Social Contract and Discourses*, translated
by G. D. H. Cole, Everyman's Library Edition, 1946, pp. 3–4, 12–13. Reprinted by
permission of E. P. Dutton & Co., Inc., New York, and J. M. Dent & Sons, Ltd.,
London.

The most ancient of all societies, and the only one that is natural, is the family: and even so the children remain attached to the father only so long as they need him for their preservation. As soon as this need ceases, the natural bond is dissolved. The children, released from the obedience they owed to the father, and the father, released from the care he owed his children, return equally to independence. If they remain united, they continue so no longer naturally, but voluntarily; and the family itself is then maintained only by convention.

This common liberty results from the nature of man. His first law is to provide for his own preservation, his first cares are those which he owes to himself; and as soon as he reaches years of discretion, he is the sole judge of the proper means of preserving himself, and consequently becomes his own master.

The family then may be called the first model of political societies: the ruler corresponds to the father, and the people to the children; and all, being born free and equal, [give up] their liberty only for their own advantage. The whole difference is that in the family, the love of the father for his children repays him for the care he takes of them, while in the State, the pleasure of commanding takes the place of the love which the chief cannot have for the peoples under him. . . .

The problem is to find a form of association which will defend and protect with the whole common force the person and goods of each [member] and in which each, while uniting himself with all, may still obey himself alone, and remain as free as before. This is the fundamental problem of which the *Social Contract* provides the solution. . . .

Each man, in giving himself to all, gives himself to nobody; and as there is no associate over [whom] he does not acquire the same right as he yields others over himself, he gains an equivalent for everything he loses and an increase of force for the preservation of what he has. . . .

Each of us puts his person and all his power in common under the supreme direction of the general will, and in our corporate capacity, we receive each member as an indivisible part of the whole.

At once, in place of the individual personality of each contracting party, this act of association creates a moral and collective body, composed of as many members as the assembly contains voters and receiving from this act its unity, its common identity, its life, and its will. This public person, so formed by the union of all other persons, formerly took the name of *city*, and now takes that of *republic* or *body politic*; it is called by its members *State* when passive, *Sovereign* when active, and *Power* when compared with others like itself. Those who are associated in it take collectively the name of *people,* and severally are called *citizens,* as sharing in the sovereign power, and *subjects,* as being under the laws of the State.

Czar Peter the Great Reforms Russia

Russia is located partly in Europe and partly in Asia. Its cultural and religious traditions came originally from Byzantium, and thus tended to be hostile to Western Christianity and civilization. For about two and a half centuries, beginning in 1237, Russia was under the domination of the Mongols, and cut off from Europe. In the sixteenth century contacts with Europe increased, but it was not until the reign of Peter the Great (1682–1725) that the "Westernization" of Russia began in earnest.

Peter was determined that Russia must learn from the West. Not that he was primarily interested in culture; what attracted the ambitious Peter were the technical superiority and material wealth of the West. By using Western technology he hoped to build a strong army and navy and expand his frontiers. Nothing could stop this extraordinary giant. So determined was he to "Westernize" Russia that he was willing to have his son put to death when he joined forces with those who threatened to undo his father's work.

In the first selection the nature of Peter's character is discussed by an English contemporary, Bishop Burnet; in the second, we learn from the writings of Jean Rousset de Missy, an eighteenth-century French historian, how Peter imposed his ideas upon his subjects.

Peter's Character

I mentioned in the relation of the former year [1698] the Czar's coming out of his own country, on which I will now enlarge. He came this winter over to England and stayed some months among us. I waited often on him, and was ordered both by the King and the archbishop and bishops to attend upon him and to offer him such informations of our religion and constitution as he was willing to receive. I had good interpreters, so I had much free discourse with him. He is a man of a very hot temper, soon inflamed and very brutal in his passion. . . . He is subject to convulsive motions all over his body, and his head seems to be affected with these. He [lacks] not [intellectual] capacity, and has a larger measure of knowledge than might be expected from his education, which was very indifferent. A want of judgment, with an instability of temper, appears in him too often and too evidently.

He is mechanically turned, and seems designed by nature rather to be a ship carpenter than a great prince. This was his chief study and exercise while he stayed here. He wrought much with his own hands and made all about him work at the models of ships. He told me he designed a great fleet at Azuph [Azov] and with it to attack the Turkish empire. But he did not seem capable of conducting so great a design, though his conduct in his wars since then has discovered a greater genius in him than appeared at that time.

He was desirous to understand our doctrine, but he did not seem disposed to mend matters in Moscovy. He was, indeed, resolved to encourage learning and to polish his people by sending some of them to travel in other countries and to draw strangers to come and live among them. . . . There was a mixture both of passion and severity in his temper. He is resolute, but understands little of war, and seemed not at all inquisitive that way. . . .

He went from hence to the court of Vienna where he purposed to have stayed some time, but he was called home sooner than he had intended upon a discovery, or a suspicion, of intrigues managed by his sister. The strangers whom he trusted most were so true to him that those designs were crushed before he came back. But on this occasion he let loose his fury on all whom he suspected. Some hundreds of them were hanged all around Moscow, and it was said that he cut off many

PETER'S CHARACTER. Source: James Harvey Robinson, editor, *Readings in European History*, Boston: Ginn & Company, 1906, Vol. II, pp. 303–04.

heads with his own hand; and so far was he from relenting or showing any sort of tenderness that he seemed delighted with it. How long he is to be the scourge of that nation God only knows.

Peter Introduces Western Customs

The Czar labored at the reform of fashions, or more properly speaking, of dress. Until that time the Russians had always worn long beards, which they cherished and preserved with much care, allowing them to hang down on their bosoms without even cutting the moustache. With these long beards they wore the hair very short, except the ecclesiastics, who, to distinguish themselves, wore it very long. The Czar, in order to reform that custom, ordered that gentlemen, merchants, and other subjects, except priests and peasants, should each pay a tax of one hundred rubles a year if they wished to keep their beards; the commoners had to pay one kopeck each. Officials were stationed at the gates of the towns to collect that tax, which the Russians regarded as an enormous sin on the part of the Czar and as a thing which tended to the abolition of their religion.

These insinuations, which came from the priests, occasioned the publication of many pamphlets in Moscow, where for that reason alone the Czar was regarded as a tyrant and a pagan; and there were many old Russians who, after having their beards shaved off, saved them preciously, in order to have them placed in their coffins, fearing that they would not be allowed to enter heaven without their beards. As for the young men, they followed the new custom with the more readiness as it made them appear more agreeable to the fair sex.

From the reform in beards we may pass to that of clothes. Their garments, like those of the Orientals, were very long, reaching to the heel. The Czar issued an ordinance abolishing that costume, commanding all the boyars [nobles] and all those who had positions at the court to dress after the French fashion, and likewise to adorn their clothes with gold or silver according to their means.

As for the rest of the people, the following method was employed. A suit of clothes cut according to the new fashion was hung at the

PETER INTRODUCES WESTERN CUSTOMS. Source: James Harvey Robinson, editor, *Readings in European History*, Boston: Ginn & Company, 1906, Vol. II, pp. 310–12.

gate of the city, with a decree enjoining upon all except peasants to have their clothes made on this model under penalty of being forced to kneel and have all that part of their garments which fell below the knee cut off, or pay two grives every time they entered the town with clothes in the old style. Since the guards at the gates executed their duty in curtailing the garments in a sportive spirit, the people were amused and readily abandoned their old dress, especially in Moscow and its environs, and in the towns which the Czar oftenest visited. . . .

The same ordinance also provided that in the future women, as well as men, should be invited to entertainments such as weddings, banquets, and the like, where both sexes should mingle in the same hall as in Holland and England. It was likewise added that these entertainments should conclude with concerts and dances, but that only those should be admitted who were dressed in English costumes. His Majesty set the example in all these changes.

The Enlightened Despotism of Joseph II

The most dedicated of all the enlightened despots was also the least successful. Joseph II (1780–1790) was determined to fashion a unified, enlightened state from the conglomeration of peoples in the Austrian Empire. His ambitious list of reforms included freedom for the serfs, religious toleration, fair taxation, and codification of the law. In his zeal and haste he managed to offend not only the upper classes but also the suspicious and ignorant masses. Adding to his troubles were his recurrent failures in foreign policy. His career demonstrated the limitations of enlightened despotism even when the despot was himself completely sincere. Joseph died believing that he had been right and convinced that he had accomplished nothing.

The following excerpts are from letters written by Joseph II on the problems of ruling and attempting to initiate reforms in his vast empire.

To Stephen Francis, Duke of Choiseul

Mon Ami:
    With the governors of the provinces I am not quite satisfied. I shall pay some attention to their mode of conducting affairs.
    The influence the clergy have hitherto exercised in the government of my mother will be another object of my reform. I do not approve that those who are entrusted with the care of our future life should take so much pains to make our existence here the object of their wisdom and solicitude.
    The state of the finances of the Austrian dominions also requires an alteration. After a short examination I find the national debt has considerably increased; the bounties, pensions, additional salaries, and the perquisites [profits] of various noblemen and persons in office have risen to rather a large amount.
    I must make retrenchments, however . . . they may be felt by some whom they will reach. . . .

Vienna, December 1780

To the Archbishop of Salzburg

Sir:
    The internal administration of my states requires immediate reform. An empire which I govern must be swayed according to my own principles; prejudice, fanaticism, partiality, and slavery of the mind must cease, and each of my subjects be reinstated in the enjoyment of his native liberties. . . .

Vienna, February 1781

To Maria Anna, Archduchess of Austria *

Madame:
    While I travel from one extremity of my dominions to the other, to inform myself about the condition of my subjects, to hear their complaints, and to enforce the observance of the laws of my Empire, you

---

* Maria Anna was the oldest sister of the Emperor.

Source: "Letters of Joseph II Written to Distinguished Princes and Statesmen . . . ," in The Pamphleteer, London, 1821, 1822, Vol. XIX, pp. 93, 95, 277, 281–83, 288–90.

214

are enjoying in your retirement that desirable lot which was designed only for the wise.

I sigh for you from a longing desire to enjoy repose, and envy your happy destiny, while the government of more than twenty million souls weighs upon me as a heavy burden, which can be felt only by monarchs. . . .

Vienna, October 1, 1782

To Count Kollowrat, First Chancellor of Austria

Sir:

For the encouragement of home productions, and in order to check the progress of luxury and fashion, my commands respecting a general prohibition of foreign merchandise have been made known.

The Austrian commerce has become more passive in consequence of the increasing consumption of foreign productions, and the funds of the state, which has thereby lost more than twenty-four million annually, would by this time have been nearly exhausted, but for the produce of our excellent mines.

Vienna, October 1784

To a Hungarian Magnate

Sir:

With respect to the new system of taxation for the kingdom [Hungary] and the German language, which I ordained to be used in the Courts of Justice, I will very briefly give you my sentiments.

The former ensures to the subject his property, fixes the taxes for the crown and those for the lords of the manor, as has been long customary in my hereditary German dominions, and prevents the nobility from making an arbitrary increase for their own profit. Is this no advantage to the common people? The peasant, who is obliged to bear the greatest burdens of the public wants, has also a special claim on the protection of his sovereign; and this, Sir, in your country is viewed with dissatisfaction.

The German language is the universal language of my Empire; why should the laws be administered and public affairs transacted in a single province in its own language? I am Emperor of the German Empire; consequently the other states which I possess are provinces which, together with the whole state form one body of which I am the head. If the kingdom of Hungary was the most important and the chief of my possessions, I would make its language the principal language of my dominions; but it is otherwise.

Although the orders which I have given in this affair clearly enough evince [reveal] my sentiments, I am nevertheless always ready, on proper occasions, to explain more fully the positiveness of my principles, even to individual subjects of my dominions. My Count, you have here a proof of it.

Vienna, January 1785

To Tobias Philip, Baron von Gebler, Austrian Vice-Chancellor

Mr. Vice-Chancellor:
The present system of taxation in my dominions and the inequality of the taxes which are imposed on the nation form a subject too important to escape my attention. I have discovered that the principles on which it is founded are unsound and have become injurious to the industry of the peasant. . . .

With this view I give you the necessary orders to introduce a new system of taxation, by which the contribution requisite for the wants of the state may be effected without augmenting the present taxes and the industry of the peasant, at the same time, be freed from all impediments. . . .

Vienna, March 1785

To ———

My friend:
. . . Since my accession to the throne, I have ever been anxious to conquer the prejudices against my station and have taken pains to gain the confidence of my people; I have several times since given proof that the welfare of my subjects is my passion; that to satisfy it I shun neither labor nor trouble, nor even vexations, and reflect well on the means which are likely to promote my views, . . . and yet in my reforms I everywhere find opposition from people of whom I least expected it. . . .

Vienna, October 1787

216

To Van Swieten

Sir:

Till now the Protestant religion has been opposed in my states; its adherents have been treated like foreigners; civil rights, possession of estates, titles, and appointments — all were refused them.

I determined from the very commencement of my reign to adorn my diadem with the love of my people, to act in the administration of affairs according to just, impartial, and liberal principles; consequently I granted toleration, and removed the yoke which has oppressed the Protestants for centuries. . . .

December 1787

The American Colonies Proclaim Their Independence from Great Britain

"There is something very absurd," wrote Thomas Paine in 1776, "in supposing a Continent to be perpetually governed by an Island." By this time revolution had broken out in the British colonies. The resistance of the Americans to any form of compromise with the British had stiffened, and the advocates of complete independence were making considerable headway. On July 2, 1776, the Second Continental Congress in Philadelphia voted for independence. Two days later the delegates adopted the famous Declaration.

This document, mainly the work of Thomas Jefferson, embodied the grievances of the colonists stated in the spirit of the Enlightenment. The ideas contained in it were not new, as Jefferson himself noted, but when they were proclaimed by a group of colonists against a powerful imperial government, they became an inspiration to people in other lands.

217

When in the Course of human events, it becomes necessary for one people to dissolve the political bands which have connected them with another, and to assume among the Powers of the earth, the separate and equal station to which the Laws of Nature and of Nature's God entitle them, a decent respect to the opinions of mankind requires that they should declare the causes which impel them to the separation.

We hold these truths to be self-evident, that all men are created equal, that they are endowed by their Creator with certain unalienable Rights, that among these are Life, Liberty and the pursuit of Happiness.

That to secure these rights, Governments are instituted among Men, deriving their just powers from the consent of the governed, That whenever any Form of Government becomes destructive of these ends, it is the Right of the People to alter or to abolish it, and to institute new Government, laying its foundation on such principles and organizing its powers in such form, as to them shall seem most likely to effect their Safety and Happiness. Prudence, indeed, will dictate that Governments long established should not be changed for light and transient causes; and accordingly all experience hath shown, that mankind are more disposed to suffer, while evils are sufferable, than to right themselves by abolishing the forms to which they are accustomed. But when a long train of abuses and usurpations,* pursuing invariably the same Object evinces a design to reduce them under absolute Despotism, it is their right, it is their duty, to throw off such Government, and to provide new Guards for their future security. — Such has been the patient sufferance of these Colonies; and such is now the necessity which constrains them to alter their former Systems of Government. The history of the present King of Great Britain is a history of repeated injuries and usurpations, all having in direct object the establishment of an absolute Tyranny over these States. To prove this, let Facts be submitted to a candid world. [Then follows a long list of grievances.]

In every stage of these Oppressions We have Petitioned for Redress in the most humble terms: Our repeated Petitions have been answered only by repeated injury. A Prince, whose character is thus marked by every act which may define a Tyrant, is unfit to be the ruler of a free People.

* **usurpations:** forcible seizures of place, power, or functions without right.

Source: *Revised Statutes of the United States*, 2nd ed., Washington, D.C.: Government Printing Office, 1878, pp. 3–5.

Nor have We been wanting in attention to our British brethren. We have warned them from time to time of attempts by their legislature to extend an unwarrantable jurisdiction over us. We have reminded them of the circumstances of our emigration and settlement here. We have appealed to their native justice and magnanimity, and we have conjured them by the ties of our common kindred to disavow these usurpations, which, would inevitably interrupt our connections and correspondence. They too have been deaf to the voice of justice and of consanguinity.* We must, therefore, acquiesce in the necessity, which denounces our Separation, and hold them, as we hold the rest of mankind, Enemies in War, in Peace Friends.

We, therefore, the Representatives of the united States of America, in General Congress, Assembled, appealing to the Supreme Judge of the world for the rectitude of our intentions, do, in the Name, and by Authority of the good People of these Colonies, solemnly publish and declare, That these United Colonies are, and of Right ought to be Free and Independent States; that they are Absolved from all Allegiance to the British Crown, and that all political connection between them and the State of Great Britain, is and ought to be totally dissolved; and that as Free and Independent States, they have full Power to levy War, conclude Peace, contract Alliances, establish Commerce, and to do all other Acts and Things which Independent States may of right do. And for the support of this Declaration, with a firm reliance on the Protection of Divine Providence, we mutually pledge to each other our Lives, our Fortunes and our sacred Honor.

* **consanguinity:** blood relationship.

The Storming of the Bastille

The fall of the Bastille echoed far and wide. A symbol of royal tyranny was destroyed by the will and power of the people. In spite of its symbolic importance, this gloomy fortress had in it at the time only seven prisoners, of whom five were common criminals and two were mental cases.

In the days before the attack, Paris was in a tense state, gripped by hunger and fear. On July 14, 1789, a mob collected before the Bastille and asked the governor for arms. At first negotiations were cordial; then, after various misunderstandings, the soldiers fired some shots at the people. The enraged mob stormed the fortress, slaughtered the soldiers, and released the prisoners. The governor of the garrison and the mayor of Paris were both murdered and their heads carried on the ends of pikes throughout the streets of Paris. The anniversary of the destruction of the Bastille has become France's major national holiday. The following account is by M. Keversau, a patriot lawyer, who participated in the event.

Veteran armies inured to war have never performed greater prodigies of valor than this leaderless multitude of persons belonging to every class, workmen of all trades who, mostly ill-equipped and unused to arms, boldly affronted the fire from the ramparts and seemed to mock the thunderbolts the enemy hurled at them. . . .

The attackers, having demolished the first drawbridge and brought their guns into position against the second, could not fail to capture the fort. The Marquis de Launay (Governor of the Bastille) could doubtless have resisted the capture of the first bridge more vigorously, but this base agent of the despots, better fitted to be a jailer than the military commander of a fortress, lost his head as soon as he saw himself hemmed in by the enraged people and hastened to take refuge behind his massive bastions, where he hoped to be able to await in safety the relief promised for that evening. . . .

The drums were beat for a parley and the white flag was raised on the tower. . . . It was too late. The people, infuriated by the treachery of the Governor, who had fired on their representatives, took these offers of peace for another trap and continued to advance, firing as they went up to the drawbridge leading to the interior of the fort. . . .

[Those below had drawn up cannons.] They were just going to fire and the ranks of the crowd had already opened to give passage to the cannonballs, when the enemy, seeing that we intended to demolish the big bridge, let down the small drawbridge on the left of the entrance to the fortress. In spite of the new danger arising from this maneuver, [sev-

Source: G. Pernoud and S. Flaissier, *The French Revolution*, translated by Richard Graves, New York: G. P. Putnam's Sons, 1961, pp. 31–37. Reprinted by permission of G. P. Putnam's Sons, New York, and Martin Secker & Warburg, Limited, London.

eral of the crowd] swarmed across it, having secured the drawbridge by pushing home the bolts. . . .

About two minutes later one of the [soldiers] opened the gate behind the drawbridge and asked what we wanted. "The surrender of the Bastille," was the answer, on which he let us in. At the same time the besiegers lowered the great bridge, on which the brave Arné leapt while it was still in motion to prevent anyone from trying to raise it again. . . .

Those who came in first treated the conquered enemy humanely and embraced the staff officers to show there was no ill-feeling. But a few soldiers posted on the platforms and unaware that the fortress had surrendered discharged their muskets, whereupon the people, transported with rage, threw themselves on the [soldiers] and used them with the utmost violence. One of them was massacred, the unfortunate Béquart, the brave soldier who had deserved so well of the town of Paris when he stayed the hand of the Governor at the moment when he was on the point of blowing up the Bastille. . . . All the officers were seized and their quarters were invaded by the mob, who smashed the furniture, the doors, and the windows. In the general turmoil the people in the courtyard fired on those who were in the private quarters and on the platforms. Several were killed. . . .

Maillard, Cholat, Arné, the grenadier, and several others contend for the honor of having arrested the Marquis de Launay. He was not in uniform but wore a grey tailcoat with a red ribbon. He had in his hand a sword stick which he wished to drive into his breast, but the intrepid Arné tore it from him. Hulin, Elie, and a few others undertook to guard him and succeeded in getting him out of the Bastille, though he was roughly handled by the people, who were calling for his death. . . .

But the fury of the crowd continued to increase and their blind wrath did not spare de Launay's escort. L'Epine received a blow on the head with the butt of a musket which would have stretched him out dead if he had not been wearing a hard round hat which saved his life. But he had no strength left and was obliged to leave the escort at St.-Gervais' Elm. Hulin himself, in spite of his vigor and his powerful frame, could no longer resist the violence of the mob. Exhausted by his efforts to defend his prisoner and overwhelmed by the rough treatment he had himself received, he had to separate from M. de Launay at La Grève in order to take some rest. Hardly had he sat down when, looking after the procession, he saw the head of M. de Launay stuck on the point of a pike. His last words had been, "Oh, my friends, kill me, kill me at once and don't keep me suffering like this!" The people, fearing that their victim might be snatched away from them, hastened to cut his throat on the steps of the Hôtel de Ville [City Hall]. . . .

In the intoxication of victory the unfortunate inmates of the dungeons of the Bastille had been forgotten. All the keys had been carried off in triumph and it was necessary to force the doors of the cells. Seven prisoners were found and brought to the Palais Royal. These poor fellows were in transports of pleasure and could scarcely realize they were not the dupes of a dream.

The National Assembly Asserts the Rights of Man

Since the French had so long been deprived of freedom and political rights, it is not surprising that the first great debate in the National Assembly was about the natural rights of man. The Declaration of the Rights of Man and of the Citizen, drawn up in August 1789, like the American Declaration of Independence, embodied the dreams and hopes of the Enlightenment. The tone of the Declaration, which was the work of well-to-do members of the middle class, is moderate and especially respectful of property.

The Declaration was read aloud everywhere and printed thousands of times. It was translated into many languages and became the hope of countless others in Europe.

The representatives of the French people, organized as a National Assembly, believing that the ignorance, neglect, or contempt of the rights of man are the sole causes of public calamities and of the corruption of governments, have determined to set forth in a solemn declaration the natural, inalienable, and sacred rights of man, in order that this declaration, being constantly before all the members of the social body, shall remind them continually of their rights and duties; in order that the acts of the legislative power, as well as those of the

Source: *Translations and Reprints from the Original Sources of European History,* Philadelphia: University of Pennsylvania Press, 1897, Vol. I, No. 5, pp. 6–8.

executive power, may be compared at any moment with the ends of all political institutions and may thus be more respected; in order that the grievances of the citizens, based hereafter upon simple and incontestable principles, shall tend to the maintenance of the constitution and redound to the happiness of all. Hence the National Assembly recognizes and proclaims in the presence and under the auspices of the Supreme Being the following rights of man and of the citizen:

1. Men are born and remain free and equal in rights. Social distinctions can only be founded upon the general good.

2. The aim of all political association is the preservation of the natural . . . rights of man. These rights are liberty, property, security, and resistance to oppression.

3. The principle of all sovereignty resides essentially in the nation. No body nor individual may exercise any authority which does not proceed directly from the nation.

4. Liberty consists of being able to do everything which injures no one else; hence the exercise of the natural rights of each man has no limits except those which assure to the other members of the society the enjoyment of the same rights. These limits can only be determined by law.

5. Law can only prohibit such actions as are hurtful to society. Nothing may be prevented which is not forbidden by law, and no one may be forced to do anything not provided for by law.

6. Law is the expression of the general will. Every citizen has a right to participate personally or through his representative in its formation. It must be the same for all, whether it protects or punishes. All citizens, being equal in the eyes of the law, are equally eligible to all dignities and to all public positions and occupations according to their abilities, and without distinction except that of their virtues and talents.

7. No person shall be accused, arrested, or imprisoned except in the cases and according to the forms prescribed by law. . . . But any citizen summoned or arrested in virtue of the law shall submit without delay, as resistance constitutes an offense.

8. The law shall provide for such punishments only as are strictly and obviously necessary, and no one shall suffer punishment except it be legally inflicted in virtue of a law passed and promulgated before the commission of the offense.

9. As all persons are held innocent until they shall have been declared guilty, if arrest shall be deemed indispensable, all severity not

essential to the securing of the prisoner's person shall be severely repressed by law.

10. No one shall be disquieted on account of his opinions, including his religious views, provided his manifestation does not disturb the public order established by law.

11. The free communication of ideas and opinions is one of the most precious of the rights of man. Every citizen may, accordingly, speak, write, and print with freedom, being responsible, however, for such abuses of this freedom as shall be defined by law.

12. The security of the rights of man and of the citizen requires public military force. These forces are, therefore, established for the good of all and not for the personal advantage of those to whom they shall be entrusted.

13. A common contribution is essential for the maintenance of the public forces and for the cost of administration. This should be equitably distributed among all the citizens in proportion to their means.

14. All the citizens have a right to decide either personally or by their representatives as to the necessity of the public contribution, to grant this freely, to know to what uses it is put, and to fix the proportion, the mode of assessment and of collection, and the duration of the taxes.

15. Society has the right to require of every public agent an account of his administration.

16. A society in which the observance of the law is not assured nor the separation of powers defined has no constitution at all.

17. Property being an inviolable and sacred right, no one shall be deprived thereof except where public necessity, legally determined, shall clearly demand it, and then only on condition that the owner shall have been previously and equitably indemnified.

Robespierre Outlines the Goals of the Revolution

Maximilien Robespierre, "the Incorruptible," was the driving force in the Reign of Terror (1793–1794) that took the lives of twenty thousand people. There is no doubt that he was an hon-

est, unselfish, and devoted patriot at a time when many citizens were busy looking after their own interests.

He dedicated himself to the establishment of a "Republic of Virtue." "Virtue" to Robespierre was essentially what it was to Rousseau — active public spirit and complete devotion to the good of the community. Dazzled by the vision of an ideal society, Robespierre was willing to go to any lengths to realize his dream; terror was but a means of accomplishing a noble end, a means of ridding the community of criminals, traitors, and even the indifferent. Like many modern dictators, Robespierre was convinced that his revolutionary regime was essential until the external and internal enemies of the state were obliterated.

In February 1794, while the Terror was raging, Robespierre outlined his aims in a speech.

It is time to mark clearly the aim of the Revolution and the end toward which we wish to move; it is time to take stock of ourselves, of the obstacles which we still face, and of the means which we ought to adopt to attain our objectives. . . .

What is the goal for which we strive? A peaceful enjoyment of liberty and equality, the rule of that eternal justice whose laws are engraved, not upon marble or stone, but in the hearts of all men.

We wish an order of things where all low and cruel passions are enchained by the laws, all beneficent and generous feelings aroused; where ambition is the desire to merit glory and to serve one's fatherland; where distinctions are born only of equality itself; where the citizen is subject to the magistrate, the magistrate to the people, the people to justice; where the nation safeguards the welfare of each individual, and each individual proudly enjoys the prosperity and glory of his fatherland; where all spirits are enlarged by the constant exchange of republican sentiments and by the need of earning the respect of a great people; where the arts are the adornment of liberty, which ennobles them; and where commerce is the source of public wealth, not simply of monstrous opulence for a few families.

In our country we wish to substitute morality for egotism, [truth] for honor, principles for conventions, duties for etiquette, the empire of

Source: Raymond P. Stearns, editor, *Pageant of Europe*, rev. ed., New York: Harcourt, Brace & World, Inc., 1961, pp. 404–05. Reprinted by permission of the publishers.

reason for the tyranny of customs, contempt for vice for contempt for misfortune, pride for insolence, the love of honor for the love of money; . . . that is to say, all the virtues and miracles of the Republic for all the vices and snobbishness of the monarchy.

We wish in a word to fulfill the requirements of nature, to accomplish the destiny of mankind, to make good the promises of philosophy . . . that France, hitherto illustrious among slave states, may eclipse the glory of all free peoples that have existed, become the model of all nations. . . . That is our ambition; that is our aim.

What kind of government can realize these marvels? Only a democratic government. . . . But to found and to consolidate among us this democracy, to realize the peaceable rule of constitutional laws, it is necessary to conclude the war of liberty against tyranny and to pass successfully through the storms of revolution. Such is the aim of the revolutionary system which you have set up. . . .

Now what is the fundamental principle of democratic, or popular, government — that is to say, the essential mainspring upon which it depends and which makes it function? It is virtue: I mean public virtue, . . . that virtue which is nothing else but love of fatherland and its laws. . . .

The splendor of the goal of the French Revolution is simultaneously the source of our strength and of our weakness: our strength, because it gives us an ascendancy of truth over falsehood, and of public rights over private interests; our weakness, because it rallies against us all vicious men, all those who in their hearts seek to despoil the people. . . . It is necessary to stifle the domestic and foreign enemies of the Republic or perish with them. Now in these circumstances, the first maxim of our politics ought to be to lead the people by means of reason and the enemies of the people by terror.

If the basis of popular government in time of peace is virtue, the basis of popular government in time of revolution is both virtue and terror: virtue without which terror is murderous, terror without which virtue is powerless. Terror is nothing else than swift, severe, indomitable justice; it flows, then, from virtue.

The Jacobins Call
for Devotion to *La Patrie*

The Jacobins, conducting a desperate and bitter war against the enemies of France, and claiming to speak for the nation, demanded the utmost devotion, sacrifice, and conformity from every individual. The ardent nationalism of the French aided them in triumphing over their more numerous and powerful enemies.

The first selection below, the Decree of Universal Conscription, drafts women and older people as well as young men into the war effort. It and the Law of Suspects which follows illustrate the nature of Jacobin nationalism.

Universal Conscription

I. From this moment until that in which our enemies shall have been driven from the territory of the Republic, all Frenchmen are permanently requisitioned for service in the armies.

Young men will go forth to battle; married men will forge weapons and transport munitions; women will make tents and clothing and serve in hospitals; children will make lint from old linen; and old men will be brought to the public squares to arouse the courage of the soldiers, while preaching the unity of the Republic and hatred against kings.

II. Public buildings shall be converted into barracks, public squares into munition workshops. . . .

III. Muskets shall be given exclusively to those who march against the enemy. . . .

IV. Saddle horses are requisitioned to complete the cavalry corps; draught horses other than those employed in agriculture will be used in the artillery and to haul munitions.

V. The Committee of Public Safety is charged to take all measures

Source: E. L. Higgins, *The French Revolution as Told by Contemporaries,* Boston: Houghton Mifflin Company, 1938, pp. 302–04. Reprinted by permission of the publishers.

227

necessary for the immediate establishment of a special manufactory of arms of all kinds to correspond to the spirit and energy of the French people. It is, in consequence, authorized to set up all the establishments, manufactories, workshops, and laboratories deemed necessary for the accomplishment of this work and requisition throughout the whole Republic the craftsmen and workers that can assist in making this a success. . . .

VIII. The levy shall be general. Unmarried citizens and childless widowers between the ages of eighteen and thirty-five shall be called first. They shall immediately assemble in the headquarters of their district to be daily exercised in the use of arms until the day of their departure. . . .

XIII. In order to gather provisions in sufficient quantity, farmers and managers of national property shall deposit at district headquarters the grain produced from these lands.

The Law of Suspects

I. Immediately upon the publication of the present decree, all suspect people still at liberty within the boundaries of the Republic shall be put under arrest.

II. Those to be considered suspect include:

1. Those who by their conduct, relations, discourse, or writings have shown themselves to be partisans of tyranny . . . and enemies of liberty. . . .

3. Those who cannot after the manner prescribed by the Law of March 21 give an account of their means of existence and their performance of civic duties.

4. Those to whom certificates of civism [good citizenship] have been refused.

5. Public functionaries whom the National Convention . . . [has] suspended or dismissed and not reinstated. . . .

6. Those among the former nobles, together with the husbands, wives, fathers, mothers, sons, daughters, brothers, sisters, and agents of [emigrants] who have not steadfastly manifested their attachment to the Revolution.

7. Those who have emigrated during the period dating from July 1, 1789, to the publication of the Law of April 8, 1792, even if

they have returned to France during or previous to the period fixed by this law. . . .

10. Individuals arrested as suspects shall first be conducted to prison at the place of their detention. If prisons are lacking, they shall be kept under constant guard at their respective dwellings. . . .

13. The prison expenses shall be charged to the prisoners and equally apportioned among them. Guard duties will be given preferably to fathers of families and relatives of citizens who are going to the front. . . .

15. If there are sufficient grounds, the civil and military tribunals may keep under arrest and send to the above-mentioned prisons those who have not been indicted for want of evidence, and even those who have been acquitted of the accusations against them.

The French Accept Napoleon as Emperor

Out of the chaos of the Revolution emerged the dictatorship and the Empire of Napoleon Bonaparte. Napoleon was an extraordinary man who created about himself a legend which has been as enduring as any of his work. He proclaimed that he was a true son of the Revolution — the apostle of liberty, equality, fraternity, and nationalism — and that he strove to achieve peace and harmony in Europe. His enemies, of course, were blamed for all his wars and troubles.

Napoleon was a tireless worker and a remarkable organizer who knew instinctively how to take advantage of a situation. Though his manners were at times hardly agreeable, he was endowed with a power to charm, persuade, and inspire. His soldiers worshiped him, and even the Czar of Russia fell under his spell. His unlimited ambitions and his arrogant self-confidence ultimately destroyed him. It took nearly all of Europe combined to crush him in war.

Mme de Rémusat, from whose Memoirs the following selection is taken, was the wife of one of Napoleon's secretaries. She had many opportunities to observe the Emperor.

The accession of Bonaparte to the Imperial throne was very variously regarded in Europe, and even in France opinions were divided. It is, however, quite certain that it did not displease the great majority of the nation. . . . The exchange of the Consulate for Imperial authority was, however, regarded with dislike by all true friends of liberty. . . . I can understand how it was that men, worn out by the turmoil of the Revolution and afraid of that liberty which had been so long associated with death, looked for repose under the dominion of an able ruler on whom fortune was seemingly resolved to smile. I can conceive that they regarded his elevation as a decree of destiny and fondly believed that in the irrevocable they should find peace. I may confidently assert that those persons believed quite sincerely that Bonaparte, whether as Consul or as Emperor, would exert his authority to oppose the attempts of faction and would save us from the perils of anarchy.

None dared to utter the word Republic, so deeply had the Terror stained that name, and the Directorial government * had perished in the contempt with which its chiefs were regarded. The return of the Bourbons could only be brought about by the aid of a revolution; and the slightest disturbance terrified the French people, in whom enthusiasm of every kind seemed to be dead. Besides, the men in whom they had trusted had one after the other deceived them; and as this time they were yielding to force, they were at least certain that they were not deceiving themselves.

The belief, or rather the error, that only despotism could at that epoch maintain order in France was very widespread. It became the mainstay of Bonaparte; and it is due to him to say that he also held it. The factions played into his hands by imprudent attempts which he turned to his own advantage; he had some grounds for his belief that he was necessary; France believed it too; and he even succeeded in persuading foreign sovereigns that he formed a barrier against republican influences, which but for him might spread widely. At the moment when Bonaparte placed the Imperial crown upon his head, there was not a king in Europe who did not believe that he wore his own crown more securely because of that event. Had the new Emperor added to

* **Directorial government:** that is, the government of the Directory, the ruling body of France from 1795 to 1799.

Source: Madame de Rémusat, *Memoirs*, New York: D. Appleton & Co., 1880, pp. 158–64.

that decisive act the gift of a liberal constitution, the peace of nations and of kings might, in sober seriousness, have been forever secured. . . .

His despotic ambition misled him; but, I say it again, he was not the only one who went astray. He was beguiled by appearances which he did not take the trouble to investigate. The word "liberty" did indeed resound in the air about him, but those who uttered it were not held in sufficient esteem by the nation to be made its representatives to him. Well-meaning, honest folk asked nothing of him but repose and did not trouble themselves about the form under which it was to be granted. And then, he knew well that the secret weakness of the French nation was vanity, and he saw a means of gratifying it easily by the pomp and display that attend on monarchical power. . . .

Bonaparte was seconded for a long time by the military ardor of the youth of France. . . . It was a long time before we recognized that each one of our conquests was a link in the chain that fettered our liberties; and, when we became fully aware of what our intoxication had led us into, it was too late for resistance. The army had become the accomplice of tyranny, had broken with France, and would treat a cry for deliverance as revolt.

The greatest of Bonaparte's errors — one very characteristic of him — was that he never took anything but success into account in the calculations on which he acted. Perhaps he was more excusable than another would have been in doubting whether any reverse could come to him. His natural pride shrank from the idea of a defeat of any kind. There was the weak point in his strong mind, for such a man as he ought to have contemplated every contingency. But as he lacked nobility of soul, and had not that instinctive elevation of mind which rises above evil fortune, he turned his thoughts away from this weakness in himself, and contemplated only his wonderful faculty of growing greater with success. "I shall succeed" was the basis of all his calculations, and his obstinate repetition of the phrase helped him to realize the prediction. At length his own good fortune grew into a superstition with him, and his worship of it made every sacrifice which was to be imposed upon us fair and lawful in his eyes.

The Grand Army
Retreats from Moscow

Czar Alexander I had never been too happy with his inferior status in the partnership with Napoleon. In December 1810 he broke his agreement with the Emperor and began to trade with England. To punish this impertinence and to bring Russia securely into the orbit of the French Empire, Napoleon in June of 1812 marched into Russia at the head of 600,000 men. He anticipated a short war with a few decisive battles.

Nothing went right for Napoleon. The Russians retreated. They seldom risked battle, concentrating instead on destroying Napoleon's supplies. When the Emperor realized that he could not humble Russia and that winter was fast approaching, he was forced to order a retreat. From October to December, in icy weather, his weary army straggled westward, harried at every turn by Russian guerrillas. By the end of the journey 400,000 men had died and 100,000 had been taken prisoner. Napoleon's Grand Army was finished. The spirit of liberation swept across Europe, and the conquered peoples prepared themselves to put an end to Napoleon's domination.

The retreat from Moscow is described by one of Napoleon's generals, the Marquis de Caulaincourt.

The following day, the twenty-eighth, we passed within sight of Mojaisk, but did not enter it. On his way by, the Emperor halted beside the road to obtain some account of the evacuation and of the distribution of supplies that he had ordered for the wounded. . . . In spite of all warnings that this would inevitably mean death, the unfortunate men who had left the field hospital to drag themselves along the road were placed, by his orders, wherever they could hang on — on the covers of wagons and even in the forage carts, or in the back of vehicles already crowded with the sick and wounded. . . . Those who did not die of

Source: George Libaire, editor, *With Napoleon in Russia, The Memoirs of General de Caulaincourt*, New York: William Morrow & Co., 1935, pp. 187–89, 223–24, 259. Reprinted by permission of William Morrow & Co., Inc., and Cassell & Company, Ltd., London.

exhaustion through the discomforts of their position, either fell victims to the cold nights or died of hunger. . . . Men in the best of health could not have endured this mode of travel and could not have held on to the vehicles in the positions in which most of them were placed. So one can imagine the state of these unhappy men when they had covered a league or two. They had to endure jolting, fatigue, and cold all at once. . . .

The country on either hand of our route had been marched over, eaten out, and left bare by the army and by the detachments that joined us. The plight of the carriages can be imagined. Having left Moscow with us, already full of refugees, women, and children, they had had to take up the men wounded at Winkovo and Malo-Jaroslawetz; and to these were added also the wounded at Mojaisk. They were put on the top seats of the carts, on the forecarriage, behind on the trunks, on the seats, in the fodder carts. They were even put on the hoods of the wagons when there was no room underneath. One can imagine the spectacle our convoys presented. At the least jolt those who were most insecurely placed fell off; the drivers took no care. The driver following, if he were not distracted or in a stupor, would not be minding his horses; or even, for fear of stopping and losing his place in the line, he would drive pitilessly on over the body of the wretch who had fallen. Nor did the other vehicles coming behind pay any heed.

Cossacks * kept up perpetual raids along the road, which they constantly crossed between one division and another — or even, when there was a gap, between one regiment and another. . . . Wherever there was no shooting to fear, wherever transport wagons were moving along in disorder or unarmed stragglers were making their way as best they could, the Cossacks improvised sudden attacks, killing and wounding, robbing all those whose lives they spared, and looting wagons and carriages when they came upon them.

It is not difficult to imagine the perturbation spread by such tactics and their effect on the army's morale. What was worse, they made communication extremely difficult, not only between one corps and another, but between one division and another. . . .

The cold was so intense that bivouacking was no longer supportable. Bad luck for those who fell asleep by a campfire! . . . One constantly found men who, overcome by the cold, had been forced to drop out and had fallen to the ground, too weak or too numb to stand. . . .

* **Cossacks:** Russian cavalry noted for their ferocity.

Once these poor wretches fell asleep, they were dead. If they resisted the craving for sleep, another passerby would help them along a little farther, thus prolonging their agony for a short while but not saving them; for in this condition the drowsiness engendered by cold is irresistibly strong. Sleep comes inevitably; and to sleep is to die. I tried in vain to save a number of these unfortunates. The only words they uttered were to beg me, for the love of God, to go away and let them sleep. To hear them, one would have thought this sleep was their salvation. Unhappily, it was a poor wretch's last wish; but at least he ceased to suffer, without pain or agony. Gratitude, and even a smile, were imprinted on his discolored lips. What I have related about the effects of extreme cold and of this kind of death by freezing is based on what I saw happen to thousands of individuals. The road was covered with their corpses.

The Political Creed of Prince Metternich

If the radical spirit of the French Revolution was to blame for the disruption and bloodshed in Europe, it was essential to suppress and eradicate that spirit in order to insure peace and stability. So reasoned Prince Metternich, the handsome and brilliant Foreign Minister of the Austrian Empire. What he considered good for Europe was crucial to the continued existence of the Austrian Empire, which contained many different cultural and linguistic groups. There, any concessions of freedom or nationality would have had a disintegrating effect. Until his fall from power in the Revolution of 1848, he was the dominant conservative force in Europe. Wherever revolution broke out, he was prepared to muster forces to crush it. Though the occasional rising succeeded, he was able to hold back the tide of liberty and nationalism for a time.

Czar Alexander I, who had entertained some hazy liberal notions in 1815, had been converted to Metternich's wisdom in 1820. At the request of the Czar, Metternich sent him a secret memorandum outlining his political creed.

Kings have to calculate the chances of their very existence in the immediate future; passions are let loose and league together to overthrow everything which society respects on the basis of its existence; religion, public morality, laws, customs, rights, and duties — all are attacked, confounded, overthrown, or called in question. The great mass of the people are tranquil spectators of these attacks and revolutions, and of the absolute lack of all means of defense. A few are carried off by the torrent, but the wishes of the immense majority are to maintain a repose which exists no longer and of which even the first elements seem to be lost.

What is the cause of all these evils? By what methods has this evil established itself, and how is it that it penetrates into every vein of the social body? . . . This evil may be described in one word — presumption; the natural effect of the rapid progression of the human mind toward the perfecting of so many things. This it is which in the present day leads so many individuals astray, for it has become an almost universal sentiment.

Religion, morality, legislation, economy, politics, administration — all have become common and accessible to everyone. Knowledge seems to come by inspiration; experience has no value for the presumptuous man; faith is nothing to him; he substitutes for it a pretended individual conviction, and to arrive at this conviction dispenses with all inquiry and with all study; for these means appear too trivial to a mind which believes itself strong enough to embrace at one glance all questions and all facts. Laws have no value for him because he has not contributed to make them, and it would be beneath a man of his parts to recognize the limits traced by rude and ignorant generations. Power resides in himself; why should he submit himself to that which was useful only for the man deprived of light and knowledge? . . .

Presumption makes every man the guide of his own belief, the arbiter of laws according to which he is pleased to govern himself or to allow someone else to govern him and his neighbors; it makes him, in short, the sole judge of his own faith, his own actions, and the principles according to which he guides them. . . .

It is principally the middle classes of society which this moral gan-

Source: Prince Richard Metternich, editor, *The Memoirs of Prince Metternich*, translated by Mrs. Alexander Napier, New York: Charles Scribner's Sons, 1881, Vol. III, pp. 455–75.

grene has affected, and it is only among them that the real heads of the party are found.

For the great mass of the people it has no attraction and can have none. The labors to which this class — the real people — are obliged to devote themselves are too continuous and too positive to allow them to throw themselves into vague abstractions and ambitions. The people know what is the happiest thing for them: namely, to be able to count on the morrow, for it is the morrow which will repay them for the cares and sorrows of today. . . .

There is, besides, scarcely any epoch which does not offer a rallying cry to some particular faction. This cry, since 1815, has been *Constitution.* . . .

The governments, having lost their balance, are frightened, intimidated, and thrown into confusion by the cries of the intermediary class of society, which, placed between the kings and their subjects, breaks the scepter of the monarch and usurps the cry of the people — that class so often disowned by the people and nevertheless too much listened to, caressed, and feared by those who could with one word reduce it again to nothingness. . . .

We are convinced that society can no longer be saved without strong and vigorous resolutions on the part of the governments still free in their opinions and actions. . . .

The first and greatest concern for the immense majority of every nation is the stability of the laws and their uninterrupted action — never their change. Therefore let the governments govern, let them maintain the groundwork of their institutions, both ancient and modern; for if it is at all times dangerous to touch them, it certainly would not now, in the general confusion, be wise to do so. . . .

Let them be just, but strong; beneficent, but strict.

Let them maintain religious principles in all their purity and not allow the faith to be attacked and morality interpreted according to the social contract or the visions of foolish sectarians.

Let them suppress secret societies, that gangrene of society.

In short, let the great monarchs strengthen their union and prove to the world that if it exists, it is beneficent and ensures the political peace of Europe.

236

PART SIX

India, China, and Japan

A Hindu View
of the Four Classes

It is a basic premise of Hinduism that men are not born the same. They differ in character, in station, and in obligations. In accordance with the doctrine of rebirth, the behavior of an individual in the previous life determines the station into which he will be born in the next. In each case, he must fulfill the tasks which are appropriate to his particular position.

Originally there were four basic classes (these were not castes) in Hindu society, as well as a large number of untouchables. Within each class there developed in time many castes. The castes did not grow out of the classes but were based on ancient divisions of tribe, profession, or religion. The untouchables, who do menial work such as disposing of corpses, have their own castes. Altogether there are now about three thousand castes in India.

The Code of Manu, the most famous of the Hindu books of sacred law, was written sometime during the first and second centuries B.C. *It outlines the duties of the four classes as seen from the traditional Hindu viewpoint.*

For the sake of the preservation of this entire creation, Purusha, the exceedingly resplendent one, assigned separate duties to the classes which had sprung from his mouth, arms, thighs, and feet.

Teaching, studying, performing sacrificial rites, so too making others perform sacrificial rites, and giving away and receiving gifts — these he assigned to the brahmans.

Protection of the people, giving away of wealth, performance of sacrificial rites, study, and nonattachment to sensual pleasures — these are, in short, the duties of a kshatriya.

Tending of cattle, giving away of wealth, performance of sacrificial

Source: Wm. Theodore de Bary *et al.*, editors, *Oriental Civilizations: Sources of Indian Tradition*, New York: Columbia University Press, 1958, p. 225. Reprinted by permission of the publishers.

rites, study, trade and commerce, . . . and agriculture — these are the occupations of a vaishya.

The Lord has prescribed only one occupation . . . for a shudra; namely, service without malice of . . . these other three classes.

The Meaning and Practice of Yoga

In the Hindu religion yoga is the training and practice which enable an individual to achieve unity with God. Because men differ by temperament, they will practice yoga in different ways — some by the use of the mind, some by emotion and love, some by work and activity, and some by rigid mental control. The yogi, by means of long and rigorous training, tries to come in contact with the divine spirit. To succeed in this quest he must first make himself oblivious of any outside influence, including that of his body. Only when this has been achieved will the yogi be in a state of pure contemplation.

In the Bhagavad Gita (Song of the Lord), one of the most popular of Hindu sacred texts, Lord Krishna, an incarnation of the god Vishnu, the Preserver, discusses the discipline of a yogi. Lord Krishna is addressing Arjuna, a member of the warrior class who is reluctant to go into battle because he is repelled by bloodshed. Lord Krishna informs him that he must do his duty, and in the course of the discussion outlines the meaning and practice of yoga.

Work alone art thou entitled to, and not to its fruit. So never work for rewards, nor yet desist from work. Work with an even mind, O Arjuna. . . . Be of even mind in success and in failure. Evenness of mind is called yoga. Far inferior indeed is mere action, O Arjuna, to

Source: *The Bhagavad Gita*, translated by D. S. Sarma, published by the *Madras Law Journal*, India, 1945, as found in *The Religion of the Hindus*, edited by Kenneth W. Morgan, New York: The Ronald Press Company, 1953, pp. 378–80, 386–88. Reprinted by permission of D. S. Sarma, the *Madras Law Journal*, and The Ronald Press Company.

equanimity of mind. So take refuge in equanimity; miserable are they who work for results.

When a man puts away all the desires of his mind, O Arjuna, and when his spirit finds comfort in itself — then is he called a man of steadfast wisdom. He who is not perturbed in mind by adversity and has no eagerness amidst prosperity, he from whom desire, fear, and anger have fallen away — he is called a sage of firm understanding. . . .

The man who gives up all desires and goes about free from any longing . . . — he attains to peace. This is a divine state, O Arjuna. He who has reached it is deluded no longer, and he who is established in it even at the hour of death — he attains to the bliss of God.

Sages look upon all alike, whether it be a learned and lowly Brahman or a cow or an elephant or even a dog or an outcaste. . . . His soul being unattached to external objects, he finds the happiness that is in himself; he is in union with God, and he enjoys undying bliss.

For the pleasures that arise from attachments are only sources of pain. They have a beginning and an end, O Arjuna, and no wise man delights in them. He who is able to resist the force of desire and anger even here before he quits his body — he is a yogi, he is a blessed man. The yogi who is happy within becomes divine, and attains to the beatitude of God.

Those whose sins are destroyed and whose doubts are removed, whose minds are disciplined and who rejoice in the good of all beings — such holy men attain to the beatitude of God. Those who are free from desire and anger, and who have subdued their minds and realized themselves — around such austere men lies the beatitude of God.

Shutting out all external objects, fixing the gaze of his eyes between his brows, and equalizing the inward and the outward breath moving in his nostrils, the sage who has controlled his senses, mind, understanding, and who puts away desire, fear, and anger, and who is ever bent on liberation — he is indeed ever liberated. And having known me who am the Recipient of all sacrifices and austerities, the Lord of all the worlds and the Friend of all creatures, he attains peace. . . .

He who has conquered himself is the friend of himself; but he who has not conquered himself is hostile to himself as a foe. The spirit of a man who has conquered himself and attained to serenity is steadfast in cold and heat, in pleasure and pain, and in honor and dishonor. He is said to be a steadfast yogi whose mind derives satisfaction from knowledge and experience, who having conquered his senses, never vacillates, and to whom a clod, a stone, and a piece of gold are the same. He who has equal regard for friends, companions, and foes, for those who are indifferent, for those who are impartial, for those who are hateful, for those who are righteous and those who are sinful — he stands supreme.

A yogi should always try to concentrate his mind in absolute solitude, having retired to a secret place, and subdued his mind and body and got rid of his desires and possessions. Having in a clean place firmly fixed his seat neither too high nor too low, and having spread over it the sacred grass, and then a deerskin, and then a cloth, he should practice yoga for his own purification, restraining his thoughts and senses, and bringing his mind to a point. Sitting firm he should hold his body, head, and neck erect and still, and gaze steadfastly on the point of his nose, without looking around. Serene and fearless, steadfast in the vow of celibacy, and subdued in mind, he should sit in yoga, thinking on me and intent on me alone.

Keeping himself ever steadfast in this manner, the yogi of subdued mind attains to the peace which abides in me and which leads to bliss. Yoga is not for him who eats too much, nor for him who eats too little. It is not for him, O Arjuna, who is given to too much sleep, nor for him who keeps vigil too long. But for the man who is temperate in his food and recreation, who is restrained in all his actions, and who is regulated in his sleep and vigil, yoga puts an end to all sorrow. When the disciplined mind of a man is established in the Spirit alone, free from the desire of any object, then he is said to possess concentration. "As a lamp in a place sheltered from the wind does not flicker" — that is the figure employed of a yogi who, with a subdued mind, practices concentration of the Spirit.

Renouncing entirely all the desires born of the imagination and restraining with his mind all his senses on every side, a man should gain tranquillity little by little, and with a steadfast purpose concentrate his mind on the Spirit, and think of nothing else. Whatsoever makes the wavering and fickle mind wander away — it should be withdrawn from that and brought back to the control of the Spirit. . . . Supreme happiness comes to the yogi whose mind is at rest, whose passions are composed, and who is pure and has become one with God.

The Four Noble Truths of Buddhism

Buddhism, the religion of many millions throughout the world, traces its origin to a handsome, wealthy young prince of a northern Indian tribe who left his family and home to live apart from the world and search for truth. Touched by human misery and suffering, Siddhartha Gautama (c. 560–c. 480 B.C.) longed to find a way to release men from pain. After rejecting extreme seclusion and self-deprivation as a possible solution, enlightenment came to him one day while he was contemplating under a tree. Thereafter he was called Buddha — the Enlightened One — or more exactly, "the One who is awake."

Buddha believed that it was his mission to enlighten the world. For about fifty years he preached his message throughout India, gaining followers and disciples wherever he went. His teachings were a reaction to Hinduism. They provided a means whereby every individual, without ritual, without a priesthood, and without supernatural aid, could attain the blissful state of Nirvana in which desire is totally extinguished and perfect peace attained.

"The Four Noble Truths" was the first sermon preached by Buddha after his enlightenment. Before an audience of five, he set forth the causes of evil and suffering, as well as the means to cope with them.

What are these Four Noble Truths? They are the Noble Truth of Suffering, the Noble Truth of the Origin of Suffering, the Noble Truth of the Extinction of Suffering, and the Noble Truth of the Path that leads to the Extinction of Suffering. . . .

What now is the Noble Truth of Suffering?

Birth is suffering; decay is suffering; death is suffering; sorrow, lamentation, pain, grief, and despair are suffering; not to get what one desires is suffering. . . .

And what is decay? The decay of beings . . . getting aged, frail,

Source: Dwight Goddard, editor, A Buddhist Bible, New York: E. P. Dutton & Co., Inc., 1938, pp. 22–24, 29–33. Reprinted by permission of the publishers.

gray, and wrinkled; the failing of their vital force, the wearing out of the senses — this is called decay.

And what is death? The parting and vanishing of beings; . . . their destruction, disappearance, death, the completion of their life period, . . . the discarding of the body — this is called death.

And what is sorrow? The sorrow arising through this or that loss or misfortune which one encounters, the worrying oneself, the state of being alarmed, inward sorrow, inward woe — this is called sorrow.

And what is lamentation? Whatsoever, through this or that loss or misfortune which befalls one, is wail and lament, wailing and lamenting . . . — this is called lamentation.

And what is pain? The bodily pain and unpleasantness, the painful and unpleasant feeling produced by bodily contact — this is called pain.

And what is grief? Mental pain and unpleasantness. . . .

And what is despair? Distress and despair arising through this or that loss or misfortune . . . — this is called despair. . . .

What now is the Noble Truth of the Origin of Suffering? It is that craving which gives rise to fresh rebirth and, bound up with pleasure, . . . now here, now there, finds ever fresh delight. . . .

But where does this craving arise and take root? Wherever in the world there is the delightful and pleasurable, there this craving arises and takes root. Eye, ear, nose, tongue, body, and mind are delightful and pleasurable, there this craving arises and takes root.

Forms, sounds, smells, tastes, . . . and ideas are delightful and pleasurable: there this craving arises and takes root.

If namely, when perceiving a visible form, a sound, odor, taste, bodily contact, or an idea in the mind, the object is pleasant, one is attracted, and if unpleasant, one is repelled.

Thus, whatever kind of feeling one experiences — pleasant, unpleasant, or indifferent — one approves of and cherishes the feeling and clings to it; . . . but lust for feelings means clinging to existence, . . . and on clinging to existence depends the . . . process of becoming; . . . on the process of becoming depends [future] birth; . . . and dependent on birth are decay and death, sorrow, lamentation, pain, grief, and despair. Thus arises this whole mass of suffering.

This is called the Noble Truth of the Origin of Suffering. . . .

What now is called the Noble Truth of the Extinction of Suffering? It is the complete fading away and extinction of this craving, its forsaking and giving up, the liberation and detachment from it.

But where may this craving vanish, where may it be extinguished? Wherever in the world there are delightful and pleasurable things, there this craving may vanish, there it may be extinguished.

Be it in the past, present, or future: whosoever of the monks or priests regard the delightful and pleasurable things in the world as impermanent, . . . as a disease and sorrow, it is he who overcomes the craving.

For, through the total fading away and extinction of craving, . . . decay and death, sorrow, lamentation, suffering, grief, and despair are extinguished. Thus comes about the extinction of this whole mass of suffering.

To give oneself up to indulgence — . . . the base, common, vulgar, unholy, unprofitable; and also to give oneself up to self-mortification — the painful, unholy, unprofitable: both these two extremes the Perfect One [Buddha] has avoided and found out the Middle Path which makes one both to see and to know, which leads to peace, to discernment, to enlightenment, to Nibbana [Nirvana].

It is the Noble Eightfold Path, the way that leads to the extinction of suffering, namely:

1. Right Understanding
2. Right Mindedness
3. Right Speech
4. Right Action
5. Right Living
6. Right Effort
7. Right Attentiveness
8. Right Concentration

This is the Middle Path which the Perfect One has found out, which makes one both to see and to know, which leads to peace, to discernment, to enlightenment, to Nibbana.

Free from pain and torture is this path, free from groaning and suffering: it is the perfect path.

An Indian Moslem's Impressions of England

Among the European states that fought one another for control of India, the British emerged supreme in the middle of the eighteenth century. The Indians reacted in various ways to the Europeans. Some admired their efficiency; others despised them for their materialism; most were indifferent.

At the end of the eighteenth century Abu Taleb Khan, a Moslem civil servant, was invited by a Scottish friend to go to Europe. For about three years he traveled extensively and recorded his observations. English society flocked to meet him, and on the whole, he seems to have had a wonderful time.

The first and greatest defect I observed in the English is their want of faith in religion and their great inclination to philosophy [atheism]. The effects of these principles, or rather want of principle, is very conspicuous in the lower orders of people, who are totally devoid of honesty. They are, indeed, cautious how they transgress against the laws, from fear of punishment; but whenever an opportunity offers of [stealing] anything without the risk of detection, they never pass it by. They are also ever on the watch to appropriate to themselves the property of the rich who, on this account, are obliged constantly to keep their doors shut and never to permit an unknown person to enter them. . . .

The second defect most conspicuous in the English character is pride, or insolence. Puffed up with their power and good fortune for the last fifty years, they are not [afraid] of adversity, and take no pains to avert it. Thus, when the people of London some time ago assembled in mobs on account of the great increase of taxes and high price of provisions, and were nearly in a state of insurrection — although the magistrates, by their vigilance in watching them, and by causing parties of soldiers to patrol the streets day and night to disperse all persons whom they saw assembling together, succeeded in quieting the disturbance —

Source: Wm. Theodore de Bary *et al.*, editors, *Oriental Civilizations: Sources of Indian Tradition*, New York: Columbia University Press, 1958, pp. 563–64. Reprinted by permission of the publishers.

yet no pains were afterward taken to eradicate the evil. Some of the men in power said it had been merely a plan of the [workers] to obtain higher wages (an attempt frequently made by the English tradesmen); others were of the opinion that no remedy could be applied; therefore no further notice was taken of the affair. All this, I say, betrays a blind confidence which, instead of meeting the danger and endeavoring to prevent it, waits till the misfortune arrives and then attempts to remedy it. Such was the case with the late king of France, who took no step to oppose the revolution till it was too late. This self-confidence is to be found, more or less, in every Englishman; it however differs much from the pride of the Indians and Persians.

Their third defect is a passion for acquiring money and their attachment to worldly affairs.

Lao-tzu's Way of Life

The birth and life of Lao-tzu, the founder of Taoism, are shrouded in legend. Whether he lived around 600 B.C., or around 300 B.C., or not at all, has yet to be determined. The writings which are attributed to him, however, are one of the most enduring monuments of Chinese civilization.

Tao means "the Way." It is very difficult to define, and Taoists themselves say that it cannot be fully understood by the mind. It may be described as the ultimate reality, the unchanging beneath all change, the all-powerful, impersonal, primary force in the universe. The mystical understanding of this force brings happiness and power.

The simple life is the best approach to the Way. Lao-tzu counseled passivity, humility, spontaneity, acceptance of life, and harmony with nature. For the ruler of a state, the Way prescribed a minimum of government direction and a surrender of ambition. The goal of Taoism was an eventual return to the happy anarchy that preceded civilization. It appealed to those who wished to leave behind the follies of the world and seek happiness in nature.

The following five selections are from the writings attributed to Lao-tzu.

Rulers

Of the best rulers
>The people (only) know that they exist;
The next best they love and praise;
The next they fear;
And the next they revile.
>>When they do not command the people's faith,
Some will lose faith in them,
And then they resort to oaths!
But (of the best) when their task is accomplished, their work done,
The people all remark, "We have done it ourselves."

Warning Against the Use of Force

He who by Tao purposes to help the ruler of men
Will oppose all conquest by force of arms.
For such things are wont to rebound.
Where armies are, thorns and brambles grow.
The raising of a great host
Is followed by a year of dearth.

Therefore a good general effects his purpose and stops.
>He dares not rely upon the strength of arms;
Effects his purpose and does not glory in it;
Effects his purpose and does not boast of it;
Effects his purpose and does not take pride in it;
>>Effects his purpose as a regrettable necessity;
Effects his purpose but does not love violence.
(For) things age after reaching their prime.
That (violence) would be against Tao.
And he who is against the Tao perishes young.

Source: Lin Yutang, editor, *The Wisdom of China and India*, New York: Random House, Inc., 1942, pp. 591–92, 599–600, 602, 607, 624. Reprinted by permission of the publishers.

Knowing Oneself

He who knows others is learned;
    He who knows himself is wise.
He who conquers others has power of muscles;
    He who conquers himself is strong.
He who is contented is rich.
    He who is determined has strength of will.
He who does not lose his center endures;
He who dies yet (his power) remains has long life.

Be Content

Fame or one's own self, which does one love more?
One's own self or material goods, which has more worth?
Loss (of self) or possession (of goods), which is the greater evil?

Therefore: he who loves most spends most,
    He who hoards much loses much.
The contented man meets no disgrace;
Who knows when to stop runs into no danger —
He can long endure.

The Way of Heaven

True words are not fine-sounding;
    Fine-sounding words are not true.
A good man does not argue;
    He who argues is not a good man.
The wise one does not know many things;
    He who knows many things is not wise.
The Sage does not accumulate (for himself):
    He lives for other people,
    And grows richer himself;
    He gives to other people,
    And has greater abundance.
The Tao of Heaven
    Blesses, but does not harm.
The Way of the Sage
    Accomplishes, but does not contend.

The Wisdom of Confucius

The greatest single influence in Chinese civilization has been Confucius (551–479 B.C.). Whereas Taoism represents the carefree side of Chinese culture, Confucianism represents the serious and disciplined side. Confucius did not found a religion; his philosophy was a way of life. Born into an age of civil war and treachery, he sought answers to the troubles of society in the traditions of the past. He traveled from state to state in China seeking a ruler who would implement his doctrines.

Confucius put great emphasis on the virtues inherent in good family life, such as order, benevolence, and respect. He abhorred force and violence and had implicit faith in the power of rational persuasion and moral example. Confucius wanted the ruler to set up a government of good men committed to sound principles. His goal was the establishment of universal harmony based on custom and tradition. In the second century B.C., Confucianism became the official philosophy of China and the subject of study for all aspiring statesmen. In later centuries the influence of Confucius spread throughout East Asia.

The sayings of Confucius were originally written down by students who had learned them from his immediate disciples.

Clever talk and a domineering manner have little to do with being Man-at-his-best.

Daily I examine myself on three points: Have I failed to be loyal in my work for others? Have I been false with my friends? Have I failed to pass on that which I was taught?

At fifteen I thought only of study; at thirty I began playing my role; at forty I was sure of myself; at fifty I was conscious of my position in the universe; at sixty I was no longer argumentative; and now at seventy I can follow my heart's desire without violating custom. . . .

Let the sole worry of your parents be that you might become ill.

Source: *The Sayings of Confucius*, translated by James R. Ware, New York: The New American Library of World Literature, Inc., 1955, pp. 21 *passim*. Copyright © 1955 by James R. Ware. Reprinted by permission of the publishers.

Today, when people call a man filial they mean that he is supporting his parents. But he does as much for his dogs and horses! If he does not show respect for his parents, how is he differentiating between them and the animals? . . .

Look at the means which a man employs; consider his motives; observe his pleasures. A man simply cannot conceal himself!

If, while being a student of the past, a man also understands the new things which surround us, he may be used as a teacher. . . .

Learning without thought brings ensnarement. Thought without learning totters. . . .

Shall I tell you what knowledge is? It is to know both what one knows and what one does not know. . . .

China without a recognized leader is preferable to foreigners with all their leaders. . . .

To live in the company of Men-at-their-best is the finest thing possible. How can a man be considered wise if, when he has the choice, he does not live in such surroundings? . . .

Great Man cherishes excellence; Petty Man, his own comfort. Great Man cherishes the rules and regulations; Petty Man, special favors.

He who engages solely in self-interested actions will make himself many enemies. . . .

Do not worry about not holding high position; worry rather about playing your proper role. Worry not that no one knows of you; seek to be worth knowing. . . .

As you serve your parents you should remonstrate with them only slightly. If on doing so you find that they are set in having their own way, be even more respectful and do not thwart them. Even though this overwhelm you with toil, do not become angry with them. . . .

When strict with oneself one rarely fails.

Great Man seeks to be slow of speech but quick of action.

Excellence does not remain alone; it is sure to attract neighbors.

A commander may be snatched away from his army, but will cannot be taken from the humblest man.

Civil Service Examinations in China

Confucius urged his followers to train themselves in the classical writings and to pursue careers in the service of the state. About the middle of the second century B.C., examinations began to be used to recruit civil servants. Thereafter, in spite of setbacks, the examination system was extended. The basis of the system was a knowledge of the classics and of Confucian principles. From time to time questions of a more practical and topical nature, such as law and current events, were included. Preparation for the examinations required years of concentrated effort, and thus could usually be undertaken only by the sons of wealthy families.

In a biography of the poet-statesman Su Tungpo, Lin Yutang gives us a vivid picture of the examinations in the middle of the eleventh century A.D.

The time for the palace examinations came. Ouyang Shiu was nominated by the Emperor to be chief examiner, together with a number of distinguished scholars as judges. The approach to this most critical moment of a scholar's life was always filled with keen excitement, tense hope, and a nervous fear of failure. It was the moment to which all his years of grinding labor and hours of burning the midnight oil were supposed to lead. The candidates had to get up in the middle of the night and come to the palace at dawn, bringing their cold meals with them, for they would not be able to leave until the examinations were over. During the examinations they were shut up in cubicles under the supervision of palace guards. There was a rigorous system to prevent bribery or favoritism. The candidates' papers were recopied by official clerks before they were submitted to the examiners, to avoid recognition of their identity by their handwriting. In the recopied papers the writers' names were taken out and kept on file. While the candidates

Source: Lin Yutang, *The Gay Genius: The Biography of Su Tungpo*, New York: The John Day Company, Inc., 1947, pp. 38–40. Reprinted by permission of the publishers.

were let out after the examinations, the judges themselves were shut up within the palace and forbidden to have any contact with the people outside, usually from late January till early March, until the papers were properly graded and submitted to the Emperor. The candidates were examined first on questions of history or principles of government. There was a second examination on the classics, and finally, after the successful ones had been graded, there was one — under the direct supervision of the Emperor — on lyrics, descriptive poetry, and again, essays on politics. Emperor Jentsung was especially anxious to recruit good talent for his government and took a personal interest in these tests. He sent out the subjects for the papers by his own personal servants and sometimes, to avoid leakage, changed them at the last moment. . . .

Tungpo wrote a paper which dealt with the principle of simplicity and leniency in the administration of a country. . . . On April 8, 1057, Su passed the examinations, and on April 14, at the age of twenty, was officially decorated, . . . almost at the head of 388 successful candidates. To obtain such an honor meant that one became at once nationally known as one of the first scholars of the land.

It was typical of the brilliant young man, however, that he took some liberties with history and invented a dialogue in his paper. He was developing the theme that in giving rewards one should rather err on the side of generosity, and in punishment one should give every benefit of the doubt to an offender lest an innocent man be killed. In the time of Emperor Yao, he wrote, a man was about to be condemned to death. "Three times the Minister of Justice said, 'Let him be killed!' and three times Emperor Yao said, 'Let him be pardoned!' " The dialogue read very well, and it seemed to support an authentic story that the sage Emperor was willing to use a bad man and give him a chance to prove his talent. The judges read the story but dared not question it, because it amounted to their admitting not having read it somewhere in one of the obscure ancient texts. So Su Tungpo was passed. After the examinations one day Mei Yaochen, one of the judges, said to him:

"By the way, where does that story occur about Emperor Yao and the Minister of Justice? I can't quite recall where I read it."

"I invented it," the young scholar confessed.

"You did!" said the old judge.

"Well, that was what the sage Emperor would have done, wasn't it?" replied Su Tungpo.

To pass an examination under a certain examiner was to place a scholar under heavy obligation to him for recognition of his talent, and establish a permanent relation between the two as "master" and "disciple." The candidates went up to pay their respects to their master and the chief judges and wrote them letters of gratitude. Ouyang Shiu was the authority on literature. He could make or unmake a scholar by a word of praise or blame. A writer of the time said that the scholars did not know the fear of punishments or the joy of promotions, nor did they value the gift of life or fear the doom of death, but they did fear the opinion of Ouyang Shiu. Imagine, therefore, the effect on the young poet when Ouyang Shiu said to one of his colleagues, "On reading Su Tungpo's letter, somehow I perspired all over with joy. My old person must give place to this young man and let him rise to the top." When such a statement was made by Ouyang Shiu, the whole capital heard about it. Ouyang Shiu was also reported to have said to his own sons, "Mark my word, thirty years from now nobody will talk about me." This prediction came true, for in the first decade after Su Tungpo's death nobody was talking about Ouyang Shiu but everybody was talking about Su Tungpo and reading him in secret when his works were banned.

Kublai Khan Holds Court

The few Westerners who came into contact with the Far East during the Middle Ages were overwhelmed by the splendor and the culture they encountered. Marco Polo (c. 1254–1324), a member of a wealthy Venetian merchant family, was one of the first Europeans to become intimately acquainted with Chinese civilization. He learned the language and the customs of the land and became a favorite and a high official in the court of the Khan. He was sent on a number of diplomatic missions to various parts of the Mongol empire and had the opportunity to observe what no European had ever seen. His experiences were recorded in his memoirs, which became very popular in Europe, though people found it hard to believe that his stories were authentic.

When his Majesty holds a grand and public court, those who attend it are seated in the following order. The table of the sovereign is placed on an elevation and he takes his seat on the northern side, with his face turned toward the south; and next to him, on his left hand, sits the Empress. On his right hand are placed his sons, grandsons, and other persons connected with him by blood, upon seats somewhat lower, so that their heads are on a level with the Emperor's feet. The other princes and the nobility have their places at still lower tables; and the same rules are observed with respect to the females, the wives of the sons, grandsons, and other relatives of the Great Khan being seated on the left hand, at tables in like manner gradually lower; then follow the wives of the nobility and military officers: so that all are seated according to their respective ranks and dignities, in the places assigned to them, and to which they are entitled.

The tables are arranged in such a manner that the Great Khan, sitting on his elevated throne, can overlook the whole. It is not however to be understood that all who assemble on such occasions can be accommodated at tables. The greater part of the officers and even of the nobles, on the contrary, eat sitting upon carpets in the halls; and on the outside stand a great multitude of persons who come from different countries and bring with them many rare curiosities.

In the middle of the hall, where the Great Khan sits at table, there is a magnificent piece of furniture made in the form of a square coffer, each side of which is three paces in length, exquisitely carved in figures of animals, and gilt. It is hollow within for the purpose of receiving a capacious vase of pure gold calculated to hold many gallons. On each of its four sides stands a smaller vessel containing about a hogshead, one of which is filled with mare's milk, another with that of the camel, and so of the others, according to the kinds of beverage in use. . . .

Officers of rank are likewise appointed, whose duty it is to see that all strangers who happen to arrive at the time of the festival and are unacquainted with the etiquette of the court are suitably accommodated with places; and these stewards are continually visiting every part of the hall, inquiring of the guests if there is anything with which they are unprovided or whether any of them wish for wine, milk, meat, or other articles, in which case it is immediately brought to them by the attendants.

Source: Manuel Komroff, editor, *The Travels of Marco Polo*, New York: Liveright Publishing Corporation, pp. 134–36. Copyright 1926, © renewed 1958 by Liveright Publishing Corporation. Reprinted by permission of the publishers.

At each door of the grand hall, or of whatever part the Great Khan happens to be in, stand two officers of a gigantic figure, one on each side, with staves in their hands, for the purpose of preventing persons from touching the threshold with their feet and obliging them to step beyond it. If by chance anyone is guilty of this offense, the janitors take from him his garment, which he must redeem for money; or, when they do not take the garment, they inflict on him such number of blows as they have authority for doing. But as strangers may be unacquainted with the prohibition, officers are appointed to introduce and warn them. This precaution is used because touching the threshold is regarded as a bad omen. In departing from the hall, as some of the company may be affected by the liquor, it is impossible to guard against the accident, and the order is not then strictly enforced.

The numerous persons who attend at the sideboard of his Majesty and who serve him with victuals and drink are all obliged to cover their noses and mouths with handsome veils or cloths of worked silk, in order that his victuals or his wine may not be affected by their breath. When drink is called for by him and the page-in-waiting has presented it, he retires three paces and kneels down, upon which the courtiers and all who are present in like manner make their prostration. At the same moment all the musical instruments, of which there is a numerous band, begin to play and continue to do so until he has ceased drinking, when all the company recover their posture. This reverential salutation is made as often as his Majesty drinks. . . .

When the repast is finished and the tables have been removed, persons of various descriptions enter the hall, and among these a troop of comedians and performers on different instruments. Also tumblers and jugglers, who exhibit their skill in the presence of the Great Khan, to the high amusement and gratification of all the spectators. When these sports are concluded, the people separate and each returns to his own house.

A Chinese Emperor Rejects Western Overtures

The Chinese conducted relations between themselves and other peoples as between superiors and inferiors, for they regarded themselves, both culturally and geographically, as the very center of the world. The Western foreigners with whom they came in contact did not always behave with propriety and tended to confirm Chinese disdain for the barbarians. Catholic missionaries, especially the Jesuits, after receiving favorable treatment in return for their military and scientific knowledge, were discredited because of theological quarrels and political intrigue. By the late eighteenth century, relations between China and the West were confined to trade in a single port — Canton.

The Chinese tended to look upon merchants as unproductive parasites. Attempts by trade-hungry Europeans to persuade the Chinese to increase trade and to treat them as equals met with no success. In 1793 Lord Macartney, heading an English delegation, arrived at the court of the Emperor Ch'ien Lung. Though Macartney refused to kowtow (prostrate himself nine times — not a dishonorable act, but symbolic of the superior-inferior relationship), he was granted an audience. The Emperor's letter to King George III illustrates China's attitude toward the West. Over the years, however, trade continued to grow in spite of Chinese restrictions.

You [George III], O King, live beyond the confines of many seas. Nevertheless, impelled by your humble desire to partake of the benefits of our civilization, you have dispatched a mission respectfully bearing your memorial. . . . I have perused your memorial: the earnest terms in which it is couched reveal a respectful humility on your part which is highly praiseworthy.

In consideration of the fact that your ambassador and his deputy

Source: Sir Frederick Whyte, K.C.S.I., *China and Foreign Powers: An Historical Review of Their Relations,* London: Oxford University Press, 1927, p. 39, Appendix I. Published under the auspices of the Royal Institute of International Affairs and reprinted by permission.

have come a long way with your memorial and tribute, I have shown them high favor and have allowed them to be introduced into my presence. To manifest my indulgence, I have entertained them at a banquet and made them numerous gifts. . . .

As to your entreaty to send one of your nationals to be accredited to my Celestial Court and to be in control of your country's trade with China, this request is contrary to all usage of my dynasty and cannot possibly be entertained. . . . If you assert that your reverence for our Celestial Dynasty fills you with a desire to acquire our civilization, our ceremonies and code of laws differ so completely from your own that even if your envoy were able to acquire the rudiments of our civilization, you could not possibly transplant our manners and customs to your alien soil. Therefore, however adept the envoy might become, nothing would be gained thereby.

Swaying the wide world, I have but one aim in view, namely, to maintain a perfect governance and to fulfill the duties of the State: strange and costly objects do not interest me. If I have commanded that the tribute offerings sent by you, O King, are to be accepted, this was solely in consideration for the spirit which prompted you to dispatch them from afar. Our dynasty's majestic virtue has penetrated into every country under heaven, and kings of all nations have offered their costly tribute by land and sea. As your ambassador can see for himself, we possess all things. I set no value on objects strange or ingenious, and have no use for your country's manufactures.

The Manners and Customs of Early Japan

Japanese records of the early history of Japan are primarily collections of legends and myths. The best sources of factual information for Japanese history before the sixth century A.D. are the histories of Chinese dynasties, which include information about the "barbarians" to the east. The Japanese owe an enormous cultural debt to China, including their written language and their introduction to Buddhism.

The following selections are taken from official histories of China for the years A.D. 297 and 630.

Japan, A.D. 297

The people of Wa (Japan) dwell in the middle of the ocean on the mountainous islands southeast of [the district of] Tai-fang. They formerly comprised more than one hundred communities. During the Han dynasty, (Wa) envoys appeared at the court; today, thirty of their communities maintain [relations] with us through envoys and scribes. . . .

The land of Wa is warm and mild. In winter as in summer the people live on raw vegetables and go about barefooted. They have . . . houses; father and mother, elder and younger, sleep separately. They smear their bodies with pink and scarlet, just as the Chinese use powder. They serve food on bamboo and wooden trays, helping themselves with their fingers. When a person dies, they prepare a single coffin, without an outer one. They cover the graves with earth to make a mound. When death occurs, mourning is observed for more than ten days, during which period they do not eat meat. The head mourners wail and lament, while friends sing, dance, and drink liquor. When the funeral is over, all members of the family go into the water to cleanse themselves in a bath of purification.

When they go on voyages across the sea to visit China, they always select a man who does not comb his hair, does not rid himself of fleas, lets his clothing get as dirty as it will, does not eat meat. . . . This man behaves like a mourner and is known as the "mourning keeper." When the voyage meets with good fortune, they all lavish on him slaves and other valuables. In case there is disease or mishap, they kill him, saying that he was not scrupulous in observing the taboos. . . .

In their meetings and in their deportment, there is no distinction between father and son or between men and women. They are fond of liquor. In their worship, men of importance simply clap their hands instead of kneeling or bowing. The people live long, some to one hundred and others to eighty or ninety years. Ordinarily, men of importance have four or five wives; the lesser ones, two or three. . . . There is no theft, and [legal action] is infrequent. In case of violation of law, the light offender loses his wife and children by confiscation; as for the grave offender, the members of his household and all his kinsmen are extermi-

Source: R. Tsunoda, Wm. Theodore de Bary, D. Keene, editors, *Oriental Civilizations: Sources of Japanese Tradition*, New York: Columbia University Press, 1958, pp. 6–8; 11–12. Reprinted by permission of the publishers.

nated. There are class distinctions among the people, and some men are vassals of others. Taxes are collected. There are granaries as well as markets in each province, where necessaries are exchanged under the supervision of the Wa officials. . . .

When the lowly meet men of importance on the road, they stop and withdraw to the roadside. In conveying messages to them or addressing them, they either squat or kneel, with both hands on the ground. This is the way they show respect. When responding they say "ah," which corresponds to the affirmative "yes."

The country formerly had a man as ruler. For some seventy or eighty years after that there were disturbances and warfare. Thereupon the people agreed upon a woman for their ruler. Her name was Pimiko. She occupied herself with magic and sorcery, bewitching the people. Though mature in age, she remained unmarried. She had a younger brother who assisted her in ruling the country. After she became the ruler, there were few who saw her. She had one thousand women as attendants, but only one man. He served her food and drink and acted as a medium of communication. She resided in a palace surrounded by towers and stockades, with armed guards in a state of constant vigilance. . . .

When Pimiko passed away, a great mound was raised, more than a hundred paces in diameter. Over a hundred male and female attendants followed her to the grave. Then a king was placed on the throne, but the people would not obey him. Assassination and murder followed; more than one thousand were thus slain.

A relative of Pimiko named Iyo, a girl of thirteen, was then made queen and order was restored.

Japan, A.D. 630

During the twenty years of the K'ai-huang era (581–600), the King of Wa, whose family name was Ame and personal name Tarishihoko, and who bore the title of Ahakomi, sent an envoy to visit the [Chinese] court. The Emperor ordered the appropriate official to make inquiries about the manners and customs [of the Wa people]. The envoy reported thus: "The King of Wa deems heaven to be his elder brother and the sun, his younger. Before break of dawn he attends the court, and, sitting cross-legged, listens to appeals. Just as soon as the sun rises, he ceases these duties, saying that he hands them over to his brother." Our just Emperor said that such things were extremely senseless, and he admonished [the King of Wa] to alter [his ways].

There are about 100,000 households. . . . Thieves are made to make restitution in accordance with the value of the goods stolen. If the thief has no property with which to make payment, he is taken to be a slave. Other offenses are punished according to their nature — sometimes by banishment and sometimes by flogging. In the prosecution of offenses by the court, the knees of those who plead not guilty are pressed together by placing them between pieces of wood, or their heads are sawed with the stretched string of a strong bow. Sometimes pebbles are put in boiling water and both parties to a dispute made to pick them out. The hand of the guilty one is said to become inflamed. Sometimes a snake is kept in a jar, and the accused ordered to catch it. If he is guilty, his hand will be bitten. The people are gentle and peaceful. . . .

As for musical instruments, they have five-stringed lyres and flutes. Both men and women paint marks on their arms and spots on their faces and have their bodies tattooed. They catch fish by diving into the water. They have no written characters and understand only the use of notched sticks and knotted ropes. They revere Buddha.

The Advantages of Drinking Tea

Buddhism came to Japan from China in A.D. 552. Attracting at first only a small group of nobles, it soon became the official religion of the land. Close contact with China was maintained, and many of the divisions in Chinese Buddhism were carried over to Japan. In the process of conquering Japan, Buddhism blended with the native culture and took on a characteristically Japanese flavor.

Zen Buddhism was brought to Japan at the end of the twelfth century by Eisai, a Japanese scholar who had studied in China. Zen Buddhism taught the value of meditation and concentration over that of book-learning and ritual. As a way of life it emphasized self-discipline, appreciation of beauty, austerity, and intuitive action.

The influence of Zen Buddhism on Japanese life may be seen in the Tea Ceremony. Eisai, who introduced tea from China, lauded the virtues of this beverage in order to help divert the Emperor's taste from alcohol. Zen monks later developed the Tea Ceremony, for which men gathered in quiet groups away from the cares of the world. Following a prescribed and graceful form of serving, they sipped tea while they meditated or admired a beautiful object. The Tea Ceremony, an expression of the ideals of Zen Buddhism, became a national institution in Japan.

Below, Eisai discusses the marvelous qualities of tea.

Tea is the most wonderful medicine for nourishing one's health; it is the secret of long life. On the hillsides it grows up as the spirit of the soil. Those who pick and use it are certain to attain a great age. India and China both value it highly, and in the past our country too once showed a great liking for tea. Now as then it possesses the same rare qualities, and we should make wider use of it.

Of all the things which Heaven has created, man is the most noble. To preserve one's life so as to make the most of one's allotted span is prudent and proper, considering the high value of human life. The basis of preserving life is the cultivation of health, and the secret of health lies in the well-being of the . . . organs. Among these . . . the heart is sovereign, and to build up the heart the drinking of tea is the finest method. When the heart is weak, the other organs all suffer. It is more than two thousand years since the illustrious healer Jiva passed away in India, and in these latter degenerate days there is none who can accurately diagnose the circulation of the blood. It is more than three thousand years since the Chinese healer Shen-nung disappeared from the earth, and there is no one today who can prescribe medicines properly. With no one to consult in such matters, illness, disease, trouble, and danger follow one another in endless succession. . . .

Yet when the heart becomes sick, all organs and tastes are affected. Then, eat as one may, one will have to vomit and stop eating. But if

Source: R. Tsunoda, Wm. Theodore de Bary, D. Keene, editors, *Oriental Civilizations: Sources of Japanese Tradition*, New York: Columbia University Press, 1958, pp. 244–46. Reprinted by permission of the publishers.

one drinks tea, the heart will be strengthened and freed from illness. It is well to know that when the heart is ailing, the skin has a poor color, a sign that life is ebbing away. I wonder why the Japanese do not care for bitter things. In the great country of China they drink tea, as a result of which there is no heart trouble and people live long lives. Our country is full of sickly-looking, skinny persons, and this is simply because we do not drink tea. Whenever one is in poor spirits, one should drink tea. This will put the heart in order and dispel all illness. . . .

Drink lots of tea, and one's energy and spirits will be restored to full strength.

The Closing of Japan

Japan's enthusiasm for trade with Europeans was somewhat dampened by the Japanese suspicion of the motives of the foreigners. They feared the spread of Christianity, which had been introduced by St. Francis Xavier in 1549 and had made several hundred thousand converts within half a century. They suspected that the Europeans harbored political ambitions in their land. The vicious commercial and religious rivalry among the Europeans also made the Japanese uneasy.

Early in the seventeenth century the Japanese, recently united under the Tokugawa Shogunate * after a period of civil war, began to persecute Christians. The resistance of the missionaries and the Japanese converts to the commands of the Shogun turned the persecutions into a campaign of extermination which was for the most part successful. By 1640 European trade was terminated except with the Dutch, who were allowed to continue only under the most careful scrutiny.

The following selection is from the Japanese government's Act of Seclusion of 1636.

* From the end of the twelfth century to 1868 Japan was governed by shoguns, who were hereditary feudal rulers. The emperors, while still supreme in theory, were in practice limited to ceremonial functions. The Tokugawa Shogunate ruled Japan from 1603 to 1867.

1. Japanese ships shall by no means be sent abroad.

2. No Japanese shall be sent abroad. Anyone violating this prohibition shall suffer the penalty of death, and the shipowner and crew shall be held up together with the ship.

3. All Japanese residing abroad shall be put to death when they return home.

4. All Christians shall be examined by official examiners.

5. Informers against Christians shall be rewarded.

6. The arrival of foreign ships must be reported . . . and watch kept over them.

7. The Namban people (Spaniards or Portuguese) and any other people with evil titles propagating Christianity shall be incarcerated in the Omura prison as before.

8. Even ships shall not be left untouched in the matter of exterminating Christians.

9. Everything shall be done in order to see that no Christian is survived by descendants, and anyone disregarding this injunction shall be put to death, while proper punishment shall be meted out to the other members of his family according to their deeds.

10. Children born of the Namban people (Spaniards or Portuguese) in Nagasaki and people adopting these Namban children into their family shall be put to death; capital punishment shall also be meted out to those Namban descendants if they return to Japan, and their relatives in Japan, who may communicate with them, shall receive suitable punishment.

11. The samurai [warrior aristocracy of Japan] shall not purchase goods on board foreign ships directly from foreigners.

Source: Y. Takekoshi, *The Economic Aspects of the History of the Civilization of Japan*, London: George Allen & Unwin Ltd., 1930, Vol. II, pp. 128–29. Reprinted by permission of the publishers.

Japan—the Land of the Gods

A return to "pure" Japanese tradition and a reaction to alien culture accompanied the unity and stability achieved in the seventeenth century. The leaders of this movement exalted the

263

ancient Japanese Shinto worship over Buddhism and Confucianism, which had been imported. They revived the study of native Japanese literature and mythology.

By the middle of the nineteenth century this movement had become ultranationalistic. Hirata Atsutane, one of its spokesmen, proclaimed the superiority of Japanese culture over all other cultures. He tried to demonstrate the antiquity of everything Japanese and insisted that Japan had invented a system of writing before China. It is interesting that he admired Western science even while he disliked the West. That Hirata's statements were not based on fact did not detract from his simple and powerful appeal. Many Japanese believed in the superiority of Japan as an article of faith.

Buddhist learning is broader in scope than Confucian, but Japanese learning is even more embracing. All the various types of learning, including Confucianism and Buddhism, are joined in Japanese learning, just as the many rivers flow into the sea, where their waters are joined. Because of the diversity and number of the different parts of Japanese learning, people are often bewildered and at a loss to evaluate it. Unless, therefore, we can distinguish accurately the elements which make up this vast amalgam of learning, the excellence of the true Way will remain obscure. . . . We must be aware of such matters in order to appreciate the pure and righteous Way of Japan. Japanese should study all the different kinds of learning — even though they be foreign — so that they can choose the good features of each and place them at the service of the nation. We may properly speak not only of Chinese but even of Indian and Dutch learning as Japanese learning: this fact should be understood by all Japanese who delve into foreign studies.

People all over the world refer to Japan as the Land of the Gods and call us the descendants of the gods. Indeed, it is exactly as they say: our country, as a special mark of favor from the heavenly gods, was begotten by them, and there is thus so immense a difference between Japan and all the other countries of the world as to defy comparison. Ours is a splendid and blessed country, the Land of the Gods beyond any doubt, and we, down to the most humble man and woman, are the de-

Source: R. Tsunoda, Wm. Theodore de Bary, D. Keene, editors, *Oriental Civilizations: Sources of Japanese Tradition*, New York: Columbia University Press, 1958, pp. 543–44. Reprinted by permission of the publishers.

264

scendants of the gods. Nevertheless, there are unhappily many people who do not understand why Japan is the Land of the Gods and we their descendants. . . . Is this not a lamentable state of affairs? Japanese differ completely from and are superior to the peoples of China, India, Russia, Holland, Siam, Cambodia, and all other countries of the world, and for us to have called our country the Land of the Gods was not mere vainglory. It was the gods who formed all the lands of the world at the Creation, and these gods were without exception born in Japan. Japan is thus the homeland of the gods, and that is why we call it the Land of the Gods. This is a matter of universal belief and is quite beyond dispute. Even in countries where our ancient traditions have not been transmitted, the peoples recognize Japan as a divine land. . . . In olden days when Korea was divided into three kingdoms, reports were heard there of how splendid, miraculous, and blessed a land Japan is, and because Japan lies to the east of Korea, they said in awe and reverence, "To the East is a divine land, called the Land of the Rising Sun." Word of this eventually spread all over the world, and now people everywhere refer to Japan as the Land of the Gods, irrespective of whether or not they know why this is true.

CONTENTS OF VOLUME TWO

THE HUMAN ADVENTURE

CONTENTS

269

PART EIGHT The Non-European Civilizations and European Imperialism

PART NINE The Rise of Dictatorships

PART TEN   Hope and Distress in the Nuclear Age